The Argo Bounce

Jay Teitel

THE ARGO BOUNCE

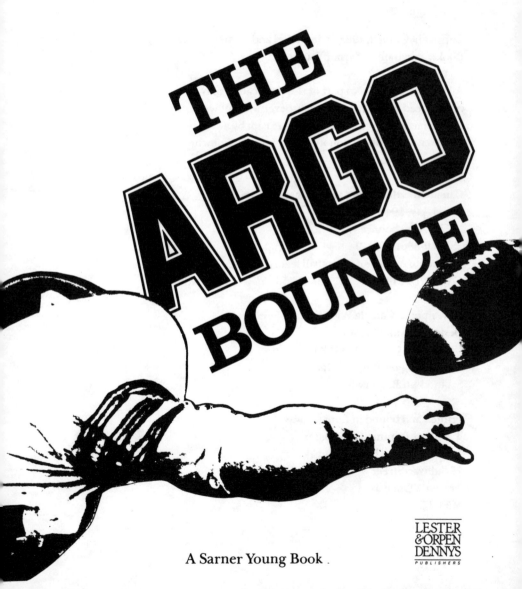

A Sarner Young Book

LESTER
&ORPEN
DENNYS
PUBLISHERS

Canadian Cataloguing in Publication Data

Teitel, Jay, 1949-
   The Argo bounce
ISBN 0-88619-033-9
1. Toronto Argonauts (Football team). I. Title.
GV948.T44 1983   796.33'56   C83-098816-5

Cover photo Canada Wide Feature Services
Design by Ivan Holmes
Cover design by Don Fernley
Typesetting by Trigraph Inc.
Set in 11 pt. Baskerville

Printed and bound in Canada by
T.H. Best Printing Co. Ltd. for
Lester & Orpen Dennys Ltd.
78 Sullivan Street
Toronto, Ontario
M5T 1C1

For Karen and Sarah; who are not fans,
but have to live with one.

Acknowledgements

As much as this book is a labour of a fan's love, it is also the history of a football team, and so could not have been written without the research that any history requires. Research is a world unto itself: fascinating, exasperating, and very easy to get lost in. For keeping their bearings and their standards in a labyrinth of dead ends and false leads—and doing it with unflagging good humour—I would like to thank Hershel Stern, Greg Ioannou, and particularly Franca Leeson.

There were also my involuntary collaborators: the voices from the sports pages. Newspapers are a fan's lifeline. No matter how many television replays of a thrilling play he sees, no matter how many diverse camera angles he sees it from, he will always read the papers the next day to make sure it really happened. It is a hopeful sign for humanity that in a world where gratification is increasingly instant, the printed word remains the only legitimate imprimatur of reality for a fan. The sources I owe a debt to are too numerous to mention comprehensively, but some names can't be overlooked. These include Bob Frewin, whose memory is as astonishing as his patience, and Annis Stukus, whose constancy is just as much of a marvel. Also Bob Hesketh, and Morley Callaghan, Jim Hunt, Milt Dunnell, Jim Coleman, and Jeff Goodman —and, especially, Trent Frayne, whose scrapbooks were invaluable, and who graciously agreed to help edit this edition. For his help on the first edition, and his unflagging support in countless other journalistic situations, I'd like to thank Don Obe. Finally, but foremost, there's Mark Sarner, who showed more talent and sensitivity in shaping this book than any editor I have known. All the nerve-racking nights beside the radio with the Argos, all the Sunday afternoons with the Cleveland Browns, are his as much as mine.

Photography credits: facing Introduction, Toronto Argonaut Football Club; facing chapters 1, 3, 6, 7, 8, 9, and 11, Toronto Star; facing chapters 4 and 5, Graphic Artists; facing chapter 10, United Press Canada.

Contents

Introduction to the Paperback Edition

> Winning is wonderful, but in a way you have to deserve it. I think the real fans are the fans of terrible teams, because they know...how far their own players fall short. The rallying cry that has always struck me as so poignant and beautiful is, "Come on, you bum!" which means, "We know you're no good, but we want to win!"
>
> Roger Angell

When I was first toying with the idea of writing this book—in the chill, pigskin-barren days of January 1982—a thought occurred to me that was obviously insane, but also so tenacious that I eventually surrendered and told it to a good friend, who also happened to be an Argo fan.

"What," I said, "if this year really *is* different? What if the Argos win the Grey Cup?"

I wish now that I'd had a camera to record the gamut of emotions that crossed his face. His final look was of an incredulity bordering on awe. "Teitel," he said, "the Argos are *not* going to win the Grey Cup."

History had the last word. The Argos didn't win the Grey Cup in 1982; they were merely in it, losing, in a strange split-personality game, to the Edmonton Eskimos, the last team they had defeated in a championship game exactly thirty years earlier. At the time of the Grey Cup *The Argo Bounce* had been on the stands in hardcover for about a month, and more than one reviewer had suggested that as a story of a doomed sports team its timing could not have been worse—the team, after all, hadn't looked this good for a generation. But they were wrong. The book's timing was perfect—what it lacked was a conclusive final chapter. The chapter I had had to close with was the 1981 2 and 14 season, undoubtedly grand in a fatal way, and containing in it the subtle glimmer of a new order, but not exactly the stuff of myth or universality. History is cyclical; to become a meaningful part of it, the Argos needed to rejoin the cycle. The 1982 season did that for them (I close my eyes as I write this)—and more. It provided an upbeat closing parenthesis for the Argos' unique, crazy story, a story unprecedented in the annals of losing, yet beloved, sports teams.

How unprecedented is that story still? Statistics rarely tell the whole story, but even including the "new-era" Argos of 1982 the figures are revealing. As of this writing, the Argonauts have not won their league championship, the Grey Cup, in thirty years. In that time they have accumulated a record of 169 games won against 259 lost. They have missed the league playoffs eighteen of those thirty years, which means they have finished in last place 60% of the time since 1952. Except for two brief oases of excellence, a decade apart—and of course 1982 itself—the Argos have been a terrible football team for the past thirty years.

Still, as long-suffering fans in a number of cities across the continent would undoubtedly argue, statistics alone aren't enough to carve the Argos an exclusive niche as professional sports losers. The contenders are legion. Baseball's Chicago Cubs last won a pennant in 1945, and have yet to win a World Series in that sport's modern era. The New York Rangers have gone forty-two years without winning a Stanley Cup, the Detroit Red Wings twenty-seven. Until the Super Bowl of 1981-82, the San Francisco Forty-Niners hadn't appeared in an NFL Championship for the thirty-one years of their existence, let alone won one. Even the Boston Red Sox, who have fielded competitive teams for most of the last two decades, have been denied a World Series victory for an incredible total of sixty-four years.

But this is where statistics begin to mislead. There are at least three areas I can see where the Argos differ significantly from any of the teams mentioned, differences that make them unique in the annals of professional sport.

The first difference is the height from which the Argos began their long 29-year slide. In three decades, the Argos have accomplished a dramatic, unprecedented reversal: thirty years ago they were a dynasty as dominant and secure as their later incarnation would be submissive and unstable. This is a fact most modern Argo fans have either forgotten, in self-defence, or never known. In 1952, the year of their last Grey Cup victory, the Argos could have been called without exaggeration the New York Yankees of Canadian football. As far as I know, no other team has fallen so far or so completely within the space of a single generation. On the list of tortures the Chicago Cubs have inflicted on their fans for more than half a century, the memory of former greatness isn't included—but for an Argo fan it turns out to be unavoidable.

The second difference is the Bounce, the Argo Bounce itself. Of all the losing teams mentioned, only the Argos boast a celebrated expression that describes their "fortune"—whether blessing or nemesis—in such a poetic way. Over the years the "Argo Bounce" has been so widely used as a piece of the Canadian sports lexicon that its origins and original nuance have all but been forgotten. Until the season of '82—or, more exactly, the last play of the second-last game of the '81 season, when the 1 and 12 Argos played the 2 and 11 Montreal Alouettes—the baby-boom meaning of the Bounce prevailed: to a spectator of that era, it was the unluckiest bounce in the world, the one that usually arose from the Argos' uncanny ability to lose critical games in the dying minutes by committing an improbable blunder (generally the flip-side of a golden opportunity) that resulted in a momentarily free football—more often than not a fumble—which then found its way into the hands of the opposition.

And from the particular the Argo Bounce moved to the metaphorical, to a description of the Argos' horrible lack of fortune in general. The Bounce was used as a synonym for the hex or jinx or "demon of the past" (in the words of Willie Wood, head coach through 1980 and half of '81) that clung to the Argos for twenty-nine years. A crazy piece of strategy, an obscure rule that cropped up perversely in a game's final moments, a terrible player deal, an optimistic comment by a coach whose team was 0 and 8, the tepidness of the grandstand coffee, the traffic jam on the way home from the game—all these, by 1982, came under the general heading of the Bounce. Where the fans of most losing teams could make do with vague generalities, Argo fans have always been saddled with the added catchiness of the Argo Bounce.

Which brings us to the third difference between the Argos and ordinary losing teams: the fans. With the exception of the New York Mets of the early and middle sixties—whose appeal as a refreshing alternative to the Yankees failed to outlive a World Series win in 1969—there has never been a consistently losing team that has commanded as large and devoted a following, or been as profitable at the box office, as the Toronto Argonauts. Between 1971 and 1981, a stretch during which they finished last eight times, the Argos led the Canadian Football League in attendance six times, and finished second in four of the remaining five seasons. By comparison, the two teams closest in total attendance to the Argos over the same period of time were the Edmonton Eskimos and Montreal Alouettes, who between them compiled thirteen Grey Cup appearances during the decade to the Argos' one, seven Grey Cup victories to the Argos' none. The fans of the winning Eskimos and Alouettes were dependable; the fans of the losing Argos were rabid, loyal, and possibly neurotic.

And afraid. So resilient and perverse was this fear that it spilled over into the rising hope of 1982, lurking like a slice of night in the hearts of fans and finally venting itself at a playoff game in November through the hoarse throat of a small, intoxicated man who looked like a miniature Ernest Borgnine in a toque—a true Argo fan.

I was sitting behind him. For twenty-one years of my life, stemming from an afternoon in front of a television set in November of 1961, I have been an Argo fan. It isn't a role I chose: it chose me. Fandom is like that, especially with a team like the Argos. I spent my pre-adolescence taking bar-mitzvah lessons and believing that an orderly intelligence ruled the world, and then one morning I woke up infatuated with a doomed sports team. Since that day I have alternately hated the Argos, and worshipped them, and sworn to turn on soccer games before I'd watch them play again. For twenty years the Argos have been a source of acute hope to me, and utter depression, and hilarity, and finally, hope again—not to mention a seasonal clock by which to remember the different years of my life.

And for six of those pre-rise years I had a slight advantage over other Argo diehards, in terms of occupation. From 1976 to 1981, I wrote a sports column for *Toronto Life* magazine. During my half-dozen years there I covered everything from dinghy-sailing to Grand Prix horse-jumping—but fate conspired to keep bringing me back to the Argos. The first column I wrote was about Anthony Davis, the highly touted running-back from the University of Southern California and the World Football League, who along with Russ Jackson was going to bring the Grey Cup to the Argos in 1976. My last column was about Cedric Minter, who came to Toronto with far less fanfare in 1980 and who turned out to be everything Anthony wasn't. And in the summer of 1982, while an unlikely offensive coach named Mouse Davis was leading no fewer than *eleven* quarterbacks through their spring training paces, I was in the process of finishing a book that I thought would for once and for all lay the spectre of that fandom to rest.

In fact, 1982 did just the opposite.

And so I submit to you the updated version of *The Argo Bounce*, with the thirtieth season since the 1952 Grey Cup included. Like the original version, this one is not a comprehensive, critical history of a pixillated franchise, or even an in-depth study of a team's front office searching for success by using the *I Ching*—either of which would have been edifying—but more a fan's view of the Argo story, the history of the Bounce through thirty years of turmoil, from ragged riches to rich rags to — I'll say it—the land of plenty again; from undeniable excellence to irresistible futility to the "run and shoot". It is still, that is, a compendium of the moments Argo fans would like to forget but never will: Leon McQuay's fumble and Leo Cahill's fall; Ronnie Knox's poetry and Wally Gabler's grin; Sandy Stephen's paunch and Vernon Vanoy's passivity and Tom Dublinski's horrible demise. It's still a litany of Argos past: Claire Exelby and John Atamian, Jim Thorpe and Wonderful Monds, Sherman Lewis, Don Paquette, and Charlie Bray. Which means that it's still the story of anyone who ever loved a losing sports team.

The only difference is in the credibility of the universal fan's whisper: "Wait till next year!"

Let's watch it now: the ovoid ball bouncing. Back, first, to . . .

1 The Last Touchdown

...to 1952. Back, more specifically, to the day a modern fan finds most haunting: November 29, 1952. Back, that is, to the day the Toronto Argonauts beat the Edmonton Eskimos to win their last Grey Cup.

Things start to come into focus with a quick review of the morning edition of the Toronto *Telegram* of that day (as opposed to the special Saturday late edition, which would include a report of the Grey Cup game itself, finished all of an hour earlier). The front page of the paper is sprinkled with (to a fan) mainly peripheral news: the Korean War winding down, Prince Charles turning four, Humphrey Bogart's long-awaited Oscar (for *The African Queen*), and a man being kicked fatally by a plough-horse in the town of Streetsville.

The sports section is the true eye-opener, the window to another world. Reading it, for instance, we discover that although the Argos are a professional football team on this day, they are owned by no trigger-happy tycoon or romantic millionaire (as will become the case for more teams than just the Argos) but by the Argonaut Rowing Club, the same amateur institution that founded the team in 1873 as an off-season rugby outlet for its more restless members. Secondly, the Argos of 1952 do not play in the Canadian Football League, but under the aegis of the Canadian Rugby Union, an umbrella organization that oversees the Big Four (the Eastern League), the Ontario Rugby Football Union (a senior league still technically in the running for the Grey Cup), and the Western Interprovincial Football Union, which includes the four Western teams. Thirdly, they do not play their home games in a stadium lost in the middle of a fairgrounds, but

The 1952 Argos celebrating the Grey Cup victory, the team's last.

in Varsity Stadium, a compact downtown gem of a football field where there isn't a bad seat in the house. Fourthly, the actual diction the *Telegram* uses to describe the Argos and the game of football is fundamentally different from what it will become, in terms of style and energy. The engaging 1952 verbs lead the way. A week ago, we read, in a game against the Hamilton Tiger-Cats, the Argos "whirred" their way to a touchdown on a 64-yard pass from Nobby Wirkowski to Rod Smylie, and Rod Smylie ran "like fury" to avoid being caught from behind.

But it isn't so much what a fan *can* find in the *Tely*'s sports section on this day that seems so unusual, as what he can't: namely, cynicism, surrender, fatalism. In fact the tenor of the Grey Cup articles is just the opposite, a tone of strange, bouncy, innocent security, the kind of blithe optimism you find in old Frank Capra films. A modern fan trying to read between the lines for something negative reads in vain. The optimism is as resilient as indiarubber. No matter what happens, it seems to say, things with the Argos will work out for the best.

And that optimism will be borne out this very afternoon. In the game against the Eskimos, with less than four minutes left to play and the Grey Cup still up for grabs, the Toronto Argonauts will come up with a play, a play called, simply, "three thirty-two across, ends cross", a play that will involve three men directly and one indirectly and will so perfectly epitomize the excellence and luck of the day that thirty years later one of the principals will walk into a bar and hear a voice call out, "Nice play, Zeke!"

This is not apocryphal.

Neither is this: on November 29, 1952, the Argos were generally considered to be the greatest money team in football.

I would love to have coined the phrase myself—"the greatest money team in football"!—but in fact Annis Stukus did, writing in the *Tely* two weeks before the Grey Cup, just before the Argos' third and deciding playoff game against the Hamilton Tiger-Cats. In a way it's perversely fitting that it was Annis, because not only had he played for the Argos—winning the scoring championship in 1938, while the team won the Grey Cup—but of all of the writers who would be raised to heights of astuteness by the Argos over the years, Annis was the least likely candidate for framing a classical phrase. I first became aware of Annis Stukus at about the same time I became a genuine Argo fan, in 1961, when I was twelve and he was appearing on television as a colour commentator for CFL games. At the time Annis struck me as a football dinosaur: he had a profile like a granite wall, and a way of talking about the game that seemed about as sophisticated. When it came to writing about the Argos, though, Annis had a strange habit of coming up with the cliché that impaled the issue through the heart. (In a similar vein, competent journalists like Bob Frewin would be consistently inspired to flashes of insight by the Argos, and excellent writers like Trent Frayne would reach peaks of ironic eloquence — more proof to me of the paradoxical effect of failure on the human imagination.)

The scenario that led up to Annis making his claim was this: the Argos, who had "struggled" through a disappointing injury-plagued season, had still managed to finish 7-4-1 on the season and had come into the two-game total-point playoff series against the Tiger-Cats as decided underdogs. They proceeded to win the first game in Hamilton, though, by a margin of 16 points. Four days later, on a Wednesday afternoon, Hamilton came into Varsity Stadium and won the second game by exactly the same margin, tying the series and dictating overtime — except that darkness had fallen and there were no lights in Varsity Stadium, football being at that time a game you played by natural light. A third game was scheduled for the weekend. It's at this point that a modern Argo fan would feel his heart begin to steel itself for the fall, but in 1952 it was at this point — in the *Telegram* of November 13 — that Annis made his remarkable statement. "On paper," he wrote, "Hamilton should win. But the Argos have two assets. One is their tradition as the greatest money club in football, a club that has a consistent record of winning the big games. The other is the ability of coach Frank Clair as a defensive strategist."

Frank Clair and his strategy we will get to shortly; at the moment what's important is that, even without the corroborating evidence of the Argos' subsequent 12-7 win over the Tiger-Cats in the third playoff game (with Nobby Wirkowski "whirring" his 64-yard touchdown pass to Rod Smylie), what Annis had written about the Argos' tradition was common knowledge.

Just how common the knowledge was is obvious as soon as you consider the record of the Argos up to that time. In fact a fan sitting down thirty years ago to write an Argonaut retrospective would have been in exactly the *opposite* predicament from me — writing about a chronic winner. Up to 1952 the Argos had won nine Grey Cups. Of those nine victories six had come within the last fifteen seasons, four within the last seven. But those nine Grey Cup victories concealed an amazing fact: since the inception in 1921 of Canadian football's "modern era", when Western teams first began contesting the championship, the Argos had never lost a Grey Cup final; having reached the vital game, that is, they had always proved superior to their opponent. The Argos of 1952 were the epitome of "Clutch".

It's difficult to try to narrow down the long list of examples that exist to illustrate this Argo phenomenon — but for facility's sake I'll cite two: the Argos' last two Grey Cup victories prior to 1952, the wins of '47 and '50. Not only are they prime examples of grace under pressure but, despite their closeness in time, they were achieved by Argo teams of two completely distinct eras: the Canadian era, and the post-American-import era. The '47 win belonged to the Canadian era, and was the third in a string of consecutive victories from 1945 on (a record at the time), all of them achieved at the expense of the Winnipeg Blue Bombers, by an Argo team *made up almost exclusively of Canadian players*. The Argos of the day, under coach Tedder Morris, were a dozen times more deserving of the label "Canada's team" than an over-slick Dallas Cowboy team would be of the name "America's team" some twenty years down the road. Although American imports were already playing a significant role on most of the other Canadian teams, the Argos still had a virtual Canadians-only policy. (Considering what would one day be a near-fatal affinity for anything with the stamp "U.S.A.", it is an item of pure irony.)

For the '47 Grey Cup the Blue Bombers had conversely arrived in Toronto with a roster bulging with large, celebrated American imports — the growing Western trend at the time. The consensus among football analysts of the day was that the Argos were about to meet their Waterloo. As Tony Allan points out in his definitive history of Western Canadian football, *Grey Cup or Bust: The Fabulous Story of the West's Eternal Quest*, "[The Bombers] wouldn't be out merely to 'make a good showing' — they would be out to win." In the first half of the game, the Blue Bombers took a 9-1 lead and looked unassailable. In the third quarter, though, Joe Krol (one half of the Argos' legendary Touchdown Twins) connected with Royal Copeland (the other half) for a touchdown pass (worth five points at the time) and kicked the convert, making the score 9-7. At that point the Bombers defence stiffened, so much so that in the fourth quarter the Argos switched to a novel strategy — playing territorial football, playing for the single point. It was a strategy based on undiluted confidence; to even consider it, the Argos had to be sure they could hold Winnipeg off the scoreboard, avoid making turn-overs, and in the meantime get possession of the ball enough times to let punting take its toll.

By the last minute, Joe Krol had kicked two singles and the score was tied at 9. With less than forty seconds showing on the clock quarterback Bob Sandberg, one of Winnipeg's Americans, inexplicably elected to call for a running play instead of a kick on third and two inside his own 40-yard line. The Argos stopped Winnipeg cold, and with just enough time left for one play Joe Krol stepped back to the 45-yard line, took the snap, and punted the ball through the end-zone, giving the Argos a 10-9 win and their third Grey Cup victory in as many years.

The 1950 win demonstrated the Argos' "Clutch" even more dramatically. In 1948 the Argos had slipped to third place, and by 1949, the watershed year of the huge influx of American players into Canadian football (due in part to the CRU's relaxing the import regulations in 1948), it became obvious that there was no way they could continue to compete with a Canadians-only policy. The course the team decided to take at this juncture was probably made easier for them by the collapse of the All-America Football Conference — along with the NFL one of the two professional American leagues — in 1949, and the subsequent availability of large numbers of quality American players. With the calmness of true champions the Argos cleaned house and hired imports of their own, men named Hirsch and Whaley and Bass Dekdebrun and Curtis. To coach the team they hired another American, the second half of Annis Stukus's equation for Argo success and one of the four men ultimately responsible for the mythical play that would electrify 27,000 people on a November afternoon in 1952 — Frank Clair.

Certain names have an immediate ring of familiar magic to a contemporary Argo fan looking back, and Frank Clair's is certainly one of them. For whatever reasons, Frank is also the first "character" in the Argo story I feel comfortable performing the fan's abbreviation on, and identifying by his Christian name only. This is the fan's equivalent of the French *tu*, and a definite problem for a sports journalist. As far as I know, it has no parallel in other arenas of North American culture. Calling Elvis Presley

"Elvis" is not the same. Calling a famous physicist by his first name — as in "Albert" or "Max" — is probably closer, in terms of eccentric affection.

No discussion of the Argo "Clutch" would be complete without a brief sketch of Frank Clair himself. After graduating from Ohio State, Frank had made his professional football debut (playing end) with the Washington Redskins in 1940, a scant seven months after they had lost 73-0 to the Chicago Bears in one of the most overwhelming, important defeats in football history. (In fact the Argos over the years would become curiously entangled with this famous NFL debacle, the game in which the Bears' quarterback, Sid Luckman, under the direction of coach George "Papa" Hallas, established — in the space of sixty minutes — the new strategic thrust of modern offensive football: the T formation.) Frank's year with the Redskins was followed by a stretch in the army, during which he apprenticed under the already legendary Paul Brown; after that came three years as an assistant coach at the University of Miami of Ohio under Sid Gilman. After Miami of Ohio Frank spent two years at the University of Buffalo, then crossed the Peace Bridge and came to the Argos in 1950.

The first thing Frank did in Toronto was to discard the old single-wing formation of Tedder Morris and Joe Krol and Royal Copeland (with its shotgun-type snap), substituting the straight T, the same one — with a man added — that Sid Luckman had used to plunder the Washington Redskins. The second thing Frank did, from all reports, was to introduce the Argos and the city to the cult of *preparation*. With all due respect to Annis Stukus and his "defensive strategist" theory, I believe that this was Frank's true contribution to the Argo Clutch of the time. His obsession with game movies was a case in point. Frank may not have been the first coach in Canada to use films, but he was the first to communicate spiritually with them. Years later, John Kerns, one of Frank's playing assistant coaches at the time, would recall watching Frank spend three hours viewing the same ten-second section from a Montreal-Ottawa game film, before Frank isolated what was bothering him: Alouette running-back Gene "Choo-Choo" Roberts was drop-stepping a count early, thus telegraphing when he would be carrying the ball. Four days later the Argos derailed Choo-Choo and beat the Als decisively. It was probably this sort of exhaustive thoroughness that earned Frank his nickname, "the Professor"; either that or the two apparently paradoxical sides of his character. "Immaculate in a business suit, wide-brimmed fedora and plastic-rimmed glasses, he looks like a professor or a lawyer," one writer observed, while another called him "a thin, nervous guy who was always in a dither." The latter description probably referred to Frank either trying to eat, or at game time, when he generally became terrifically excited, so much so that his two assistant playing coaches, Kerns and Buckets Hirsch, ended up doing most of the actual game coaching themselves. A picture of Frank holding the Grey Cup after the 1950 victory, with Joe Krol's arm around him, shows an exhausted, smiling man with a boyish, wet face, all but lost inside his overcoat. From Monday to Friday, though, he was brilliant.

Nowhere did Frank's preparedness and the Argos' Clutch mesh more effectively than during the 1950 Grey Cup game. The horrible conditions the game was played under provided a perfect test for the "marriage". It had snowed all week prior to the Cup, and the groundskeepers at Varsity Stadium, apparently unfamiliar with an American innovation called the tarpaulin — or perversely opposed to it — had let the snow pile up, only to try to remove it with bulldozers two days before the game, in thawing temperatures. They eventually got rid of the snow, but in the process reduced the field to a rutted quagmire, the basis for the game's eventual historical label, "the Mud Bowl".

From most reports the condition of the field didn't seem to bother the Argos. They weren't bothered either, apparently, by the fact that Winnipeg was led by one of the great passing quarterbacks of all time, Indian Jack Jacobs. If the Bombers had Indian Jack, the Argos had that intangible, the Argo instinct for exactly what it would take to win. They also had Frank Clair. All week Frank had scoured various sports stores and athletic facilities in the city, searching for a possible Argo edge, until at the University of Toronto's athletic department he finally unearthed a set of what Argo trainer Walt Huntley called the "biggest, longest, danged cleats I ever saw." The cleats worked, as did the thumbtacks that Argo quarterback Al Dekdebrun, recruited by Clair from Buffalo, taped to the fingers and thumb of his throwing hand.

The Argos won the game 13-0, providing a neat reversal — in terms of astute, critical equipment selection — for a playoff game against Russ Jackson and the Ottawa Roughriders in 1968, when the Roughriders would use broom-ball shoes to sink the traction-less Argos. In fact the reversal would be just one part of a perverse Argo pattern that would ultimately emerge: for every disaster the Argos would fall prostrate in front of in the lean years to come, you could find a similar predicament they had somehow managed to scale in the old days. It was as though there were a mirror-image cabbala at work.

But the most revealing incident from the 1950 Grey Cup was also the most famous image of that game. In the middle of the second quarter a player was knocked unconscious and fell, face down, in a pool of water and ooze. He lay there, ignored for a long count, and the consensus of opinion is that if referee Hec Crighton hadn't finally noticed him and rolled him over he would have drowned. At the risk of sounding callous, a very pertinent point for an Argo fan looking back is not so much the personal identity of the endangered player—his name was Buddy Tinsley—but his affiliation: Buddy Tinsley played for Winnipeg. The point is, he wasn't an Argo.

The overall point is, as of 1952 the Argos were a classic example of one of the two basic species of teams that consistently win in professional sport. One of these is the genus of the "powerhouse", teams like the Montreal Canadiens of the late fifties, or the New York Yankees of several eras, that dominate through sheer talent. The other species is the more interesting and rare: the team whose greatest plus is no particular player, but an intangible quality: the instinctive knowledge of what is required to win. The Boston Celtics have traditionally been this sort of team, with John Havelicek coming off the bench with his unlikely gait, or Bill Russell frustrating an awesome Wilt Chamberlain with his defensive guile—but it's difficult to imagine a team that knew how to win more than the Argos of the early fifties. They were the consummate professional team, the team that would ultimately figure out a way—orthodox or not—to beat you. They were canny, resilient, maddening.

They were also the team that Trent Frayne wrote about in September of 1951 in *Maclean's* magazine, in an article entitled, "Why They All Hate the Argos". For a modern fan, the article is a voyage backwards in time. Accompanying the text is a colour picture of a row of Argonauts (with brush-cuts) down on one knee on the turf at Varsity, in pale blue uniforms with navy stripes on the arms. The colour of the photograph is over-vivid, as is the sense of innocent optimism in the young Argo faces looking out at the camera. At the same time, these Argos somehow seem more solid to me, more like *men*, than any of the Argos I would personally watch after them. Under the photograph is the caption "Almost everyone who knows football will tell you that the Argos are lucky, stuffy, and stingy." In the body of the article itself we can read, "This is the time of year to say that the Argos are the luckiest team that ever fumbled a football and recovered it while looking the other way"; and then, farther down the page, there it is, perfectly matter-of-fact, with no irony whatsoever: "The Argonauts have done so well over the years with loose balls which take weird bounces and wind up in Argonaut arms that they have injected a new phrase into the language; nowadays, when a team — any team — fumbles the ball and recovers it, that team is said to have been saved by the Argo bounce."

The Bounce.

The Grey Cup of 1952 began at 1:32 p.m. On the opening kick-off, Joe Krol — now a kicker only, a shadow of his former self — toed a high deep one to the Edmonton nine, where it was caught by Rollie Prather of the Eskimos and returned to the 36. Rod Pantages took a handoff from Claude Arnold, the passing Sooner, and rammed for three up the middle. Rollie Miles, the great "coloured flash", stumbled on the next play, but had no hole anyway, and the Eskimos were forced to kick, which they did, to Ed Soergel, the great Argo end, who ran it back a scant three yards to the Argo 36. Billy Bass, one of the two black players on the Argos at the time, went nowhere off-tackle on the first play, and on the second, a long Wirkowski pass to the other, more celebrated black Argo, Uly (Ulysses) "Crazy Legs" Curtis, was tipped away at the Edmonton 25 — and Joe went back to kick again.

Over the next ten minutes the game lapsed into a kicking contest, with neither team going anywhere. The Eskimos were completely nullifying Uly Curtis, the brilliant, elusive-legged halfback out of Florida A. and M. (Curtis was believed by some to be the best all-round back ever to play for the team; "In my opinion," Nobby Wirkowski would say, "Dick Shatto couldn't have carried Uly Curtis's jock-strap.") The Argos, aided by the erratic passing of Claude Arnold, were doing an equally good job on Rollie Miles and "the China Clipper", Normie Kwong. One of the most effective runners in the early going was Doug Pyzer, a little "fireplug" of a scatback who had just come off the Argo bench the game before. Like another fireplug who would take to the field a decade later for the Argos, a player named Bobby Kuntz, Doug had a stocky Clutch all his own. At one point, with the Argos mired at their own 16, Doug "*beetled* wide for 12" (the *Telegram*'s verb again) for the team's initial first down of the game.

The Eskimos drew first blood. Just before the end of the quarter the official attendance was announced — 27,391, a new Grey Cup record. Rod Smylie, the hero from the Hamilton playoff, was knocked cold, and Claude Arnold connected with Rod Pantages for a 63-yard pass and run to the Argo 11. The play actually went 73 yards to the Argo 1, but Pantages fumbled out of bounds at that point, incurring a 10-yard penalty (a perfectly logical punishment, the elimination of which has never been properly explained beyond the fact that it coincided with American rules). Two running plays later, from Kwong and Miles, the Eskimos led 5-0.

But now the Eskimos' place kicker, Wilbur Snyder, missed the convert. It was a small mistake, the kind that generally only fuzzes the sharp edges of elation for the erring team, but that happened so often to teams that played the Argos. On the first series of downs following the Edmonton kick-off Nobby Wirkowski found Doug Pyzer alone in the flat. Doug ran and ran down the sideline like a blurred mite, to the Edmonton 15, where he swivelled 360 degrees to avoid one Eskimo back, ducked three more, and was finally knocked down on the 1-yard line. Nobby snuck over on the next play. Red Ettinger did not miss the convert, and the Argos led 6-5.

And then the teams changed ends for the second quarter and the game seemed to speed up as the Argos came on. The quarter was *all* Argos, as fast and pell-mell as a sportswriter's fingers on a typewriter's keys. Who says that television is the next best thing to being there? Consider the *Telegram*'s line-copy:

> Miles got open in the flat for a pass, evaded Bass and gained 13 before Karrys smothered him with a jump. King made two on a draw play. Arnold just got the pass away but missed Miles by miles. Pantages kicked, dropped the snap again but again saved Edmonton to kick to Copeland who was downed on the Argo 35.

Missed Miles by miles? And Copeland? Yes, it was Royal himself, relegated to playing defensive back and returning the odd punt, but still comporting himself like one of the "Touchdown Twins". Half-way through the second quarter he came within inches of intercepting an Arnold pass. Shortly thereafter Red Ettinger kicked a field goal to make it 9-5. And on the next Argo possession Wirkowski hit Al Bruno, who carried the ball all the way down to the 10-yard line. Bill Bass ran it in two plays later, giving the Argos a secure lead of 15-5 at the half.

At least the lead seemed secure. The teams came out for the second half, and Edmonton almost immediately stole back that translucent cliché, Momentum. To their credit they did it the hard way, with an incredible goal-line stand in the second minute of the half, stopping the Argos three times from the 3-yard line. Another touchdown would have finished the Eskimos, but now instead they were revitalized. The spectre of a comeback was in the air. (The Eskimos had only reached the Grey Cup, the fans at Varsity were no doubt remembering with paranoia, by pulling off two pure Hollywood come-from-behind playoff victories over the Calgary Stampeders and the Winnipeg Blue Bombers.) Half-way through the quarter the Eskimos put together a 62-yard march, with Normie Kwong scoring his second touchdown of the game on a slashing 8-yard run to make it 15-11.

The quarter ended, and still the Eskimos kept coming. The only thing stopping them from taking the lead seemed to be the incredible luck of the Argos—that and the Eskimo's own ineptitude inside the 20-yard line. In *Grey Cup or Bust*, Tony Allan would later claim that "if Filchock [Frank Filchock, the Eskimos' playing coach] had been out there directing traffic, they'd have run the Argos clear into Bloor Street." The truth is that, even without Frankie Filchock's direction, an Edmonton touchdown seemed like a foregone conclusion—several expert observers had already conceded it to them, and were also in the process of conceding the Grey Cup. With seven minutes left the Eskimos moved to the Argo 17, only to have Art Scullion knock down a third-down pass attempt.

On their very next possession—six minutes left now—the Eskimos moved, in three plays, to the 17 *again*. This time Arnold threw a screen pass on first down that fell short. At the time, though, any pass thrown behind the line of scrimmage, forward or not, was a live ball (another exciting rule gone by). The Argos recovered—Scullion again. The Argos went nowhere. Krol had to kick on third down, and except for a desperation tackle by Don

"Shanty" McKenzie at the 36 the Eskimos might have scored on the punt return. Incredibly, instead of running the ball at the decimated Toronto line, Claude Arnold — spooked maybe by a particular species of Argo voodoo that had appeared before and would continue to hand the Argos wildly improbable chances to win in the years to come — threw on first down, to no nearby Eskimo, but directly into the hands of Ed Soergel, the Argo end.

Over the stadium the blue of the sky was darkening, and reality was threatening to crack. Three times in a row the Argos, hopelessly on the ropes, had been saved by miraculous turn-overs. It couldn't last. The next time Edmonton got the ball they would certainly score, and take a lead the exhausted Argos would never overcome. The string had run out. There were four minutes left in the game. It was time.

What happened next has that suspended quality of certain moments in sport, frozen motion, events excised out of time. Possibly this has something to do with the numerical simplicity of the moment: there were only four minutes left on the clock at this point, and for all intents and purposes there were only three players left on the Varsity Stadium field.

Two of them were bent over in the Argo huddle; the third was standing on the Edmonton side of scrimmage. The shorter of the two Argos, the man about to call the play, happened to be playing in his first full season as a professional. The year before, in the middle of the 1951 season, Frank Clair had noticed while studying game films (where else?) that Al Dekdebrun, the quarterback he had brought from Buffalo, was favouring his throwing arm. Getting rid of Dekdebrun, Frank would later claim, was the hardest thing he'd ever done as a coach. To replace Dekdebrun Frank had gone back to his coaching Alma Mater, and from a graduating class that included three men named Ara Parseghian, Woody Hayes, and Bo Schembechler (a kind of patriarch's row of crazy coincidence) he plucked a stubby, blunt Polish quarterback named Nobby Wirkowski. Nobby had played the rest of the season with the Argos, helping them rally to a 7 and 5 record and a share of first place. In the off-season George "Papa" Halas of the Chicago Bears, who had pursued Nobby out of College, had finally offered him as much money as the Argos were paying him — but Nobby decided to reject the overture on the grounds that it could have come earlier and more forthrightly. He stayed with the Argos.

What would a fan have noticed about Nobby if he had slipped into the huddle now, in the pause before Nobby called the play? Most likely he would have noted his size. Listed at 5'11 in the program, Nobby was nowhere close. In years to come his size or lack of it would follow him like a bad cloud, although Nobby, being Nobby, would never blink at it. "He was terribly small," one writer would remember. "When he had to come out of the pocket it looked like he was running on his knees." And from one of his colleagues: "Nobby? He had an exceptionally fine arm, and he was a pretty good play-caller; if only he'd been a bit taller. . . ." At the moment, however, in the huddle, Nobby's size probably had more defiance than pathos to it. As a rookie, Nobby had already started to grow the armour he would need to deal with a hundred late hits and other blows — among them the charge that he was the greatest *practice* quarterback in the history of football, and conversely terrible in games.

Now, with four minutes left to play in the game, the whirring slot machine that was Nobby's mind finally came to rest on a play: three thirty-two across, ends cross. "Three signified that it was a pass," Nobby would later explain, with characteristic economy, "thirty-two meant that it came off a run, it was a play action pass, one fake outside, one inside. End cross meant that the ends crisscrossed: Al Bruno, the primary receiver, went down about ten and then cut left to right, and O'Connor cut from right to left about five yards underneath him as a decoy."

The O'Connor Nobby referred to was hunched over in the huddle to his left. Half a foot taller than Nobby, Zeke O'Connor was an urbane articulate American tight end (at least the big, slow 1952 equivalent) who had the kind of nasal, perennially youthful American-accented voice that would have been at home in a J. D. Salinger short story. He had played his college ball with Notre Dame and played professionally with the New York football Yankees and the Cleveland Browns. When he came to the Argos in the spring of '52 he enjoyed the large field and most of the rule changes (although he would never be sure about three downs) and the small but enthusiastic crowds. He liked Toronto itself so much that, although he would only play for the team for two years, he would continue to live in the city and become the vice-president of a department store chain. In that capacity he would meet the British climber Sir Edmund Hillary and become good friends with him, travelling to Nepal six times to visit the Sherpas and the base camp of Everest. None of those visits to the foothills of the gods would be more vivid in his mind, however, than the Argo play that was about to unfold.

Nobby brought the Argos out over the ball. The sound of the crowd was steady and agonized — but not too loud for Nobby to call the signals. The snap came back; he spun, executed his fakes to Billy Bass and Doug Pyzer, dropped back, looked up, and saw something remarkable.

On the Eskimo side of scrimmage Al Bruno, the "more famous" receiver (in the *Telegram's* words), had gone down his ten yards and started his cut from left to right. The Eskimo back responsible for covering Bruno, Bob Paffrath, had started to go with him, that was clear. But it wasn't the back on that side who was important at the moment, but the man covering the other side, the man covering Zeke O'Connor — Frankie Filchock. Frankie, the third man. Frankie Filchock, not only the playing coach of the Eskimos on this particular day, I should point out, but also the Frankie Filchock who twelve years earlier, on a November day in 1940, had played by crazy coincidence on the Washington Redskin team that had been on the losing end of the 73-0 Chicago Bear annihilation. It was the same Frankie Filchock who had been implicated, then cleared, in a $100,000 betting scandal in 1946 while preparing with the New York Giants for yet another championship game against the Bears; who had found refuge in Canada, first in Hamilton, then in Montreal, before finally being brought to Edmonton by the coach he would replace, Annis Stukus himself; who, maybe in one final attempt to wipe out the last traces of suspicion that still lurked in the minds of men — it's an Argo fan's point of view, tragic but plausible — would now immortalize himself by having an inspiration and calling for a "switch" to Bob Paffrath, indicating that Paffrath should ignore Bruno and pick up coverage of O'Connor, while Frankie himself went after the more famous Bruno. Except that Paffrath didn't hear him — maybe it was the crowd — and Zeke was in the clear.

Standing in the crowd, writer Bob Frewin felt the lady behind him suddenly begin to pummel him on the back, pointing and wailing, "O'Connor! Look at O'Connor!" The crowd was on its feet, pointing, imploring, with disbelief and excitement and that fan's anxiety that maybe the most important person wouldn't notice in time. "Zeke! Look! He's *open!*" And as a tag end to the scene, like something small in the midst of largeness to uplift or break your heart (depending on whom you were pulling for), Al Bruno himself slowed down and tapped Frankie Filchock on the shoulder and pointed to Zeke as well.

It was about now that Nobby did notice, and threw.

What eludes a modern Argo fan are the details. What was it really like in Varsity Stadium, with Nobby's pass looping out to the left and the crowd on its feet at the peak of that collective hopeful inhalation? How perfect was the ball's spiral, how crisp was the air, how long was it going to take to get home after the game? I probably wonder about these things because an Argo fan learns to be distracted by style over the years, so that he doesn't have to dwell on the ruins of the content. But it was 1952, and Nobby's pass came arching down into Zeke's hands.

Even here there was some controversy. The *Telegram* has Zeke "stumbling" as the pass reached him, but Zeke himself would remember it as a deliberate stutter-step to adjust to the ball ("a beautiful pass nevertheless"), which was a bit high and behind him. "*Behind* him?" Nobby would say. "If anything it was in front of him; I remember that he had to go for it a little more." Stutter-stepping, stumbling, Zeke reached back and in front of him for his nevertheless beautiful pass, and caught it, and held it, and turned, and ran down the sideline into the south-eastern corner of the end-zone for the touchdown that made the score 21-11, and sealed the Grey Cup victory for the Argos.

Four minutes later the fans were chanting "Number Ten!" (for the tenth Argo Grey Cup win in their last ten attempts) and surging onto the field like old, delirious hands to tear down the goal-posts. Who could blame them? In the fan's scheme of things they had something to tell their grandchildren: they had seen Zeke O'Connor's catch.

As it turned out they had also seen the last offensive touchdown the Argos would score in a Grey Cup Game for at least twenty-nine years (the last Grey Cup touchdown *altogether* until a linesman named Roger Scales picked up a fumble in 1971). They had seen the end of the Argos as they were. They had watched the last benign journey of the Argo Bounce.

2 You Are My Sonshine

In 1953 the Argos slipped to a 5-9 record and last place in the Eastern Conference. It was an unquestionable comedown for a team of pride, but the remarkable thing about it was the public reaction: never had fans or press been more understanding. "Like Jack and Jill the Argonauts went over the hill together," wrote Bob Frewin in the *Telegram*. "There was one difference: the Argonauts never returned." What was happening to the Argos, it was generally held, was a by-product of the natural ageing of champions. To my mind this was as impenetrable a piece of sports wisdom in 1953 as it is now — how do two dozen superbly conditioned, alert athletes turn frail and uncertain in the space of a year?

But with the Argos there *was* some fairly convincing evidence in the ageing theory's favour. Of the twenty-eight men listed on the Double Blue roster for the '52 Grey Cup, fourteen would be gone by the end of the '53 season, and another six by the end of '54. Ed Soergel, the great defensive halfback who made the critical interception that led to Zeke's catch, would not even make it into the '53 season; Zeke himself finished 1953 with the team, then joined the retail world.

And at half-time of the last Argo game of the 1953 season (a 27-8 loss to the Alouettes) Joe Krol, aged thirty-four, officially retired from football. The picture of the ceremony says it all: Joe, unhelmetted but in uniform — sweater number 55 — beside his wife and son, in front of the round-nosed double-blue Oldsmobile the team had given him in honour of his already legendary career.

All three Toronto papers ran feature stories on the event, and buried in the stories were a number of items, particulars of Joe's

Harry Sonshine, the fan who took over the Argos.

history and testaments to his greatness, that to me still sport an aura of football magic. Joe's famous last-second kick to win the 1947 Grey Cup was completely overshadowed, for example, by a description of an earlier kick in the '46 Cup victory: in the third quarter of that game, with the Argos ahead 16-0, Joe had dropped back to the Winnipeg 50 on third down, and calmly toed a coffin-corner punt, high enough and pinpoint enough that Royal Copeland—who had been onside at the time of the kick—had time to run underneath it and *catch it on the fly* between two Winnipeg defenders, falling out of touch on the 1-yard line. It was the equivalent of a fifty-yard pass, "thrown" with a *foot*, released with the eventual receiver of the pass still parallel with the quarterback.

There was also the story of Joe's brief foray into American professional football, a story that involved the Detroit Lions (the same team Royal Copeland had an abortive tryout with) and that once again seemed to reinforce the notion that the Argos as a team have been magnetically drawn over the years to peaks of American football legend. During the Second World War, while Joe was attending the University of Western Ontario, intercollegiate play in Canada was suspended briefly, forcing colleges like Western, that continued to field teams, to play exhibition games with American schools. The games were generally mismatches in favour of the Americans, and a game Western played against the University of Detroit in 1940 was no exception—except that during the trouncing Joe scored three touchdowns, distinguished himself as the best player on the field, and caught the eye of the Detroit coach, Gus Dorais. When the same Gus Dorais became coach of the National Football League's Detroit Lions three seasons later, he invited Joe to try out with the NFL team, which Joe finally did in 1945. Joe's brief stay with the Lions is shrouded with conjecture. According to some reports he got tired of sitting on the bench and departed himself; according to others, his loping and effortless style of running was *so* loping and effortless that Gus Dorais mistook it for loafing. "I was at the Lions' camp, and asked Gus Dorais what he thought of Krol," recalls Annis Stukus. "Dorais said, 'He's the second-fastest runner on the team; he's the best passer I've got; the best runner, and one of the best pass-receivers. He's the best *kicker* I've ever seen in my life. And I'm going to cut him. He won't hustle.'" If Annis's story is correct, it was a premature illustration of a pattern that would surface again with the Argos: the clash of American and Canadian legends. Joe Krol was Joe Krol, and Gus Dorais was not only the Lions' coach, but also the first man in football history anywhere to have thrown a forward pass — to a receiver named Knute Rockne.

In 1953, though, Joe's departure from the Argos wasn't considered particularly ominous, at least according to the newspaper reaction. The team had survived greater traumas — the wholesale restructuring of 1950 was one — and emerged with their tradition intact. There seemed to be no plausible reason why this situation should be any different.

The 1954 season started under the same arch of grace. Times being what they were, the sports pages generally didn't turn to the Argos until the last week in July, by which time fans were probably hungering for news of the team, as opposed to fearing it. (The lure of football in the summer in Canada is probably closer to the spring-training lure of baseball for Americans than to anything else. No equivalent exists for hockey — who craves winter?) So it is that the Argos don't surface on the sports page until July 31, with Frank Clair giving a characteristically modest interview in which he says the same thing three different ways, and makes one interesting prediction — that, in view of the team's youth, the Argos will be strong in the *second* half of the season — interesting to me because, in the years to come, I would rarely have the patience or the mental serenity to wait for the second half of the season. Aside from Frank's interview, the only mildly Argoish item on the sports page was the news that the Argos had signed Billy Cross, or "Bitsy Billy" as he was known, a 5'6 150-pound "pony-back" who had played three years with the Bears and Cardinals of Chicago in the NFL and had never been hurt. A good pass-receiver and a so-so runner, Billy had in fact been about to retire to run his sporting-goods store in Amarillo, Texas, when the Argo call for help came. "The Cardinals won't sue," the story continued. "They aren't interested in small halfbacks this year."

But Rule Number One of modern Argo fandom — and fandom in general for that matter — could be this: nothing is as dangerous as serenity. Two weeks after Frank Clair gave his interview, on a night when the air at Varsity Stadium was, in the words of Trent Frayne, "heavy with humidity and derision from the stands", the Argos lost their opening exhibition game, "amateurishly", by a score of 18-7, to the same Edmonton Eskimos they had out-clutched less than twenty months before to win the Grey Cup.

From the crow's nest of the present the game sounds like a minor catastrophe at worst. The margin of loss was small, and on the Argo scale of abuse "amateurishly" is pretty mild. But three nights later, in Winnipeg, where the team had gone for another exhibition game against the Blue Bombers, four men met in a suite of a Winnipeg hotel with a theatrical name, the Royal Alexandra.

The meeting (which was eventually described in a *Maclean's* magazine article, by Trent Frayne again) had been called by Bill Ross, the president of the Argonaut Rowing Club, which at this point still owned the Argos. Present were three other men, two of them fellow executive members with the rowing club, Joe Wright and Ted Punchard. For the first five minutes or so the three "sombre executives paced and fretted, until Bill Ross took it on himself to bring things to a head. 'We can't have our own fans down on us like this. We're off $40,000 in season-ticket sales and we won no friends against Edmonton.'" And then Bill Ross did the one small thing that, without too much overstatement, may be said to have sealed the fate of the Argos and the legion of unfortunates who would love them for ever.

He turned and said, "You got any notions, Harry?"

The man Bill Ross was addressing, the fourth man in the room, was not an Argonaut Rowing Club executive. He was, though, a man who had played for the Argos himself between 1937-39, who had once disguised himself as a University of Michigan freshman at that team's training camp at Ann Arbor to spy on the Blue Bombers' plays for the Argos, and who at the age of forty-one had amassed enough money to enable him to accompany the Argos on most of their road trips, even as far as Winnipeg and the Royal Alexandra Hotel.

His name was Harry Sonshine.

"I'm sick to death of seeing us get kicked around," said Sonshine bluntly (Trent Frayne's words). "'The trouble, I'm convinced, is our material—the imports just don't measure up. Would you fellows, for example, *trade our Americans for Montreal's?*'

"The three of them reluctantly agreed that they'd not hesitate to make the swap.

"'Well,' said Sonshine, 'it's not too late. If Frank agrees, I'll try to help.'

"'We'll spend a hundred thousand dollars if we have to,' Ross told Sonshine. 'I've had enough of this kicking around.'"

Any fan considering the story to this point would probably have his curiosity pricked by one pivotal item: the question of Bill Ross's state of mind at the moment he made his decision. Anxiety is an outside possibility, maybe even panic. It was true that the Argos had won two Grey Cups in the last four years, and that they had lost a total of a mere nine regular-season games since their last Grey Cup victory—but it was also true that the '53 season was, amazingly, only their *fifth* losing season since 1921 and the beginning of the "modern era". Only twice before had the Argos ever had back-to-back losing seasons. Faced with that prospect, maybe Bill Ross decided extreme measures were necessary.

Another possibility that would gain a following over the years was that Bill Ross was trying to take the Argos back in time—to "steal" the team back from Frank Clair and the new American import influence, and return to the days when the Argos were Canada's team. Given this scenario, what better aid could Bill Ross enlist than that of someone who had played for the Argos of the old era? This theory seems unlikely to me (not to mention ultimately ironic in the Argo scheme of things), but you can never tell with owners.

Panic-stricken, or maybe blinded by nostalgia, Bill Ross handed the Argos (and my fate as a fan) to Harry Sonshine.

To an Argo fan of any era, Harry Sonshine has to be acknowledged as the first light of craziness on the Argo horizon. Harry's story is so compellingly crazy that it may be unique in the history of professional sport. As a sports journalist in the 1970s I certainly never came across anything like it. When I did encounter it for the first time, I was absorbed enough in its engaging unlikeliness that I tended to completely overlook Harry's role as a principal guide in leading the Argos down the garden path they've followed for the last quarter-century. But Harry's is a guilt that even the most generous football analyst could not airbrush completely. Harry's best friend would have trouble denying it. "Sonshine was well remembered as a player", wrote Gordon Currie in his history of the CFL, "who when he played for the Argos . . . usually refused to wear a helmet: his unprotected head could often be seen butting into the opposing linemen, clearing a path for his teammates. Such tactics, when applied to the tasks of a team executive, were notably less successful and Sonshine is credited with much of the blame for the Argonauts' dismal record for nine of the next fourteen years." Gordon Currie's claim is probably an understatement. For one thing, he wrote his book in 1968—the Argos still had at least thirteen more years to let Harry's magic work its wonders. For another thing, Currie failed to mention that Harry created his legacy of doom in exactly *eighteen* official months with the Argos.

To try to understand what it was about Harry Sonshine that qualified him for his role as saviour-scourge of the Argos in 1954, and ever since, you have to look first at his background. The son of Ben Sonshine, a manufacturer of interior fixture fittings, Harry went to Queen's University and, despite his 140-pound weight, starred at wingback there on the Varsity team. After graduating with a Bachelor of Commerce degree he signed to play for the Argonauts under Lew Hayman (ironically the single other name most commonly linked to the Argos' demise). He subsequently played three years with the Argos, including the Grey Cup-winning seasons of '37 and '38, when the team was in the midst of establishing itself as a dynasty.

Prophetically, Harry's greatest service to the Argos as a player was rendered off the field, not on. Prevented by a broken jaw from playing in the 1937 Grey Cup, Harry travelled to Ann Arbor, to the football fields of the University of Michigan where the Winnipeg Blue Bombers, the Argos' oppponents in the Cup that year, were training. Putting a University of Michigan's freshman tam on his head—disguising himself as an American student, that is—he struck up a conversation with Fritz Hanson, a renowned Winnipeg halfback from North Dakota. "Hey, this game's not so different from our game, is it?" Harry is said to have remarked to Hanson. "Fundamentally, the same game," said Hanson. Harry politely asked what the difference was, and Hanson just as politely embarked on a detailed discussion of the singularities of Canadian football, using the Blue Bomber offence and game plan as illustrations. When Hanson trotted out onto the field at Varsity Stadium the next week, the first person he saw was the freshman from Michigan, sitting on the Argo bench beside Lew Hayman. It was a perfect illustration of the mettle of the old Argos. Using Harry's inside information, the Double Blue neutralized the Bomber attack and won the game and the Grey Cup, 4-3.

Harry finished his career with the Argos in 1939, at the outbreak of the war, and in the five years that followed he worked as a stockbroker, salesman, and general superintendent of a truck transport company, a job he would one day describe as invaluable experience: "The guys driving inter-city trucks in those days," Harry was quoted as saying in a magazine article, "were the toughest, shrewdest bunch of bandits in the world. Handling them was a murderous job because if one of them figured he could beat you he'd steal your socks." Most likely Harry used a word other than socks—he was no shrinking violet. In 1946 he went from trucking to plastics with his friend Harry Tepperman and spent $100,000 to buy the first plastic press for making table tops in Canada. He proceeded to work an average of seventeen hours a day, often coming out of the factory and dropping into the car beside his wife at 2 a.m., and falling asleep immediately. Business came Harry's way. By 1954 he owned a plywood-door manufacturing company, a steel-door company (doors were big in his life), and a bowling alley in Niagara Falls. By his own estimate he was a millionaire three times over. He was a pure entrepreneur, shrewd, hard-working to the point of obsession, and confident. He weighed 260 pounds, was six feet tall, and couldn't shave often enough. He was a Jewish businessman with a secret dream. He was a tough operator with the heart of a Shakespearean lover. He was a fan.

This was probably the single critical reason why Harry was so perfectly imperfect for the job he was about to undertake: his fandom. Actually Harry was more than a fan—he was the ultimate fan, a kind of early super-groupie who had realized the fan's dream: to travel with his team. He would in fact later be called "the fan who came out of the stands to run the Argos". "We'll see," Harry is reported to have said prior to the 1955 season. "We'll see this fall. The one guy in all this fuss who isn't being overlooked is the fan." One of Harry's first stipulations to Frank Clair for the same season was that quarterback Nobby Wirkowski had to go because of his lack of "colour". "It was nothing personal," Harry said. "We were simply convinced that he was colourless and our fans were down on him."

In the picture accompanying Trent Frayne's article in *Maclean's*—called "The Fan Who Took Over the Argos"—Harry is shown standing ahead of two of his burly American recruits, Bill Albright and Gil Mains, in the east bank of seats at Varsity Stadium. It may seem fanciful, but it's always struck me as significant that the photograph wasn't taken on the field, the scene of the action. Even subconsciously Harry may have brought the players into the lair of the species closest to him. He was a barometer acutely tuned to the passions of the crowd, Harry, the one thing every diehard dreams of, and consequently the one thing that can spell trouble for a sports team in the blink of an eye: a fan at the top.

The early part of 1954 Harry spent getting in training: this meant perfecting his shopping style and alienating Frank Clair. Spending $15,000 of his own money in travel expenses (Harry was never paid by the Argos), he flew to the States nearly every weekend to scout players in the National Football League, an institution whose glamour was apparently almost as irresistible to him as his allegiance to the Argos. (Although he was using his own money for travel, he had at his disposal the $100,000 Bill Ross had promised in the Winnipeg meeting, a huge sum of money in those days. In 1950 Bob Masterson, the Varsity coach at the University of Toronto and another alumnus of the 1940 Washington-Chicago NFL Championship game, had said, "Give me $96,000 and I'll buy you the Grey Cup.") Every week or so, another Sonshine-procured American recruit would arrive at the Argo camp—only to be snubbed by Frank Clair as though he were an untouchable. The first American was a former Washington Redskin end named Frank Polsfoot who got to the Argos while they were still preparing for the season opener. After three days of Argo workouts Frank Clair hadn't even looked at Polsfoot. Harry demanded to know why. Frank replied that it would take six weeks for a player to learn the Argo system, and that he was too busy getting the team ready for the season to spend time on newcomers. When Polsfoot headed south, and a week later scored two touchdowns for the Chicago Cardinals, Harry's answer was sharp and Harry-ish: "It didn't take him six weeks to learn Cardinal plays."

A week later, after a Philadelphia Eagles exhibition game in Rochester, Harry lined up Ken Snyder, Adrian Burk, and John Palmer, all proven NFL stars. On the phone from Toronto, though, Frank Clair once more demurred, claiming it would take the Americans six weeks to learn the Argo system. "Six weeks" seemed to have become his magical formula in his war with Harry, a kind of incantation to keep the barbarians at bay. It's difficult to blame him for trying. For a brief moment in history Harry was pulling one of the reversals that would be his trademark: Frank, the American, was cautious, modest, with pragmatic aims and ulcers; Harry, the Canadian, was daring, extravagant, full of vinegar and vision. Frank thought it couldn't be done; Harry *knew* it could.

Still, in spite of all the reported tension between Harry and Frank, the Argos didn't do all that badly in the '54 season. Bitsy Billy Cross turned out to be a pleasant surprise, a tiny flanker with moves and valour, as did a promising, versatile rookie from the University of Kentucky named Dick Shatto. In the last game of the season (the Argos' Achilles' heel in years to come) they lost to Hamilton by the respectable, hard-fought score of 15-9, finishing 6-8 and in third place, just out of the playoffs. It was pretty well where Frank had said they'd be.

On December 13, 1954, Harry announced the firing of all thirteen imports who played for the Argos.

It hit the papers like a thunderbolt. "Revenge Burns In Fired Argos", the *Tely* trumpetted. Nothing like it had ever happened before — not with the Argos, not with any professional team in the country. When has any other team anywhere ever cut thirteen veterans at once, even on the peewee level? It went beyond insanity to a kind of crazy consistency. Gone in the same fell swoop were not just Bitsy Billy but Nobby — one of the critical links — and Uly Curtis, and Art Scullion, all the remaining members of the Grey Cup team of a scant two years before. Gone, too, was Frank Clair. Shaken by the purge, and already hamstrung by half a dozen incredible "Sonshine" clauses inserted into his 1955 contract (among them the stipulation that Harry would name the starting line-up to each game and have the authority to phone down from the spotter's box to make sure certain Canadians got onto the field), Frank resigned from his $12,500-a-year job with the Argos and fled to the University of Cincinnati for $5,000 less and "better security". In the *Argo Fact Book* you can look them all up today and see their careers truncated cleanly at 1954; there's a flat understatement to the numbers — '50-'54, '49-'54 — that completely belies the melodrama of the story underneath.

The awesome thing about the firings was that they turned out to be just the tip of the iceberg, the result of what Harry had already quietly wrought on all his weekend jaunts to the States. At the same time that he announced the firings, Harry also announced that to replace the banished players he had either signed or "given his bond" to seven National Football League players, *not one of whom was in the process of playing out his option year.*

What ensued was a conflagration that threatened to turn into an all-out continental football war.

A little background may be helpful here. As hard as it may be to believe—considering the smoothly oiled, Bismarckian juggernaut it is today—and in spite of Harry's enchantment with its American glamour, the National Football League was in 1954 anything but a stable, professional sports institution. Compared to the Canadian Rugby Union, in fact, the NFL was a paragon of instability, a shaky league spooked by the spectre of college football competition (the league's Sunday scheduling was originally an attempt to avoid going head to head against the Saturday college games) and unsure of its fan support. In his book *A Fan's Notes* Frederick Exley tells how the Polo Grounds (then home of the New York Giants, one of the best teams in the league) was never completely full. Zeke O'Connor himself would recall playing for the Cleveland Browns against the Bears in Chicago's Soldiers' Field with all of 3,000 people in the stands. Even the addition of the three viable teams (one of them the Browns) from the collapsed All-America Conference in 1950 failed to alleviate the fundamental shakiness of the league.

In terms of charm the NFL was probably far superior to the seamless combine it would become, but it paid for its charm with paranoia. In 1954 franchises still had a habit of winking in and out of the league like spaceships navigating time warps. The year before, for example, the Baltimore Colts, a team that had already folded once in 1950, re-entered the NFL by dint of being awarded the holdings of the recently folded Dallas Texans, who had been through various incarnations before that: the New York Yankees, the defunct New York Bulldogs, and the Boston Yanks. So the NFL had had its fill of traumas by the winter of 1954-55; and then Harry arrived on the scene with his Argo bankbook and stole seven of the best players in the league out from under the noses of their owners.

Not that the same thing hadn't happened before: in 1953 the Edmonton Eskimos had made headlines by snaring the season's number-one American college prospect, Billy Vessels. Nor that it wouldn't happen again: some twenty-eight years later a man named Nelson Skalbania would hire a trio of NFL stars in an ill-fated move that would create its own share of headlines. But compared to Harry, Nelson Skalbania would be a dilettante, a fan not of football but merely of glamour. Skalbania hired three NFL players, all of whom would have question-marks beside their star quality. Harry hired seven with impeccable credentials. The four most noteworthy were: Billy Shipp, Bill Albright, Gil Mains, and Tom Dublinski. Shipp and Albright were both huge, agile linemen from the New York Giants (a team Harry positively ravaged), while Gil Mains and Tom Dublinski hailed from the Detroit Lions. Mains was a celebrated and crafty tackle. Dublinski was the quarterback of the future, the young, brilliant heir apparent to the great but ageing Bobby Layne. With 17,500 of Harry's above-par Canadian dollars in his pocket, Dublinski was the most highly paid quarterback anywhere. Besides towering over Nobby, he was considered to be the possessor of skills perfectly suited to the Canadian game. If any single American was going to save the Argos, it would be Tom Dublinski.

The four players mentioned above are singled out not simply on the strength of their reputations; they also turned out to be the Americans Harry was allowed to keep after all the dust (and bodies) had settled. Comments from the States were the quickest to come, and the most vitriolic. Reading them is a rare pleasure for a modern Argo fan. "Disastrous," said George Preston Marshall, owner of the Washington Redskins (who knew about disaster, after all). "We'll drive these Canadians out of business," said Timothy Mara, owner of the New York Giants. The Detroit Lions sued over Dublinski—the case revolved around the ubiquitous option-year controversy and they eventually won $6,950 (Canadian) in damages on appeal (The Detroit Football Club vs. Dublinski, Ontario Court of Appeals, 1957, J. A. Roach presiding). Harry insisted that the Argos pay the damages, as well as all of Tom's court costs. He probably would have done it even if it had been his own money. One thing you could never deny about Harry was his sense of *noblesse oblige*.

In the end, though, for all its thunder, the NFL was hamstrung, and it was the nervous voice of the Dominion that managed to slow Harry down. "A terrible black eye to Canadian football," said Leo Dandurand, president of the Alouettes, "I do not hesitate to indict Mr. Sonshine." "He's trying to price the rest of us right out of business," said the president of the Hamilton Tiger-Cats, Jake Gaudaur; "To up salaries is suicidal, yet if we don't keep pace on the field our fans will desert us and that'll be suicidal. I do not hesitate to condemn everything Sonshine has done."

It would have been futile at the time to try to convince Leo Dandurand and Jake Gaudaur that their dual failure to hesitate really didn't matter; that they could leave the issue of suicide to Harry Sonshine, who was about to skipper the Argos into a fog of failure more dense than they could imagine. Jake Gaudaur and Leo Dandurand didn't have today's historical sports perspective; to them the Argonauts were still the Argonauts, the team you couldn't turn your back on, the team who would nudge the ball a few inches towards your goal-line while you were taking a huddle. Two weeks later, at the Big Four's annual meeting in Montreal, the CRU owners passed a statute declaring any player currently under contract or *option* to an NFL club—which meant all seven of Harry's Americans—ineligible to play in the Big Four in 1955. Harry insisted that he was bound by his bond to pay the seven players, and that he would, even if it meant playing a whole season of exhibition games. The Big Four backed down. Harry could keep four of his players but he had to make his choice secretly, and send it to the league office in a sealed envelope. It was as though the other owners were trying to cloak themselves in some sort of mystique in order to combat Harry's.

But even with just the four players he was allowed to keep— Billy Shipp, Bill Albright, Gil Mains, and Tom Dublinski—Harry was taking the Argos into the 1955 season with a team that was considered near awesome, a team of "supermen", one that most experts agreed was as close to a sure thing as was possible in professional sport. To round out the complement Harry turned again to the New York Giants, and for $14,000 hired Bill Swiacki, the brilliant young coach who had devised the complex, dazzling Giant offence; to help Swiacki he spent another $20,000 to bring in assistants from the Detroit Lions and Notre Dame. To the objection that Frank Clair had never needed a non-playing assistant (until Chuck Klein came along, and that had been a disaster), Harry had a ready answer. "The game has become so complicated," he said, "that one man simply can't handle all the details." And so now Harry had his selected coaches, and his team, and his vision. The date was May 15, 1955.

By November the Argos were 4 and 8, and in the playoffs only because the Ottawa Roughriders had a more dismal record. They flared briefly, beating Hamilton in the semi-final on total points 32-28, but then in the final lost a 38-36 cliffhanger to the Alouettes that was as revealing as it was thrilling. It was exactly the type of game the old Argos had never lost. By March Bill Ross and the Argonaut Football Club had sold the team to a consortium of businessmen and sportsmen, including John Bassett (the publisher of the *Toronto Telegram*) and Lew Hayman (a man whose association with the team would touch four separate decades). In the space of a single football season an era had passed. And something else had passed too; Harry Sonshine was gone.

The question that will most likely occur to you at this point is one that fans of losing teams are not unaccustomed to asking: what had happened? What had happened to turn a team that couldn't lose into one that all too obviously could? What had happened to Tom Dublinski that, by November 2, 1957, no one less than Morley Callaghan would be moved to write in the *Telegram* (including Tom with Hank Greenberg, Howie Meeker, Sugar Ray Robinson, and the Brooklyn Dodgers' fans as the year's great losers in his weekend sports column, "Callaghan in the Gallery"):

> Think of what happened to Tom Dublinski this year. At the beginning of the season he was the real prize package with Detroit and Argos having wrangled in court over him, and so many of his fans believed he was the greatest quarterback in the east. What a year it was for him. If he met with Robin Roberts, could they tell each other what went wrong? And Howie Meeker?

One possible answer to the question "What had happened?" was that nothing had. "It is the tradition in sport that losers have no story," Morley noted in the same column. The claim is a shaky one in my opinion: from a fan's point of view losers may have the *only* story.

But it's true that a shroud of mystery does hang over the fall of the '55 Argos.

Ordinarily, when any team — let alone the Argos — begins to lose for a second or third season in a row, you sense a growing cynicism on the sports pages, at least a touch of wryness. As the Argos started to lose in '55, though, the tone that predominated in the sports section was closer to generous. Take the first game that Harry's Argos played and lost that year, an exhibition game against the B.C. Lions. It was the Lions' second victory, not of the season, but of their *history* — they'd only entered the league the year before, and had lost seventeen of their first eighteen games.

Still, the headline read "Lions Field Powerhouse To Upset Argo Supermen"; it had to be the Lions ascending, as opposed to the Argos falling. "By Labour Day and the Big Four opener," Bob Frewin wrote under the headline, "Argos will mature. They will be in this football season with an explosive wide open style and a club which will never quit." What Bob Frewin failed to note was his very own description in the same article of the play of Gil Mains, the highly touted former Detroit tackle: "Argos vaunted line was not the super wall expected. . . . Gil Mains was disappointing. He seemed dazed and indifferent." Separately the two adjectives are fathomable, it seems to me — Mains could have been "dazed" by a blow on the head or "indifferent" to an exhibition game. But dazed *and* indifferent? Something was growing inscrutable in the world of the Argonauts.

In sport, when a team hits a dry, inexplicable slump, the traditional therapy is a return to the fundamentals. The same approach might work here with the main character in the 1955 Argo drama, Harry Sonshine. Going back to basics with Harry means retreating a year and a half to the meeting Bill Ross had convened at the Royal Alexandra Hotel. A closer examination of the meeting reveals that with the very first suggestion he uttered, Harry had made a critical omission. Asked by Bill Ross to suggest ways to save the Argos, Harry had asked Ross if he'd be willing to trade the Argos' *Americans* for Montreal's — but he made no mention of their Canadians. Taking into consideration that the Canadian Rugby Union at the time had a rule restricting each team to a maximum of eleven Americans on a 28-man roster, this was no small oversight. But it was typical. In his year and a half with the Argos, operating on behalf of a team that a scant six years before could have billed itself as Canada's team, Harry Sonshine failed to make a single important manoeuvre that involved a city named Sudbury or Moosonee or Galt — instead he made headlines with Philadelphia, New York, and Washington, D.C.

This preoccupation — or infatuation — with the National Football League, and American football in general, was a part of the Sonshine legacy that would linger with the Argos long after Harry was gone, and rarely do them any good. In years to come the obsession would combine with certain realities of the Canadian game of football (three downs instead of four, a mandatory number of Canadians on each team) to produce a kind of Argo schizophrenia that wouldn't be that different from the schizophrenia of the team's home country: Canada itself. More important to a fan, it would present a possible explanation for the Argos' travails. According to this argument, from the time of Harry Sonshine the Argos ceased to be interested in cultivating Canadian talent—which has always been the single most critical prerequisite for success in Canadian football—in favour of running around bedazzled and importing a long line of glamorous American stars who would almost invariably prove disappointing. What's difficult to deny is that the more glamorous the stars grew over the years, the worse the Argos became. The "Argument from America" also goes a long way towards explaining a rumour that started to circulate a few years after Harry's departure: that from that first night of the meeting in Winnipeg, Harry's intention had been to secure a National Football League franchise for Toronto, to take the Argos into the NFL—a league he believed would one day be a gold-mine—and retain a piece of the action for himself.

But in the end, I think, like most of the theories about Harry and the Argos, the Argument from America is too specific. The truly revolutionary thing Harry introduced to the Argos wasn't a country, but a concept: the idea that winning might not be enough. As important as winning was, from this point on, the manner of winning, the *style*: specifically, big-league style. It was only coincidence that in mid-fifties Toronto "big-league" happened to mean American; if it had meant Hungarian the team would have recruited in Budapest and instructed their half-time marching bands to play in a minor key.

But where did this concern with style come from? How did the staple of fashion magazines come to dominate the front-office strategy of a professional sports team? Ironically, there's a good chance it came from the history of the Argos themselves, as a function not of their recent feebleness in the '53-'54 seasons, but of their dominance up to that point.

Success in sport is often its own worst enemy. A winning team has two choices: it can go downhill, or it can move onto a different playing field, trying to hone the way it wins towards the edge of perfection. Just to keep on winning with the same level of incompetence is to court boredom and ennui. New York Yankee owner George Steinbrenner, for all his boorishness, knows this, and Harry knew it too. The Argos had already won ten Grey Cups with canny pragmatism—to win another the same way would be standing still. The fans would grow restless. The only alternatives left were to either slide backwards towards sports oblivion, or move ahead into the glossy frontier of style.

It's a mark of his unique genius that Harry Sonshine managed to do both at once.

TRANS-CANADA
AIR LINES

TCA

AIR CANADA

3 The First Fall

From 1956 to 1959, under their new owners and the general managership of Lew Hayman, the Argos finished dead last four years in succession, with identical 4-10 records. Never again would the Argos be so neat in their manner of loss. In the same four-year stretch, the "First Fall", you might call it, the team not only went through three head coaches and seven quarterbacks, they also introduced most of the Harry Sonshine-derived Argo syndromes that would eventually attain a kind of reverse legendary status themselves. In a way the Argos seemed to be institutionalizing Harry's approach to football, experimenting with the various forms of practice — or malpractice — that might fit it best.

One of the more classic of these forms was the Overnight Visitor: the Argo whose brilliance would only be matched by the brevity of his stay in Toronto. (This was a natural offshoot of Harry's impatience, if not his preoccupation with style.) The best example I can think of was a quarterback named Arnie Galiffa, who played during the 1956 season when both Tom Dublinski and his back-up Gerry Doucette (the first French-Canadian quarterback in pro football) were sidelined with injuries. In a twelve-game career with the Argos, Arnie managed to accomplish enough on the field that twenty-five years later, in the 1981 *Argo Fact Book*, he would appear as one of the top five Argo quarterbacks of all time in no fewer than eleven individual passing categories (including "Most 300-Yard Passing Games Career" where his 7 was second only to Tobin Rote's 10). And Arnie, in his "Overnight Visitor" status, was anything but alone. Over the years the Argo record-book would come to be populated by a dispro-

Overnight visitor; quarterback-poet Ronnie Knox
arrives in Toronto with his sister "The Starlet".
Ronnie stayed thirteen games.

portionate number of Arnie Galiffas — to the point where a fan looking through the record-book would have the feeling he was reading the register of a rooming-house for famous commercial travellers.

In the "Most 300-Yard Passing Games Career" category, the five quarterbacks listed in the 1981 *Argo Fact Book* — Tobin Rote, Arnie Galiffa, Joe Theismann, Nobby Wirkowski, and Tom Dublinski — account among them for a total of fifteen seasons, an average of just three seasons per quarterback. Using actual games played as the yardstick, and postulating an average fourteen-game season, the career average of the five drops to approximately 2.2 seasons. Cookie Gilchrist, who played for the Argos for three seasons, appears in seven point-scoring categories. Al Bruno, the intended receiver on the play that produced Zeke's touchdown in '52, played two seasons for the Argos, and appears in five lists in the pass-receiving department, topping two. It could be argued that some of these categories pertain to single seasons, or even single games, and that consequently a player would only have to play one game or season to set the record, but that only hatches a more baffling question: *how could the Argos let a player like that get away?*

A fan is forced to arrive at one of two conclusions: either every excellent player the Argos unearthed turned out to be hiding a tragic flaw that mere numbers don't reveal; or every time the Argos got hold of a player with genuine promise they made sure to get rid of him as quickly as possible, before he had a chance to infect the rest of the team. So — to get back to 1956 — it seems to have been with Arnie Galiffa. That year, playing for an Argo team that had a record (that still stands) of having 413 points scored against it, Arnie threw thirty-two touchdown passes, to go with 256 completions for the season (an Argo record) and a 58% completion average. In the final game of the season, a 41-27 upset of the Eastern champion Montreal Alouettes (who were quarterbacked by Sam Etcheverry), Arnie was particularly brilliant, throwing three touchdown passes to an Argo end named Al Romine. At one point Al carried three Montreal tacklers from the 8-yard line into the end-zone. A quarter later Arnie himself scored on a quarterback sneak from the 15. It was an exciting, remarkably gritty performance, the kind that ordinarily assures a player of career security. But by the beginning of the next season both Arnie and Al Romine (who played a grand total of seven games for the Argos) were gone and virtually forgotten – the '57 Argo yearbook didn't even mention their names.

One result of the Overnight Visitor syndrome over the years has been a kind of reverse fan haunting. Normally a fan looks into the record-book of his team expecting to find his favourite, celebrated star's name under a certain category, only to discover that the record is held by some obscure workhorse who laboured away for years in near anonymity. An Argo fan approaches the Argo record-book *expecting* to find the name of some relatively unknown player because he knows that with one or two exceptions none of the memorable Argos stayed remotely long enough to hold records – only to find these short-lived stars staring back at him from every list. The whole process verges on eeriness for a fan; it's a twilight zone of the familiar.

Besides the Overnight Visitor, the most dramatic of the set pieces that emerged during the four years immediately following Harry Sonshine was the Argo Tease. Actually, Arnie Galiffa himself had been an early purveyor of the Tease with his final-game heroics against Montreal. Ordinarily a heartbreaking team will start the season with a fanfare of hope, then get steadily worse as the days lengthen, until by Labour Day (or Columbus Day) what you're watching resembles the last scene from *Hamlet*. Later Argo teams would follow this pattern, but the Argos of the First Fall had a refinement. The 1958 season is a perfect example: coming off two 4-10 seasons and two consecutive last-place finishes, the team somehow managed to beat the Winnipeg Blue Bombers (Kenny Ploen, Eagle Day, Leo Lewis, *et al.*) 22-15 in their first exhibition game, on a balmy first night in August at Varsity Stadium. "Man Oh Mann!" (i.e. Dave Mann) ran the headline in the *Tely*, "Argos Lick 'Pegs 22-15". "No More Patsys, THESE Argos Know How to Fight!" proclaimed a caption over a photo. "The comeback of a summer night is the keynote for the Argonaut autumn," wrote Bob Frewin. "This may come as something of a startler, but Toronto has a hustling ball club," opined George Dulmage, the *Tely*'s editor of sports, "and *not* the Toronto baseball Maple Leafs." "They're lean and hungry," offered Bud Grant, coach of the Blue Bombers. "They hustle." But by October second, when the Argos were dissected 20-9 by the Tiger-Cats in front of a crowd of over 23,000, all the enthusiasm had turned to pathos. "Somebody Hand Pool A Bromo", ran the headline this time (Pool as in

Hampton, coach of the Argos). "The Argonaut invalid raised himself painfully," wrote Frewin. "Once, twice, seven times he kicked," while across the page in his "gallery" Morley Callaghan had completely given up on the Double Blue and was writing essays about the Big Four's rumoured plans to do away with the American import quota, and the inflated reputation of American imports in general.

Then, just when the last crystal of hope was crumbling to dust, the Argos reversed form and barely lost to the league champion Montreal Alouettes, 14-12, in Montreal after actually leading 12-0 in the fourth quarter on a field goal, two singles by Dave Mann, and a touchdown pass to Tex Schriewer from a young blond quarterback named Ronnie Knox. It wasn't the first time Montreal had fallen victim to the Argos' terminal stand: the year before the Argos had beaten them 27-0 in the final game, shutting out Sam the Rifle and the rest of the Alouettes for the first time in more than fifty games. The year before that the valour of Arnie Galiffa and Al Romine had sunk them. It was pure tease—the Argo Tease, the football equivalent of the classic GI dream about Betty Grable. Half-mad with loneliness and libido, the GI has Betty Grable backed up against a tree, a smile of a thousand prospective delights on her lips—when he wakes up. The Tease was just such a siren song, a taste of what could have been in the Argo universe, if only a fan hadn't woken up too soon. Maybe the Argos were actually a good team, who had been inexplicably cursed for the first nine-tenths of the season. Attached to this was the corollary that has seduced sports fans ever since a Roman charioteer lost a wheel on the last turn at the Colosseum: the whisper, "*Wait till next year.*"

Another classic Argo twist that first came to light in the dog-days from '56 through '59 was another one that Harry Sonshine had personally laid the groundwork for, and that would have the highest profile of all over the years: the (American) Saviour of the Year. The only things that would change about the Saviour from one year to the next would be his skin-colour and the position he would play. At the time of the First Fall, with the possible exception of Al Pfeifer, the talented Argo end sometimes called the "Fordham Flash" (who along with Dick Shatto had mysteriously managed to manoeuvre his way back onto the team after Harry's axe had fallen in the purge of '54, and who seemed to oscillate in status between hero and goat on a yearly basis), the Saviours were white quarterbacks and white head coaches. The quarterbacks were more numerous but, again, short-lived: Arnie Galiffa lasted those twelve games, Al Dorow seven, Dave Doane just *two*.

It may be a function of maturity, or their slightly longer stays with the Argos, but over the years the coach-saviours have been the most interesting. A prime example of these was Hampton Pool, the man who arrived from the Chicago Bears to coach the team in 1957 after Bill Swiacki was fired. *Hampton Pool* — has there ever been a more tranquil football name? It was like a mixture of an estate on East Egg and a Greek myth starring wood-nymphs. If Hampton's name wasn't enough, there was the coincidence that was starting to become commonplace for the Argos: Hamp Pool had played in none other than the legendary 1940 Washington-Chicago NFL championship rout (as an end for the victorious Bears), the one Frank Clair had just missed, and Frankie Filchock had suffered through on the Washington side. To magnify the coincidence, Hampton's first game as Argo coach in 1957 came on an August first, pre-season summer night against the Saskatchewan Roughriders, who were coached by none other than Frankie Filchock himself. The Argos lost 30-9, and in the process were involved in the two brawls that became instant footnotes to Argo history: the first one featured Dick Fouts, the Argos' tackle, chasing Regina's Ron Atchison across the field to the Roughriders' bench, where he (Fouts) was knocked down and kicked anonymously in the groin; the second highlighted Bobby Kuntz flailing away at a Rider from behind with his helmet.

In a historical context the brawls aren't all that surprising. Losing teams tend to get frustrated, and over the years the Argos would erupt from time to time in an orgy of piling on, when things got particularly gloomy. But Hamp Pool was amazed — at both the football and the fights. The press was just as mystified by Hampton. "Under interrogation in the catacombs," Bob Hesketh wrote in the *Telegram*, "Pool conducted himself admirably, almost phlegmatically. He demonstrated one characteristic which is unique, particularly among coaches who have been defeated 30-9. He didn't raise his voice above its usual gruffness. He did not refuse to talk about anything. 'It seemed that the backfield forgot all the footwork they've been taught,' he said. 'Some of those plays out there tonight I've never seen before. When the guards were pulling they were stepping all over the quarterback's ankles.'" Later Hampton was quoted as saying, "I didn't expect we would beat them. But I was embarrassed by our offence. I thought we'd be better on offence," and another writer was quoted as saying, "I've studied Pool closely, and I have yet to find anything wrong with him." If all this sounds hauntingly familiar to a modern Argo fan, it should. Twenty-three years later another exemplary, painfully honest, American human being, who had played on the winning side in another mythic football game, would be brought to the same level of mystification by the Argos — Willie Wood. The major difference between the two coaches — besides the fact that Willie was black — was in the quality of their exit lines. Hampton's, before his last game in 1959, was perfect: "I looked around the dressing room at these guys," he said, "and I knew our goose was cooked."

While the Argos were floundering, the rest of the football world was moving onward and upward. Two tremendous rivalries in particular were staking out the second half of the fifties as their exclusive territory — Edmonton vs. Montreal, followed by Winnipeg vs. Hamilton. From the Montreal point of view the first rivalry was a kind of elevated version of a familiar frustration; the Argos' own, but in more elevated circumstances. Three years in a row, from 1954 to 1956, the Alouettes, with the explosive passing attack of quarterback Sam "The Rifle" Etcheverry and "Prince Hal" Patterson and Red O'Quinn, and running-backs Alex Webster and Pat Abbruzzi, reached the Grey Cup only to be beaten by the immutable ball control of the Eskimos: Johnnie Bright and Normie Kwong and a quarterback/defensive-back nicknamed "Spaghetti-Legs" — one Jackie Parker.

It was in the first of those Grey Cups, the 1954 game at Varsity Stadium, that the Eskimos beat the Alouettes 26-25 as a direct result of possibly the most famous single play in the history of Canadian football — Hunsinger's Fumble. The situation was this: leading by a score of 25-20, with less than six minutes remaining in the game, the Alouettes had moved to the Edmonton 10-yard line, where an apparent game-clinching score — a touchdown or at least a field goal — seemed certain. Even if the Alouettes had turned the ball over on downs at this point, they would probably have succeeded in holding the Eskimos off for the win. On first and goal, though, Sam Etcheverry handed the ball off on a sweep to one of his halfbacks, Chuck Hunsinger, and Hunsinger, turning the corner, lost control of the ball. In a kind of horrible slow motion the ball bounced onto Chuck Hunsinger's knee, then the grass, at which point Jackie Parker picked it up going the other way and ran ninety yards down the sideline with his fractured gait to win the game.

The second Montreal-Edmonton Grey Cup was the first one ever played in the West, in Vancouver, away from Varsity Stadium. The third, back in its ancestral home, is noteworthy because it was a rout, 50-27, and also because it tied a record for consecutive Grey Cup victories—the Argos' own record, the one they'd set from '45 to '47. In winning their trio of Cups the Eskimos forged for themselves a reputation as one of the great football teams of all time, a record they would supersede themselves by winning four Grey Cups in a row in the late seventies and eighties—and one only the Winnipeg Blue Bombers would approach in the interim, playing in five out of six Grey Cups from 1957-62 and winning four of them. With Bud Grant coaching, Kenny Ploen passing, Farrell Funston and Ernie Pitts catching, Leo Lewis and two-sport Gerry James running, the Blue Bombers would become a football team that would invent ways to win if necessary, a team of supreme opportunists that, a decade earlier, would have been dead ringers for a squad in double blue. . . .

Meanwhile the Argos, moving further into the First Fall, were becoming firmly entrenched as the clown princes of football. "Can't anybody here play this game?" you can almost hear Casey Stengel asking. By 1959 the Argo style of football was more like basketball played by a practising high-school team when the coach was out of the gym. To win the Argos would try anything—anything short of real football, that is. It was an early example of the future Argo tendency to opt for the gimmicky and the experimentally suspect at times of crisis. As 1957 limped into '58 and '59, the games at Varsity burgeoned into jamborees of jump passes and "Statues of Liberty" and "flea-flickers" and even, on one occasion, a tackle-eligible play designed by *Hampton Pool*. I include the italics because Hampton was widely known in football circles as a purist of purists, a man who would drink hemlock before he'd try anything remotely questionable on a football field. But Hampton had a large talented tackle named Pete O'Garro who could catch a football as well as block, and with O'Garro in mind he inserted a tackle-eligible play into the Argo offensive repertoire for a critical game against the Hamilton Tiger-Cats.

But these were the new Argos; O'Garro broke his leg on the third play of the game and Jim Trimble, the Hamilton coach, stole the idea and used the play to win the Eastern championship in 1962.

And then there was Ronnie Knox. Certain names are pure magic to a sports-fan: mention them and you rocket backwards in time; either that or a totally forgotten ambience suddenly surrounds you, so rich that you can taste it. Mention Joe Pepitone to a New York Yankees fan of a certain vintage, K. C. Jones to a Boston Celtics fan, Frank Mahovlich to a Toronto Maple Leafs fan, and that fan is transported through time.

But it's difficult to imagine a player evoking a particular time and style more strongly than Ronnie Knox for any Argo fan who can remember him. Three days after he joined the Hamilton Tiger-Cats from UCLA, the story goes, Ronnie was on a bus to Toronto for his first game (against the Argos), sitting beside the Hamilton coach Jim Trimble, who was feverishly going over a play-book with him. Finally Trimble looked up and asked him if he had any questions. "Coach," Ronnie said, "am I good-looking?"

When Ronnie eventually made his way back to Toronto half-way through 1958, this time to play for the Argos, it was as though he was coming home. He brought his family with him, maybe in honour of the event; his father-agent Harvey (known widely as a "loud, bombastic son-of-a-bitch") and his sister Elise (known widely as the "starlet"). As part of Ronnie's scholarship deal at UCLA Harvey had insisted on an extra fifty tickets per game, which he had proceeded to sell for thirty dollars apiece. Ronnie was less materialistic. He wrote poetry—free verse devoid of capital letters, like e. e. cummings (with a suntan)—and threw jump passes. The jump pass was Ronnie's trademark. It was most effective in publicity shots: Ronnie aloft, without his helmet, smiling his blond, indecently good-looking smile at the camera. In games, on the other hand, he had a fragile, vulnerable look up in the air, like A. E. Housman's athlete dying young—"And round that early-laurelled head"—with a suntan.

The thing fans tend to forget in all the looniness surrounding his career, though, is that Ronnie was an extremely talented athlete. Even now, writing this, I have trouble believing it. But it was true. In his thirteen-game career with the Argos across the '58-'59 seasons (just one more game than Arnie Galiffa), Ronnie inscribed himself into the Argo record-book in five separate passing categories. His 60.1% completion average in 1958 is the third highest for an Argo quarterback ever, and the 522 yards he passed for in the October 25 game against Ottawa that season ranks second, behind Tobin Rote's 524. With receivers like Dave Mann, Dick Shatto, and Tex Schriewer, Ronnie was on occasion the most exciting passer in the CFL. But his heart was elsewhere. At the beginning of September '59 he sold a poem called "Scarecrow" to Bob Frewin for twenty-five dollars (he never cashed the cheque) and two weeks later, having jump-passed the Argos to ten losses and three wins, he was gone, heading for Hollywood and the movies. Ronnie's parting words comprise one of the more famous farewells in Argo history. "Football," he said, "is a game for animals."

It certainly wasn't a game for the Argos. Football the way the Argos played it at the time was more hilarious than tragic; it was the sort of spectacle you squinted at, like ballet performed by transvestites, as opposed to something you brooded about and became suicidal over. This was probably its saving grace. Being an Argo fan was trying, but not without its zanier compensations. From most reports, watching the Argos in the late fifties was like going to New York Mets games in the early sixties. The Argo Bounce may no longer have been the Bounce of Joe Krol and Royal Copeland and Zeke O'Connor, but it wasn't the Bounce of sheer perversity either—it was the jester's bounce, sometimes going your way, sometimes theirs. It was the bounce of forty undergraduates in a phone-booth, of Argos named Knox and Muckles and Kuntz and Fouts, and Rountree and Shatto and Corky Tharp.

There is one more element that has to be included in this portion of the Argo story, something else that was coming into focus at the time of the First Fall. A day arrives in the lives of some boys when sports cease to be peripheral to life, and become life itself. This transformation is most likely to happen to a boy between the ages of six and ten, which is exactly the span I covered from 1956 to 1959.

I didn't actually become an Argo fan during this period, I should point out, but simply a fan of football. The games I remember most vividly had nothing to do with previous partisanship or loyalty. The earliest of these was the 1956 Edmonton-Montreal Grey Cup, which I listened to on the radio in my sister's bedroom. I have no idea what I was doing in my sister's bedroom in the first place—there was a much better radio in my parents' room—and I'm even less sure why I was cheering for the Alouettes. At that point in my life Montreal meant nothing to me outside the Canadiens. The Alouettes were an exotic, racy, but obscure sports team that my father got excited about. For all that, I have a perfectly clear, technicolour memory of holding the edge of my sister's white school-desk, rocking back and forth, saying, "Let's go, Sam, let's go, let's *go!*" Prophetically, Sam (Etcheverry) and the Alouettes went nowhere, and the Eskimos won the game 50-27.

The second football game I can remember with complete clarity was the NFL championship game of 1958, the classic which saw the Baltimore Colts defeat the New York Giants in overtime, with Alan "The Horse" Ameche taking a hand-off from Johnny Unitas and diving into a snow-covered end-zone to win the game. I not only heard this particular game but saw it, in a Bathurst Street delicatessen. I sat beside my father while he crumbled halvah, and stared up at a television set perched on a shelf over the front door. The greyness of the day outside, I remember, matched the greyness of the weather in New York. There was no question in my mind which greyness was preferable—I was an instant Colt fan. And this time the good guys won.

My experience of the Argos at the time was far less significant. Although I knew who they were, naturally, the Argo games I remember came later. But considering the seductiveness of losing teams, it's not impossible that the Argos were already making their impression on my subconscious. For certain kinds of fans, age—tender or advanced—is no defence against certain kinds of sports teams.

I don't think I realized this in a complete sense until the fall of 1972 (the Argos were 3 and 11 that year, with Leo Cahill coaching) when I read a book by Frederick Exley called *A Fan's Notes*. *A Fan's Notes* was an autobiographical novel which used as a metaphor the author's eccentric but doomed passion for the New York Giants, in particular their great halfback of the fifties and early sixties, Frank Gifford. One passage I have never been able to get out of my mind. Near the beginning of the book Exley told a story about Steve Owen, the coach of the powerful Giants' team of the early fifties, the man who invented the "Umbrella" pass defence and who made the Giants legendary enough to match Gifford's own celebrity. The story hinged on two "meetings" Frederick

Exley had with Steve Owen. The first took place when he was eight years old, in a hotel lobby in New York City when Owen asked his father about him: "Is he tough, Mr. Exley?" The second "meeting" was some fifteen years later, in 1955, at the last game Owen coached for the Giants (against Bobby Layne and the great Detroit Lions, as it happens, minus Tom Dublinski). It was also, coincidentally, the first game that Frank Gifford was starting at halfback for the Giants, and in his mind Frederick Exley had devised a fantasy of justice whereby Gifford would win the game against all odds and save Steve's job. It didn't work out that way. Gifford was stopped on the 1-foot line by Les Bingaman on New York's final series, and Owen was fired the next day. As Exley himself put it:

> Frank Gifford went on to realize a fame in New York that only a visionary would have dared hope for; he became unavoidable, part of the city's hard mentality. I would never envy or begrudge him that fame. I did, in fact, become perhaps his most enthusiastic fan. Undoubtedly he came to represent to me the realization of life's large promises. But that is another part of this story. It was Owen who over the years kept bringing me back to life's hard fact of famelessness.... After that day at the Polo Grounds I heard of Owen from time to time, that he was a line-coach for one NFL team or another, that he was coaching somewhere in Canada — perhaps at Winnipeg or Saskatchewan. Wherever, it must have seemed to him the sunless, the glacial side of the moon....

But in 1959 Steve Owen wasn't on the glacial side of the moon. He wasn't in Saskatchewan either — not yet. He was with the Argos.

And true darkness was about to fall.

4 Faloney's Run

In 1959, while Ronnie Knox was still with the team, the Argos moved from Varsity Stadium to a new expanded home field, the Canadian National Exhibition Stadium. The CNE Stadium had a seating capacity of 35,000 to Varsity's mere 25,000; it afforded half its customers an impressive vista of Lake Ontario if play on the field palled; and it was located in the heart of the largest annual fair in the world.

But for the fan it turned out to be a complete mistake. What any sporting arena requires, first and foremost, is insularity, even coziness; this probably accounts for the popularity of the "bowl" shape for arenas and stadiums, regardless of the sport. And while Varsity Stadium was by any criteria a gem of a bowl — insular, cozy, and theatrical — CNE Stadium was anything but. The new stadium consisted of two apparently unrelated banks of stands: one open to the elements, and one covered by an overhanging roof that had support columns placed in strategically maddening places, and a narrow horizontal topping of lights and press boxes that looked like the leading edge of a flying saucer. Both end-zones, which would have been safely encompassed by a bowl, were open as far as the eye could see. Looking left from the covered side through the east end-zone, a fan could gaze at a wire fence, and past the fence a cluster of blue-painted wooden sheds that housed equipment from the midway, and above the sheds the skeleton of the CNE's roller-coaster, the Flyer, and beyond the Flyer various turrets and roofs of the exhibition. To the right, through the west end-zone, he could see past the Exhibition grounds to the curve of Lake Ontario. It was as though the stadium had been built prefab, in pieces, then set down on the shore of the lake. It was a

Then general manager Lew Hayman chats with
Tobin Rote, Argos' first truly accredited quarterback
Saviour-of-the-Year.

stadium without a frame of reference. Possibly Albert Camus would have felt comfortable in CNE Stadium, but what chance did a fan have?

On sunless October days in years to come the wind would sweep uncontested up the field, bringing the chill of the infinite and the inevitable, even before the game began. Marching bands who played at half-time would have entire overtures literally blown away; they would turn smartly towards you in the covered stand and...nothing. Nothing but a faint, delayed whisper of brass, like the distant ragged playing of a Scottish infantry company limping home from a terrible battle. The only times the stadium wasn't desolate in my experience were balmy summer nights during the pre-season. On those nights, perversely, everything seemed to work: the walk in from Dufferin Street, under the spare arch and through the closed Ex (waiting itself to erupt in excitement in August), the rising anticipation. But then, that was the Tease. CNE Stadium was the perfect set-piece for the Tease. To the generation of Argo fans who would live through the next twenty-two years of drought, it would also be home.

At the time the move to the new stadium was considered one of the more important things to have happened to the city since the opening of the Yonge Street subway. Hal Walker, writing in the *Tely* on August 7, 1959, the day after the first game played there, said, "...it was, nevertheless, what old Stone Face [Ed Sullivan] would call a r-e-a-l-l-y big 'shew'. There was a genuine big-league atmosphere about it. The new stand looked glittering under the brilliant glare of the mazdas, and customers in the covered stand could look beyond the field to the lake and glory with the dinghy sailors as they sailed home in the gathering dusk." There were also backs to the seats on the covered side, Hal Walker pointed out, whereas Varsity Stadium's benches had none.

Twenty-seven thousand, seven hundred and seventy fans attended that first game at CNE, a figure that not only exceeded the total ever to attend an exhibition game in Canada, but also broke the single-game Eastern Conference attendance mark, one that had been set at the 1956 Grey Cup between Edmonton and Montreal. It wasn't surprising. The game that night pitted the Argos against the Chicago (soon to be St. Louis) Cardinals of the National Football League. The only sports event I can think of to compare to it for sheer curiosity would be the initial Russia-Canada hockey series of 1972: it was a similar sort of mysterious meeting of worlds, although without quite the same trauma attached to the possibility of the home team losing.

Part of this was due to the fact that in 1959 it was the visiting Cardinals who were the genuine big-league component in the match-up; no football analyst with his faculties intact gave the Argos the slimmest chance of winning. This may be why the press surrounding the game was so casual. The *Star* ran one small item on the day of the game; the *Tely* included a picture of four large Cardinals in uniform doing the cancan with the Argonaut Shellettes. This was in spite of the fact that no Canadian professional team had ever met an American one, let alone a team from the NFL, a league which by 1959 was finally attaining a public image to match its excellence of play. It was in spite of the fact, too, that coaching the Cardinals was none other than Pop Ivy, the man who had led Edmonton to its three consecutive Grey Cup victories over Montreal in the mid-fifties; and in spite of the fact that the improvised rules for the game were a football fan's delight, an amalgam of three-down Canadian rules and four-down American regulations that shifted every time the ball changed hands.

The game itself started off like a dream. The first time the Argos got the ball they went fifty yards in four plays, with Ronnie Knox faking a jump pass on the fourth play, rolling to his right, directing Dave Mann to cut behind a Cardinal defender into the end-zone, then calmly flipping the ball ("a la Otto Graham", as the papers put it) over the Chicago back's head into Dave's arm for a touchdown. A few plays later Toronto's Bob Dehlinger intercepted an M. C. Reynolds pass and went seventy yards for another touchdown, giving the Argos a 13-1 lead. It couldn't last, of course. By the end of the game the Cardinals, who outweighed the Argos by an average of at least twenty pounds per man, were ahead 55-26, and the Argos had lost four players to broken bones — including Norm Stoneburgh, their all-star centre, out with a leg fracture. The post-game reports dealt almost exclusively with the list of Argo injuries, and the ensuing traffic tie-ups on Lakeshore Boulevard.

The regular season of 1959 was the last of the Argos' four consecutive 4-10 seasons. The only thing to recommend it was the CFL-leading seventy-five points scored by a bull-like newcomer to the Argo backfield, Carlton Chester "Cookie" Gilchrist. Cookie would become one of the mainstays of the Argo team of the next two years and we can't really proceed without at least a short testament to his uniqueness. Born in a less than genteel ghetto suburb of Pittsburgh — McKeesport, Pennysylvania — he had attended the Cleveland Browns' tryout camp as a "kid" fullback at the age of eighteen, fresh out of high school, and had made it to the last cut. At that point Paul Brown had recommended Canada, and Cookie had subsequently ended up playing for the Sarnia Imperials of the old Ontario Rugby Football Union. A short, turbulent career with Sarnia was followed by a shorter and more turbulent career with the Hamilton Tiger-Cats of the Big Four (1956-57) and one spectacular season with the Saskatchewan Roughriders, when he ran for 1,254 yards (some 150 yards more than any Argo running-back would ever gain).

It was after his season with Saskatchewan that Cookie came to the Argos. At the time of his arrival (1959) the Argos' annual Saviours were still white quarterbacks rather than black running-backs, which was ironic; compared to the touted, often pampered black Hopes who would arrive to rescue the Argos in years to come, Cookie was in another universe of talent altogether. His versatility, for one thing, was extraordinary by any standards — for a black player at the time it was unheard of. Where some of the Argo running-backs to come would be able to run with the football and sometimes even catch it, Cookie, at 6'2½, 252 pounds, could run, catch, kick, *and* tackle. One thing that always galled Cookie was the unconditional attention lavished on Jimmy Brown, the Cleveland Browns' fullback and a contemporary of his, whom he considered a less rounded ball-player than himself. "I respected Brown, but I thought I was the more complete ball-player," Cookie said. "His offence was set up so he didn't have to block. To me blocking was just as important. I was 252 pounds. I moved well. I ran hard. Even big men feared me." As a member of the Cleveland Browns of the early 1960s, Jimmy Brown occupies a special niche in my fan's heart, but considering the record, it's difficult to argue with Cookie.

In 1956, when he was still playing for Hamilton, Cookie was named to the Eastern All-Star Team at both fullback and middle-linebacker. In 1959 and 1960, running and place-kicking, Cookie won the league scoring championship. In a mere three years with the Argos, '59-'61, he scored enough points to place him sixth in the all-time Argo scoring list, just forty-odd points behind Joe Krol, who had played *ten* seasons with the Double Blue. In 1960, when the Argo defensive line was decimated by injuries, Cookie bailed the team and Lou Agase out by playing a little defensive tackle (the position he first played with Sarnia) just for a change.

This isn't to say that Cookie didn't have his detractors. There were those who questioned his judgement off the field as rabidly as they cheered his performance on it. Cookie tended to have a different interpretation of team rules from management, as well as an occasional aversion to taking the same plane home as the rest of the team, and a generally quixotic approach to money. (When Cookie was eventually acquired from the Argos by the Buffalo Bills of the American Football League in 1962, the Bills first paid off a $5,000 debt he owed the Argos.) Cookie was also outspoken in ways that no black player in the city had been before him. But where the volatile temperaments of future American running-backs would seem arbitrary and sometimes unjustified (to me, at least), Cookie had a very good historical reason for his. "Cookie was coloured," Bob Frewin would later explain, "and he felt he had no allegiance to whites. It was a different kind of attitude from a Negro athlete than people were used to at the time. The reason Cookie had this attitude was that he felt the only reason whites had any interest in him was because of what he could do on the football field. He was probably right." As Cookie himself put it, "I believe half of what I see and none of what I read and hear....I haven't been the run-of-the-mill Negro athlete who accepts the crumbs offered. I felt that I produced better than the white athlete and I wanted to get paid better." Of the white athletes on the Argo team at the time, the one Cookie most liked and respected, apparently, was Nobby Wirkowski. Cookie and Nobby. If there was justice in the world — or just in sport — neither of them would have had to live through what was to come.

But then, neither would the other Argo light in the barren-ness of 1959 — Dick Shatto. It's probably criminal to try to sum up the career and significance of Dick Shatto in this cramped con-text, as a short detour on the road to catastrophe — but there's no better place to do it. In fact, this may be the only place Dick *can* go, because a roomier berth would only end up being filled by what Dick was: ten per cent taste and quiet elegance, ten per cent statistics, and eighty per cent clear and colourless vapour. If Cookie was blessed with a surfeit of colour, Dick was cursed by a terrible lack of it. Over his twelve-year career with the Argos ('54 to '65, second in longevity in the modern era only to Danny Nykoluk's fifteen years) Dick set fifteen Argo records, including the most touchdowns (ninety-one, second in CFL history only to George Reed), most points, most carries, and most yards gained. He led the team in rushing five times and in pass-receptions five times, combining these feats in three seasons. In the process he also spanned three eras, managing to survive Harry's purge and Hampton's honesty and the disaster yet to come, and he even lasted half-way through the Second Fall and the era of the Airlift. He was an intelligent, durable runner, a gifted pass-catcher, a passable quarterback, and a decent kicker.

But unfortunately Dick Shatto is also a classic example of that sports phenomenon: the statistical cipher. Dick Shatto is the only major figure I could excise completely from the history of the Argos, and not really miss at all. As a fan moving into my early teens I saw Dick Shatto play on television more times than I can count, but Cookie Gilchrist, whom I saw play exactly twice, is much clearer in my memory. The face of Dick's daughter Cindy, who became a world-class diver and whom you had to look at upside-down fifty per cent of the time, is clearer to me than Dick's. Certainly he was well groomed, and he had dignity, but what else? "He was the quintessential white player," one former teammate would point out in retrospect. "He was the victim of his own versatility," another would say, "playing flanker, halfback, even a little quarterback. Today if he came up they'd make a flanker out of him and he'd be a star." "He was an innocent...boy, from the University of Kentucky," a writer would say, "who left school early, came up here, got married, and spent his whole career with the Argos. He suffered with dignity. What do you want, fireworks?"

That season of 1959 Dick ran for 950 yards and caught forty-six passes to go with Cookie's seventy-five points, but the Argos still finished 4 and 10, and dead last for the fourth year in a row. The only other notable event of the season took place exactly at its half-way mark. At that point, with the Argos 2 and 5, Hampton Pool was fired as coach and his assistant line-coach, Steve Owen — the same Steve Owen as in Frederick Exley's story — was promoted to replace him. The record shows that Steve lost as many games as Hampton and by the end of the season was gone too, heading for Calgary and Saskatchewan and various other dark, Exleyian sides of the moon.

The man who fired Hampton and allowed Steve to escape — or who at least oversaw the proceedings in an official capacity — was Lew Hayman, the Argos' general manager, one of the men who had purchased the team from the Toronto Rowing Club in 1957. In doing so Lew Hayman had actually returned to the Argos after a fifteen-year intermission which included a dazzling nine-year stretch as, variously, general manager, coach, and part owner of the Montreal Alouettes. It was Lew who had coached the Argos from '33 to '41 (the Argos of the "Stuki" brothers, Annis, Bill, and Frank, as well as Harry Sonshine), leading the team to three Grey Cup victories and compiling a 40-15-2 record, a winning percentage of .727 over nine years. By comparison Frank Clair's winning percentage was .500, Tedder Morris's .580, and Leo Cahill's—Leo being technically the "winningest" coach in Argo history (in terms of total victories)—.500, to match Frank Clair's. Statistically Lew Hayman had been far and away the most successful coach the Argos had ever had. In view of all this, and his success at Montreal as well—two Grey Cup appearances with Sam Etcheverry, Hal Patterson, *et al.*—Lew seemed to be the perfect candidate to lead the Argos out of the wilderness, back to dignity and the Bounce of old.

And it was Lew who added the final ingredients to an Argo lineup that already included Cookie and Dick Shatto, rounding out the team that would take the field for the 1960 season. It was a collection of unique football talents, a team that would ride the eclectic brilliance of four men in particular—Dick and Cookie were two—to within scant millimetres of the summit; a team that would have a championship in its sights; a team that would instead blow it in impossible fashion, killing one Argo fan outright and breaking the hearts of a legion of others in the process.

For a coach, Lew Hayman looked south and west to Michigan State University and chose a man named Lou Agase. Lew and Lou. Legend has it that Agase was referred to Hayman by a Chicago variety columnist named Irving Cupsonet, who also happened to be an avid football fan. The story is not all that unlikely. Of the handful of expert assessments available nowadays concerning Lou Agase's coaching credentials, the most flattering is that he was a good "kaffeeklatsch coach"—which means that on Saturday afternoons when the alumni had gathered at the campus practice field to watch a languid workout, when balding ex-ends from '38 in tweed sports jackets wanted to talk football, Lou was their man. Such a talent—the ability to look and sound like a coach without really being one—can't be taken too lightly when you're speaking of the Argonauts: more than one coach would be hired who had exactly that quality (and one, Leo Cahill, would elevate it to an art). Lou's speciality was looking terrific on the sidelines; he may have looked better in headphones than any other coach the Argos ever had. A classic newspaper photo exists of Lou on the sidelines in the first game he coached for the Argos, wearing a suit and headphones, bent over slightly at the waist with his hands splayed open in front of him, apparently showing a quarterback on the bench something about taking a pass from centre. With his blunt head, his nose hooking down from his forehead like an apostrophe, his short neck, his thinning dark hair swept wetly back, Lou looks every inch the tough but dapper strategist. He looks like a Mediterranean Hank Stram. It's only on closer examination of the photograph that it becomes obvious that the quarterback Lou is talking to isn't really paying any attention to Lou; the player's gaze is directed at the field, and verges on an eye-roll.

The quarterback's name was Tobin Rote. Another of Lew Hayman's additions to the Argos, Tobin was the first truly tested, famous, professional version of the quarterback Saviour-of-the-Year the Argos had ever acquired. Tobin represented a definite step up the Harry Sonshine ladder of big-league Style; he was the costliest, most *American* American yet. A balding realist who smoked cigars in the shower and looked like a weary, philosophical hit-man (the kind who might commiserate with you about your bunions and your wife before he dropped you into Lake Michigan), Tobin had played college ball in his native Texas, and then distinguished himself as a canny, classic drop-back passer with the Green Bay Packers and Detroit Lions of the NFL (at Detroit, just before coming to the Argos, Tobin had led the Lions to the NFL Championship in 1957, a resounding 59-14 trouncing of the Cleveland Browns). The only other quarterback I can think of who was stylistically—and baldly—comparable to Tobin was Y. A. Tittle of the New York Giants and the San Francisco Forty-Niners, but it's doubtful Y. A. had Tobin's constitution. Before one particular Sunday game in Montreal, in September of 1960, the story goes, Tobin stayed up all night Saturday touring Montreal's bistros; Dick Shatto, coming into the clubhouse early the next morning, found Tobin stretched out on his back on a bench, his arm covering his eyes. "I'm not sure I can get through the game, Dick," Tobin said, and Dick replied, "Sure you can,"—and Tobin went out onto the field and completed nineteen of twenty-two passes for an 86.4 completion average, an Argo record that stands to this day. In his career with the Argos, Tobin also set team records for most completions in a game (thirty-eight, also a CFL record), most completions in a career (662), most touchdown passes in a game (seven), most touchdown passes in a career (sixty-six), most yards passing in a career, season, or game (9,872; 4,247; 524), most touchdown passes in a season (thirty-eight), most 300-yard passing games in a career (ten — Arnie Galiffa, remember, was second with seven), and the longest completed pass, a 108-yard touchdown bomb to Jim Rountree against the Saskatchewan Roughriders on September 10, 1961 (a scant sixty days before *the* game). Tobin accomplished all this in just three seasons with the Argos. Considering what happened one afternoon in November, two thirds of the way through his Argo sojourn, the wonder is that he stayed that long.

The first game Tobin played as an Argonaut was the opening preseason game of the 1960 season, an exhibition game against the Pittsburgh Steelers of the National Football League (the Argos' second exhibition game in a row against an NFL team). It turned out to be just as one-sided on the scoreboard as the Argo-Chicago Cardinal contest had been — 43-16 for Pittsburgh — but fortunately for the Argos it wasn't as traumatic physically. The only injuries of note were suffered by Tobin himself — a slightly bruised knee that kept him out of most of the game and caused several near coronaries in the front office boxes — and Dick Shatto, who sprained his thumb and tore rib cartilage. Otherwise the Argos escaped from the game in good health. Their next exhibition game was against the Hamilton Tiger-Cats, their first legitimate test. The Argos won. As August cooled into September and the regular season, they kept winning. And slowly the fans took note, and began to watch, with surprise and that fatal, feathered thing: hope.

What they were watching, specifically, was the forward pass. It was the season of the pass, an aerial circus ring-mastered by Tobin and unequalled in Argo history. Six times during the season Tobin threw for more than 300 yards. Three times he threw for five touchdowns or more, twice for seven. By the end of the season he'd thrown for thirty-eight altogether (second highest for a season in CFL history, behind Pete Liske), and for 4,247 yards.

Meanwhile, Cookie Gilchrist was scoring eight touchdowns on the ground, and adding forty-three converts, nine singles and five field goals to lead the CFL in scoring with 115 points; Dick Shatto was gaining over 1,200 yards on passes and runs combined; and Dave Mann was leading the league in pass-receptions with 1,382 yards (an Argo record) on sixty-one catches. Danny Nykoluk was catching four passes on the tackle-eligible play. Lou Agase was looking terrific on the sidelines. From the tone of the reporting in the press, and the general fan reaction, 1960 was obviously an unexpected season in the sun, a bonus of a season for an Argo team that hadn't had a winning record since the Grey Cup Year, 1952.

The 1960 Argos finished the regular season 10-4—the exact reverse of the 4-10 rut they had fallen into—and in first place. It was when they came up against the Ottawa Rough Riders in the Eastern playoff final—the Riders having beaten Montreal—that their luck ran out. Unlike other Argo post-season collapses to be, this one was not really a collapse. The Argos had for once been blessed by unusual luck all season long—Ottawa was actually the better team. A major reason for Ottawa's superiority was a daring managerial decision Ottawa had made prior to the 1960 season. At that point they had opted to bench their veteran quarterback Frank Tripucka and go instead with a young Canadian named Russ Jackson. Jackson proceeded to demonstrate a panache at the position that only a handful of Americans throughout the league had ever come close to showing. From the Argo point of view there was also a more haunting possible reason for the Rough Riders' success: the Rider coach, the man who had decided to give Russ Jackson a chance, and who had laboured the last four years building Ottawa into a contender—Frank Clair. Having Frank meet Lou Agase in a coaching duel has always struck me as a bit like pitting Robert Oppenheimer against Mr. Wizard for the Nobel Prize in Physics.

Even with Frank, though, the Riders might not have won without a sleeper play. In the days of Joe Krol and Royal Copeland, the Argos had used this particular play to win games themselves, but until its abolition in 1961 it drove me crazy. One of the redeeming features of spectator sports, especially football, is their creation of a universe of *order*, to counter the arbitrariness of the world at large. The sleeper was on the side of the arbitrary. (It could also only be used effectively on a Canadian-sized field;

American gridirons were too narrow for the prerequisite subterfuge.) There were two classic ways the sleeper play could be executed. In one a player sauntered towards the sidelines as though he was about to leave the game, but didn't quite make it; in the second a player who found himself close to the sidelines at the end of one play would simply stay on the sidelines—maybe prone with an ostensible injury—hoping no one on the opposition had noticed him. In the Argo-Ottawa final game it was the latter version: with under seven minutes remaining and the Argos down by less than a touchdown, an Ottawa end named Bob Simpson ghosted around at the sidelines at the end of a play, and continued to loiter there while the Rough Riders huddled up. Then he took off down the line, gathered in Russ Jackson's pass, and made it inside the Argo 10 before he was tackled. A moment later the Rough Riders had the clinching score, and the championship of the East. Even Frank Clair was surprised. "I didn't see Simpson and I didn't know what he had pulled off until he came running past our bench on his way into Argo territory," Frank said. "Imagine that. A sleeper play!"

Still, it was by no means a devastating loss. The Argos had played valiantly, coming back from behind on the arm of Tobin, and only losing because of a trick play that had no right being in a self-respecting rule-book. The fans who had seen it happen had no valid reason to complain. From all indications, the Argos could only get better. If the ancient whisper rose, it did so with some justification: "Wait till next year!"

The next year was 1961.

The beginning was not auspicious, which for most teams would have been a warning. (With the Argos, the Tease always made promising starts more ominous than terrible ones.) In their August 1 opener the Argos, for the third year in a row, were beaten badly by an NFL team, losing this time by a 35-7 score to the St. Louis Cardinals (the Chicago Cardinals of 1959, transplanted). In the opening half of the game the Argos' defensive unit— anchored by Billy Shipp, Jim Andreotti, and Jim Rountree— actually held the St. Louis offence, considered one of the NFL's strongest, *scoreless*. The man who finally did get the Cardinal offence untracked in the second half—their new first-string quarterback—was none other than Sam Etcheverry, the Rifle himself, who had defected to the Cardinals in reaction to a notorious off-season trade the Alouettes had made with the Hamilton Tiger-Cats: Sam and Hal Patterson, for Hamilton's Bernie Faloney and Don Paquette. This trade would come to be known in Montreal as the plague trade, a blunder as famous as Hunsinger's fumble and as notorious as National Hockey League president Clarence Campbell's suspension of the Canadiens' superstar Rocket Richard in March, 1955. Twenty-one years later in a column designed to plumb the pathos of Nelson Skalbania's Alouettes the *Toronto Star's* Jim Proudfoot would cite the Etcheverry-Patterson trade, amazingly, as the beginning of Montreal's troubles. I say "amazingly" because by the time Jim Proudfoot wrote his column Montreal would have played in six more Grey Cup games, actually *winning* three—so where were the troubles? Of much greater, ironic interest, it seems to me, was the fact that but for a legal technicality the Montreal trade might have saved the Argos. Hal Patterson went readily to the Tiger-Cats but Sam Etcheverry, who had a no-trade clause in his contract, cited the Alouettes for breach and headed for St. Louis and the Cardinals instead—leaving in Hamilton a quarterback named Bernie Faloney.

Another noteworthy item from the Argo-St. Louis game was that it marked the last appearance in Argo colours of Norbert Wirkowski, himself the last remaining link to Zeke and Frankie Filchock and the afternoon of November 29, 1952. After being swept away in Harry's purge Nobby had played in Hamilton and then Calgary, until Lew Hayman summoned him back to Toronto in 1960 to back up Tobin and help Lou Agase with the coaching. As of the first game of '61, Nobby wasn't even supposed to be in uniform, let alone on the field against the Cardinals. He had been hurt earlier in training camp, and at the opening kickoff was safely ensconced high above the field in the spotter's booth; Nobby was the voice sifting drily into Lou Agase's headphones. By half-time, though, with the Argo offence having recorded minus 22 yards rushing and three first downs, Lou wanted more than the voice. (Of all of Lou Agase's coaching moves, this one strikes me as the most typical, a mixture of a kind of simplicity and surrender.) "At half-time," Nobby would remember, "our quarterback was doing so badly Agase called me up in the spotter's booth and said, 'You want to try?' So I went down and dressed and got in in the second half. I didn't do too badly either. I completed eleven out of twelve before Henke hit me, and the twelfth one Shatto dropped on me." It was the perfect Nobbyish epitaph for a career of courage: what obviously bothered him wasn't so much that Dick Shatto (a man Nobby would never be quite sure of) had dropped the twelfth pass, but that he had dropped it "*on me*", on *Nobby*. Pride may be the seventh deadly sin, but it's infinitely more forgivable in an athlete than apathy, in my opinion. How much less would Nobby have been if he'd said, "and someone dropped the twelfth one, I forget who, not that it matters, that's the way it goes," or "and Dick Shatto dropped the twelfth one on *the team*." Unfortunately for Nobby his knees weren't as durable as his honesty. On his thirteenth pass attempt, the Cardinal's swift tackle, Ed Henke — a former teammate of Nobby's at Calgary — hit him while his right cleated foot was planted firmly in the soft CNE turf, and Nobby went down, his knee unhinged from its moorings. He would not play football again.

Meanwhile the Argos were limping into the regular season as a group. Dick Shatto and Cookie were less than a hundred per cent, and Tobin had been stricken by another one of his chronic injuries — this time an injured thumb. The thumb injury had kept Tobin out of the pre-season games, and was still troublesome enough by the time of the regular-season opener that he was unable to start. His replacement was the 27-year-old rookie black quarterback Nobby had taken over for in the St. Louis game, John Henry Jackson. By taking the field for the Argos at CNE John Henry gave the team the distinction of having black players performing the three functions that had traditionally been the iron-clad preserve of white players in football (to an extent they still are): quarterbacking (John Henry), place-kicking (Cookie Gilchrist) and punting (Dave Mann). It was an anomaly of professional football, and its shame, that at the time not a single one of those jobs was held by a black player on any other football team on the continent. (By contrast, the modern Argos have always been at the vanguard of social progress in football, for greater reasons, I like to think, than just the fact that they're willing to try anything to lift the curse.)

As a starter for the Argos John Henry had everyone pulling for him and the Cinderella possibilities of the situation — the fans, the press, possibly even Tobin. It was an unreasonable burden for any athlete to bear. By the end of the first quarter John Henry was battling his own nerves more than the opposition, and Lou Agase was forced to take him out of the game (giving him the regular-season Overnight Visitor record of fifteen minutes played). Tobin had to go in at quarterback, too early, it transpired, for the season as well as the game. The only thing I can remember about the dozen games that followed, aside from the frustrating balkiness of the Argos' play, was the name of a new Argo punt-returner, Lynn Bottoms. Lynn, and maybe Stan Wallace, an inventive, extremely intelligent defensive back Lew Hayman had recruited the year before from the Chicago Bears to call the Argos' defensive signals; which Stan did, with an independence that was fortunate for Lou Agase. Half the signals Stan called were for formations that weren't even in the Argo play-book. With two games left in the season the Argos, who had been 10 and 4 in 1960, had a 5-6-1 record and were wallowing in mediocrity.

And then it all suddenly came together. The catalyst was an unlikely offence introduced by Lou Agase: the shot-gun. The shot-gun was an offence even more pass-oriented than the Argo attack of 1960: it called for Tobin to stand five yards behind the centre, take a medium-deep snap, and then pick out one of five or six or sometimes *seven* potential receivers who were describing various posts, patterns, comebacks, and loop-the-loops down-field. The shot-gun was exciting—something would happen on every play—but also extremely nerve-racking to watch, with Tobin standing completely alone behind the line, and his receivers fleeing downfield and the blocking in front of him threatening to break down at any moment. There was also the question of frequency. Years later the Dallas Cowboys and a quarterback named Roger Staubach would employ another form of the shot-gun with exemplary effectiveness—but Dallas wouldn't use it on every play. The Argos essentially did. It was another example of Lou's singular all-or-nothing philosophical outlook.

With Tobin passing, and Dick and Cookie running (occasion-ally), and Bobby Kuntz blocking, and Stan Wallace inventing defensive signals, the Argos won their last two games of the season, finishing with a record of 7-6-1 and, more important, earning the right to meet the Ottawa Rough Riders—the very team that had "sleepered" them out of playoffs the year before under the dual guidance of Russ Jackson and Frank Clair—in the Eastern semi-final. But this year things were different. When the game was over Tobin had thrown four touchdown passes to Ron Morris, a journeyman Canadian receiver the team had recently acquired from the Calgary Stampeders, and the Argos had won the game 43-19. "If the Argos play the way they did against us,"

Frank Clair himself said looking ahead to the finals, "they'll beat anybody."

The Argos didn't have to beat "anybody". Instead they had to beat the Hamilton Tiger-Cats — in a two-game *total-point* series. In future years the Tiger-Cats would come to haunt the Argos (especially on the last games of countless seasons) as doggedly as death — but in 1961 the tradition of the Hamilton nemesis was still in its embryonic stages. Not that the Hamilton team of 1961 wasn't a formidable one. In many ways it may have been the most formidable Hamilton team that had ever played in the Big Four. It was the Tiger-Cat team that had played in three of the last four Grey Cups, the Tiger-Cats of coach Jim Trimble, the man who would one day invent the phrase "We'll waffle 'em," as well as the futuristic single-support goal-post standard that would become common in football everywhere. It was a team anchored by its "Steeltown" defence, cast with ingots named John Barrow and Ralph Goldston and Zeno Karcz; the Ti-Cats of Garney Henley (the antelope in glasses), the transplanted, elegant Hal Patterson, and Bernie Faloney himself.

The first game of the total-point series took place at CNE Stadium, in brilliant sunshine — and the Argos were flawless. Jim Trimble used the word himself, with, if you took the time to read between the lines, discernible awe. The Argos held the Tiger-Cat offence to one single and an unconverted touchdown in sixty minutes, and scored three touchdowns themselves, added a field goal and a single and won the game by a score of 25-7, emerging with a lead of eighteen points. All they had to do was avoid losing the second game by eighteen points or more, and they would go to the Grey Cup. Eighteen points. Eighteen, twice nine, root of the magic square. Eighteen, the numerical equivalent of the letters in the Hebrew word *chai*, meaning "life". Even cabbalistically, it later occurred to me, the omens for the second game could not have been better.

I watched the game in the den of my parents' home in Bathurst Manor, a Jewish suburb north of the city. The Argos were very big in Bathurst Manor — probably because, with their swoon in the latter half of the fifties, they had gradually taken on the mysterious aura of what I would one day label, for want of a better term, a "Jewish" sports team: a team whose ambience of doom would prove more irresistible to the fatalistic Jewish sensibility than a pure winner. There were other "Jewish" athletes who had a high profile in the Manor at the time: Frank Mahovlich, Gump Worsley (hockey), Jimmy Piersall (baseball); and even other teams: the Boston Red Sox, the New York Rangers; and even other subgroups within teams, for example all small Montreal Canadien defensive specialists who jumped over the boards to get *onto* the bench—but no single person or organization ever caught the general mordant fancy of the Manor the way the Argos did.

There were two other people in the den with me at the time of the Hamilton game: my father, and an uncle, both fans, but of very different stripes. My father was a "polite" fan—he affected a civilized indifference towards the Argos, as though he could take them or leave them. My uncle was more forthright, but all his loyalty had turned to bile: he referred to the Argonauts as "bastards", a word that usually comprised his entire commentary for the games I watched with him; at strategic moments he would stare at the screen and emit a single understated, contemptuous "Bastards."

I was not an Argo fan. Not yet. I liked the Argos, and I knew the names of most of their players, but this didn't constitute real fandom, any more than the fact that I had been excited by games before—the '56 Grey Cup Game and the '58 NFL Championship, to name two. As a fan I was a *tabula rasa* at the start of the second Hamilton-Argo game, waiting to be inscribed with my fate.

The Argos came out passing. Of all the strange patterns that held during the game, this was the first and fundamental one, the one that would be at the top of the list in most perplexed post-game analyses. Even granting Lou Agase his lack of sophistication, it was a baffling piece of strategy. Ralph Goldston, the Hamilton great who played both ways for the entire game, noted afterwards, "They didn't play the game right. . . . If I'd been Agase I'd have put Cookie Gilchrist, Mann, and Shatto in the backfield to run. . . . They'd have to make some yards and they'd have run out the clock. After all, they had eighteen points, and it should have stood up. But they kept passing and giving us the ball. I didn't understand it." "Why did Faloney pass," Annis Stukus started his list of questions the morning after the game, "What happened to the Argos' running game; why didn't they kick on first down...?" Annis's first and last questions were basically unanswerable, and the second was the same one that mystified Ralph Goldston. The reason the Argos had no running game was that they had the shot-gun. From the opening kick-off there was no one in the backfield to do the running. Cookie Gilchrist and Mann and Shatto were where everyone else on the team was, where Lou Agase had sent them—out on the flanks, running downfield to catch Tobin's passes. The trouble was, the Hamilton line was breaking into the Argo backfield on every other play, and Tobin was throwing the ball with a spooked lack of accuracy even when they weren't. The Argos coming back to the huddle seemed to be physically fading under the pressure. I remember having the feeling that there was something wrong with the television set —we were getting ghosts, but only on the Argo side of scrimmage.

In the growing glaze of unreality the Tiger-Cats, the most solid of teams, scored first on a single point. They scored another two points in the second quarter on a safety touch after Ron Morris—playing defence now—intercepted a Bernie Faloney pass on his own 3-yard line and fell into the end-zone. (Even the *way* the Ti-Cats were scoring was unreal.) That only made the score (counting both games) 25-10 at the half; the Argos were still ahead by fifteen points. But in the third quarter Faloney hit Garney Henley for a touchdown and the Tiger-Cats were only down by eight. It was as though Hamilton was playing in a vacuum: the Argos had yet to put a *point* on the board in nearly forty-five minutes of play; *they had yet to move past Hamilton's 35-yard line*. At the end of the third quarter Faloney passed to Ralph Goldston for another touchdown. Argos 25-Hamilton 24. In the first two minutes of the fourth quarter Don Sutherin kicked a field goal: Hamilton 27-Argos 25. The Argos had done it; against all odds they had collapsed completely, squandering their eighteen-point lead and being outscored on the day 20-0.

But now, with time running out, the Argos suddenly revived. With seven and a half minutes left in the game Dave Mann kicked a 47-yard single, and five minutes later, after making a brilliant catch and run to the Hamilton 35, he kicked another single, this one a towering spiral that carried twenty yards into the end-zone. With the score tied now, 27-all, the Tiger-Cats took the ball on their own 25.

And this is when it happened. On first down Bernie Faloney, maybe infected by the waves of illogic the Argos had been generating all day, but more likely distracted by the ghost of the Bounce past—of opposing quarterbacks calling suicidal plays in the last two minutes of a championship game (it had happened in

1946, you'll recall, as well as 1952)—called a *pass play* on first down, dropping back and throwing the ball over the middle. He was aiming at a crossing Hamilton flanker, but instead it was caught by Stan Wallace, who on one of his inspired whims had wandered over from his outside position and stepped in front of the Hamilton receiver. Stan was tackled on the Tiger-Cat 27-yard line, giving the Argos a first down there with just ninety-one seconds left in the game.

No one who saw this part will ever forget it. In our den in Bathurst Manor, it took a moment for the action on the television screen to register as reality. With a minute and a half left in the game, with the day's score standing at 20-2, after putting on one of the most horrible displays of football I would ever see, the Argos had truly done it. They had snatched victory from the jaws of humiliating defeat. The game had come down to a mere formality. The way Dave Mann had been kicking all day (averaging forty-eight yards per punt), chances were good he could kick the ball completely out of the end-zone from the 27. In our den, opinion was divided: my uncle thought the Argos should kick on first down and not risk a fumble; my father, more fastidious, less paranoid, thought they should run out the clock first so Hamilton would have no chance to come back. (I was standing behind the couch—my traditional position for watching sports—and for the moment said nothing at all.)

On the field in Hamilton the Argos came out of the huddle with Tobin tight behind the centre—they were going to run out the clock. It was spine-tingling strategy, but by no means insane (although Zeke O'Connor himself would later make the claim that Lou Agase, an American coach under pressure, had actually *forgotten about the single point*, a strictly Canadian rule). The first play made sense too—a quarterback sneak by Tobin—but the Argos went offside. On first down over again, from the 32-yard line, Tobin carried *again*, gaining three yards. On second and seven, the Argos tried a draw play. A *draw* play? "The only way [a draw] could possibly work is if the opposition suspects a pass play," a bemused Annis Stukus would write, "and not even Tobin Rote could take a chance on a pass then." The draw went to Bobby Kuntz, the last time he would touch a football as an Argo, and lost two yards. But that was irrelevant; what mattered was that the Argos hadn't fumbled. They had the ball, and a down left, with twenty-eight seconds on the clock, and they were on the 31-yard line—a range that for Dave Mann meant a practically automatic single point. Dave had almost kicked the ball beyond the dead-ball line on his last single, from the 35, four yards back. And without blocking on punt returns (the rule would not change for another decade) Hamilton had almost no chance of running the punt back even if Dave's kick was a bit short.

The Tiger-Cats appeared to be acknowledging defeat themselves. In a move of pure desperation, Jim Trimble sent Don Sutherin and Bernie Faloney, both kickers, deep into the end-zone, with instructions to *punt* the ball back out if they got the chance. Not only was it a desperate tactic, it was a purely Canadian one—in American football there was no such thing as a single point (a rouge), and no one had kicked a ball out of an end-zone for fifty years. It's doubtful, though, that too many Argo fans were thinking about technical points, or the irony of the last play of a modern football game coming down to a rule left over from basic rugby. Most likely they were thinking about Dave Mann, dropping back now some twelve yards behind scrimmage in his familiar punting position; Dave Mann, the fourth dominant Argo of the era (along with Cookie and Tobin and Dick Shatto), the mysterious, virtuoso black player in a city white to its bones (if Cookie was Satchmo in a bad mood, Dave Mann was Charlie Mingus); Dave Mann, who until he came to the Argos had laboured in the shadow of the great running-back Ollie Matson, first with the University of San Francisco, then with the Chicago Cardinals; Dave Mann, who after he came to the Argos was dogged by another shadow, criminal charges concerning marijuana allegedly found in his car, a charge that was eventually dropped, but not before he missed the entire 1959 season. Dave Mann, who—more important—could kick punts that would draw you to your feet as they spiralled up into the night air, arcing past the lights, breaking scale altogether with the play on the field, while far below the punt-returners fell back and tried to gauge just where the ball would re-enter the atmosphere. Dave Mann, who would kick the ball out of the end-zone now and win the game for the Argos.

The snap came back. Dave stepped forward and kicked. It was his worst punt of the day, a wobbly forty-yarder, but it still carried eight yards into the end-zone. It came down to Don Sutherin, who somehow, surrounded by blue shirts, managed to execute a panicky stutter-step and actually *kick it back out*. The camera swung back crazily, tennis-style, catching Sutherin's kick coming down just past the 30-yard line into the hands of, amazingly, Dave Mann again, who hesitated, then stepped forward and *again* kicked it back towards the end-zone. Dave's second kick landed on the goal line, and bounced into the hands of Bernie Faloney. And Faloney began to run.

In the panelled den of a stately home in Rosedale, a man whom I will call Mr. Stanley was watching the game on television. As Bernie Faloney started to run Mr. Stanley rose slowly out of his chair as if, the people around him reported, something was drawing him up, making him lighter than the surrounding world. When Faloney reached mid-field Mr. Stanley pointed a finger at the set and said, "Look at that Faloney run!" Then Mr. Stanley keeled over, dead of a heart attack.

Faloney ran and ran. For the first thirty yards or so he wove in and out of would-be Argo tacklers at a leisurely, hypnotic speed, so that as he moved up the field he seemed to be passing the same players twice and even three times. Even when he'd passed mid-field, and there were no Argos left to weave around, he wove. It was one of the strangest runs ever made on a football field. The last forty yards he ran incoherently, exhausted, in another dimension. He ran 111 yards in all, into the Argo end-zone for a touchdown, and he probably would have kept on running if a Hamilton fan hadn't leapt out of the stands into the end-zone and knocked him flat by way of celebration.

The irony that usually gets lost in any retelling of the story of Faloney's run is that the play was eventually called back. Hamilton's Grant McKee bumped Bobby Kuntz illegally on the Tiger-Cat 46 and so nullified the entire run. But it didn't matter. It was Faloney's run that had killed Mr. Stanley; and it was Faloney's run that had given birth to the new Argos. In the thirty-minute overtime period the Tiger-Cats scored four unanswered touchdowns, taking the game 48-2 and the series 55-27, and qualifying to meet the Winnipeg Blue Bombers in the Grey Cup.

The Argos had finally done it. They had snatched defeat from the jaws of certain victory; they had moved firmly into the realm of unreality. When the final gun went off, the twelve players in double blue remaining on the field stood stock still for a moment, victims in a tableau that would become familiar before long. It was as though they were starting to realize that there was something larger than themselves controlling their destiny.

Actually there were thirteen victims. The extra one was me, standing by the door of the den. Faloney's run had hooked me. I would spend no small part of the next twenty years trying to figure out how. If a fan has a soul, though, mine was lost to the Argos from that fatal moment on.

5 The Second Fall

In 1962, just a year after coming within twenty-eight seconds of a Grey Cup appearance, the Argos finished last with a 4-10 record. It was their fifth 4-10 record in the last seven years (a 4-10 percentage from 1956 of .714). Three games into the season, John Bassett—now the principal owner of the team—had had enough, and Lou Agase was fired as coach. His replacement was none other than his assistant, Nobby Wirkowski. It's interesting to speculate what Nobby might have done in a coaching position with a normal team during a normal season; with the Argos in the year following Faloney's Run it was all he could do to keep the shock waves to a minimum. By the end of the season Tobin Rote, who had been playing less-than-inspired football, was conducting a public newspaper feud with Annis Stukus, who had been citing Tobin's play selection as one of the major causes for the Argos' demise. The *Telegram* played the feud to the hilt, giving Tobin equal space for rebuttals under his own by-line and publishing adjacent pictures of both contestants with their responses: Tobin in his baldness, and Annis in his playing days, in his crazy-looking leather helmet and bare shins. Annis's main point was that Tobin did not seem to be mixing his plays as well as he had in the heady period before the second game of the '61 final. Tobin's thesis was that Annis didn't seem to know anything about the game of football. As a bonus Tobin threw in the same opinion about the departed Lou Agase—confirming the suspicions of thousands of fans (me included) and finally explaining Tobin's rolling eyes in the sideline photograph of August, 1960.

But it was Annis, with his dictionary of vague generalities,

Quarterback and airlift passenger Sandy Stephens.
The "can't miss" Stephens lasted eight games.

who had the last word. Tobin led the Argos through the final game of 1962, a 32-8 loss to the Montreal Alouettes on a rain-soaked mud-bowl of a field (another Argo tradition: the wet or windy goodbye) and immediately left town, heading south towards sanity, the San Diego Chargers of the fledgling American Football League, and the waning years of a distinguished football career. Cookie Gilchrist had already jumped to the Buffalo Bills of the AFL at the start of the season, after being put on suspension by the Argos for various pieces of eccentric, Cookie-esque behaviour. (A story describing Cookie's departure would eventually appear in a book called *The Running Backs*, to the effect that when a Buffalo scout named Harvey Johnson arrived with Buffalo news-paperman Jack Horrigan at the CNE to first talk to Cookie, their car was immediately surrounded by an angry mob that shouted, "Here come the carpetbaggers. They're coming to steal Cookie!" — and then proceeded to attack the car, pounding on the roof and threatening its occupants. The story doesn't strike me as quite convincing. Argo fans — and the fans of losing teams in general — tend to be more private and complex when they get angry. A losing fan is more likely to assault his own car than anyone else's.)

So Cookie was gone now too, along with Tobin. That left only Dick Shatto and Dave Mann as the remaining stars from Lou Agase's team to suffer through what was to follow.

Over the next four years the Argos finished last four times, making their string in the cellar five consecutive seasons long and breaking the four-year record stretch of 1956-59. Over the five seasons — the "Second Fall", you might call it — the Argos averaged 3.8 wins against 10.2 losses a year. They scored 1,079 points while having 1,597 scored against them, approximately the same point totals that they would have compiled if they had lost every game in those five seasons — seventy games in all — by a score of 23-15. In certain ways the Second Fall might have had a less debilitating effect on Argo fans if they had.

During the Second Fall most of the now established Argo syndromes — the Tease *et al.* — were honed to perfection, and two important new ones were introduced. One of these was the Annual Theory for the Existence of Doom. In this case, I admit, the Argos were not at first glance all that unique — the theories to account for the doom of any doomed sports team usually multiply till their number reaches the number of fans who are doomed along with it.

But the Argo theories always seemed to me to be tinged with something special. At the end of the 1963 season, an open letter of advice to the Argo management appeared on the sports page of the *Telegram*. The letter had been written by an Argo fan named Mike Steers; every second instruction was, "Don't panic":

1. Give the Coach the best contract available, more money than the players.
2. Don't panic.
3. Discard the Sonshine formula of airlifts, quarterbacks who write poems or columns, fading NFL greats and clipping-laden All-something-or-others.
4. Don't panic....

The official theories for the Argos' failure that began to appear in the early days of the Second Fall tended to be derivatives of Mike Steers' letter. One that was slightly different, and that would gain a considerable following over the years, was the Quarterback-Coach Timing Jinx. Every time the Argos had managed to land a coach with offensive acumen, went the argument, they were saddled with an impostor for a quarterback. Conversely, every time they fluked onto a decent quarterback, the head coach was a Lou Agase. Lou had been contemporaneous with Tobin, after all, while Hampton Pool had had only Tom Dublinski, Al Dorow, and Ronnie Knox to work with. The only trouble with the Quarterback-Coach theory was that it was only loosely supported by future pairings. These would include Nobby Wirkowski and Sandy Stephens (possibly good coach, impossibly hopeless quarterback), Leo Cahill and Joe Theismann (questionable coach, good quarterback), Forrest Gregg and Tony Adams (pompous coach, terrible quarterback), and Condredge Holloway and Willie Wood (penitent quarterback, humble coach).

You see the problem.

Another theory that cropped up around this time was one of the slew of explanations that centred around Lew Hayman—in this case the Franz Kafka metamorphosis of Lew. Shortly after he returned to Toronto in the mid-fifties, this theory held, Lew had awakened one morning to find himself transformed into a kind of Harry Sonshine, a spooked wraith who was preoccupied with trying to find a weekly newsworthy titillation for the mob at the CNE. This theory would have impressed me more in the long run if Lew—who always reminded me of a world-weary uncle I had in the garment business—had been patently oblivious of the fans before his return to Toronto, in the style, say, of Frank Clair. But in 1954 Lew had engineered a television contract with NBC for the showing of CFL games in the States (*before* the NFL had a network contract), not to mention initiating in 1946 the playing of games on Sunday in Canada, the first night games ever played, and the first use of black players. Public relations was obviously already in his blood. Much more convincing to me was a simpler Lew theory—his ubiquity. Harry might have instigated the fall, but Lew was the single managerial constant who had been there for its entire first decade.

But all these early theories were in my opinion secondary to another Argo-inspired theory at the time, a unique theory that had less to do with the reasons for doom than with its effects. I know the theory was unique because it was mine. From 1962 to 1966—from the year of my bar mitzvah to my second-last year of high school—my identity as an Argo fan was consolidated. Over that apprenticeship period I got to know not just the idiosyncrasies of the Argos, but the rhythms of losing fandom in general. Like most aficionados of teams that do not win, I gradually became obsessed with the hypothetical opposite—I started to become keenly aware that somewhere there had to be a team that did win. Somewhere there was a sports universe where success was possible, a mirror-image dimension where all the scores were reversed.

I didn't develop this theory on my own, as it happens. I was helped out by the Cleveland Browns.

It was all an accident of timing and the signing of a television contract. In 1961 the National Football League reached an agreement with the Columbia Broadcasting System involving the telecast of all of its regular-season games—on a *regional* basis, on the assumption that local loyalty was the best vein to tap. This meant that if you lived on the west coast you saw the Los Angeles Rams (or the then-hapless Forty-Niners); on the east coast you might pick up the New York Giants; in the centre of the continent, the Chicago Bears. And if you were somewhere between east and centre, you got a team that hailed from a city where a river would one day ignite of its own accord, a team that had one of the most illustrious histories of any ever to play the game. The eastern

Great Lakes was Cleveland territory, and so on Sunday afternoons in Toronto—while the Argos were idle, naturally—we watched the Cleveland Browns.

The Browns. The Browns, specifically, of the early and mid-sixties, the near-great team that with a few propitious breaks might have attained the greatness of the Browns of a decade and a half earlier. As it was, in a five-year span the Browns of the sixties era finished in second place three times and in first once, winning the NFL Championship in a stunning 27-0 rout of Johnny Unitas and the Baltimore Colts in 1964, and losing 23-12 to the Green Bay Packers of Bart Starr and Paul Hornung in '65 in a game whose first five plays are inscribed on my consciousness the way the first five Commandments might have been on Moses'.

But the Browns were so much more than a mere football team to a Toronto fan—especially a thirteen-year-old recovering from the debacle of November 25, 1961—that it's almost impossible to convey the difference to anyone who wasn't there. They were a list of ineffable names that would live in a fan's memory for ever: Frank Ryan, the skinny quarterback with the doctorate in math; Gary Collins, the slow but uncanny split end, the master of the post pattern and the down-and-out; Bobby Mitchell, the flanker with a penchant for describing dazzling ziggurats up the field (two steps sideways, one step forward); Lou "the Toe" Groza; Bernie Parrish; *Jimmy Brown.* Jimmy Brown, slouching back to the huddle with guarded, painstaking slowness, then carrying five Detroit Lions across the goal-line on the next play. They were the Browns, the team with the deceptively simple name and the uniforms as sepia-toned as history. They were the miniaturized TV distillation of the thing that could always banish boredom. They were Harry Sonshine's vision, big-league glamour American-style, come to the small screen.

They weren't the Argos.

To begin to appreciate the phenomenon of a Toronto fan watching the Browns, you have to go back first to the day before Sunday, Saturday afternoon, and a television program of the time called *Countdown to Kickoff.* Broadcast on CBS (Channel 4 in Toronto) every week, wedged between the bank of morning kids' shows—*My Friend Flicka, Circus Boy, Sky King*—and the afternoon's tacky midway of programs, the shadowy schedule of freaks—*Shock Theatre*, professional wrestling from Chicago or Buffalo, and *Roller Derby*—*Countdown to Kickoff* consisted of a slim, half-hour run-down of highlights from the previous Sunday's NFL games. There was nothing *but* the highlights: after a brief, breezy introduction done by an affable announcer—the antithesis of Howard Cosell and his momentous monotone—the highlights would come on, embellished by an up-tempo sports tune, something like the "To Look Sharp" theme from the Gillette Friday-night fights. And embellished, too, by slow motion.

This was the critical ingredient. As far as I've been able to determine, *Countdown to Kickoff* was the first television program on which slow motion was used regularly to illustrate the raw and lyric savagery of the game of football. In their imitations of American TV in years to come, Canadian networks would try to use slow motion in televising CFL games—including those of the Argos—but they would never get it quite right. Either the camera angle would be wrong, or they would use it too much (a classic shortcoming, slow-motion orgies), or the speed wouldn't be quite correct—it would be a shade too fast, or a tad too slow. *Countdown to Kickoff* established two perfect speeds for football slow motion that set the standard for ever. The first was *minimal* slow motion, a slowing down so slight you weren't exactly sure it *was* slow motion; it was just enough that the sharp edge of jerky reality was oiled into fluidity, so that when Johnny Unitas was dropping back into the pocket with his shoulders hunched up around his neck, his chunky sideways scurry actually looked smooth. The second kind was *extreme* slow motion, usually reserved for close-ups of acts of prodigious strength or balance—New York Giant linebacker Sam Huff steeling himself like a Neanderthal for an annihilating hit; Raymond Berry reaching up skinnily over his shoulder for the spot pass Johnny threw for two touchdowns a week—or sometimes, on rare occasions, the actual flight of the ball.

This was another thing the Canadian camera would never capture properly. Part of it had to do with the ball itself: the Canadian football—the J5V—was plump (a legacy of the kicking game) and striped. The NFL ball—called the "Duke"—was needle-nosed and stripeless. Thrown expertly, and caught against the sky in extreme slow motion, it had a spiral so perfectly uniform it was almost impossible to tell it was spinning at all: it was like my conception of America in general—incisive, effective, as smooth as silk. Even when it was thrown with a wobble, the American ball in extreme slow motion had a definite gyroscopic allure; it became a kind of lean, perfect error. The girthy Canadian ball, on the other hand, wobbled as a matter of course, and in slow motion the stripes created an exaggerated schoolyard effect that was actually embarrassing.

As American as *Countdown to Kickoff* was (with its NFL ball and extreme slow motion), the Browns on Sunday were triply so. I generally watched them not in the den — which by 1962, the year following Faloney's Run, my sister had appropriated for a bedroom — but downstairs in a dim recreation room my parents had furnished for my subterranean adolescence. (I wasn't alone — dozens of other teenaged Argo fans, I later discovered, were watching in similar grottoes scattered through Bathurst Manor.) Actually, to say I went down to watch the Browns is inaccurate; I went down, bored, sedated by Sunday, to watch *television*, and at one o'clock the Browns were suddenly there. In my years of watching the Argos I can't recall ever being surprised by a televised Toronto game; with the Browns in my recreation room, I was never anything but.

As far as the other obvious differences between the two teams went there was, first of all, Municipal Stadium, the Browns' home field. No matter how many times I saw it, the initial camera shot of Municipal was always unreal, in a paradoxically *super*-real way. The stadium rose endlessly up from the field, its decks layered like an ocean-liner's on a grey autumn day (the traditional Brown weather). Added to this vertical awesomeness — the same no matter which way the camera swivelled — was the crazy consistency of the attendance figure: 70,000. In years to come sell-outs in the NFL would become as predictable to football fans as Super Bowl hyperbole, but on those Sundays the 70,000 people who weekly packed Municipal Stadium and turned it into one dense vault of sound were a complete revelation to me. They had absolutely *nothing* in common with the crowds at Argo games, which, although sometimes large, were still in the early sixties anything but consistent. The Sunday 70,000 were a new kind of crowd, an American crowd that turned Municipal Stadium into an inescapable cocoon, a fortress of excitement. It was fantastic: there was no way out. At the CNE, when your gaze swung to the end-zones there were always those wide-open spaces dissipating cheers and passion. It was the same with most Canadian fields. At Taylor Field in Regina the television camera provided glimpses of station wagons rolling serenely past the end-zone, a little residential side-show. In Ottawa there were trees, stoplights. Calgary had a pre-fab clubhouse and the ubiquitous emergency vehicle. But at Municipal Stadium there were only people; it was a vertical Manhattan on a raw day. It was an American way of looking at the universe.

And then, of course, there was the American game itself, with its liberal rules: time-outs, the lack of even a millimetre between the offensive and defensive lines, and most critical of all, four downs instead of three. This last was at least partially responsible for the greatest difference I detected, over those Sundays, between the Browns and the Argos: the relative efficiency of their offences. No Argo team I'd ever watched could put together the kind of laboratory-precise, twelve-play march that Frank Ryan orchestrated at least twice a week. When had I ever seen a down-and-out used to set up the down-out-and-down? When had I ever seen a true screen play? The Browns' offensive drives sometimes went beyond good form to perfect show-biz. It was almost as though they were fixed. But they weren't, of course, and the fact that they weren't led me dangerously close to one inescapable suspicion: if football was meant to be more like art than chance, then football the way the Browns played it was very possibly football the way it was supposed to be played. What the Argos played was a unique sport that followed star-crossed rules all its own.

And finally, on Sunday with the Browns, there was the sound. Even before Faloney's Run, I had a vague suspicion that there was something wrong with the sound of Argo games on television — of all Canadian games for that matter — but it wasn't until I watched the Browns that I knew what it was. Again, it had to do with gaps: on Sunday afternoons with the Browns, there were none. The din of the crowd was a steady swath, and when the announcers cut in to speak the sound engineers dropped the crowd rumble but never wiped it out completely; the sound of life was always there; there was always a *background*. But too often, in Argo telecasts, when Fred Scambatti took a breath what you heard was the aural equivalent of the open CNE end-zones: space, silence, a two- or three-second gap. The moments tended to be so naked that they produced a tangible discomfort. Maybe in reaction to the uneasiness, when Fred came back on his voice was sometimes much too bright — it tended to fill the room.

In years to come I would resign myself to the peccadilloes of Canadian football broadcasts — I would even come to value them. But I could never get used to the sound. It was something I would bore editors with, and try to sneak into too many articles. If only they could get the sound right.

But even when I was thirteen I think I knew that they never would, that the lack of background in Canadian games was chronic and unavoidable. In a way it was too real; it left no gaps for daydreams, or the call of the loon. Or the Argos.

In 1963 Lew Hayman initiated a series of managerial moves which seemed to indicate he'd been watching the Browns and *Countdown to Kickoff* too—maybe in his own basement. Actually, what Lew was inventing (or perfecting—Harry Sonshine had been responsible for the prototype) was the final major Argo pattern of the era, the Airlift. The scenario for the Airlift was relatively straightforward: it involved the Argos falling into a state of acute anxiety following a limited number of losses—usually two, at the outside three—in the first quarter of a given season, and proceeding to fly in squadrons of Americans: late American cuts from the National Football League, or similar cuts from the American Football League, or Americans cut from other CFL teams, or Americans who had been out of football for two years and were working at putting decals on trucks in Fort Worth, Texas. It was characteristic of an Airlift that the players involved had to jet into town as opposed to arriving by any other mode of transportation (a busload of NFL cuts just wouldn't have been the same), that the vast majority of them did not last past their first game in Argo uniform (assuming that they even made it through their five-day trial), and that they had to be tragically flawed. This last was not Lew's prerequisite, or the fans'—it belonged to the Bounce.

Two of the most famous of the Airlift's passengers from the '63 season were Jackie Parker and Sandy Stephens. Both were quarterbacks, a problem-laden position for the Argos over the years. After the '62 season, Nobby, still ensconced as head coach, had stated publicly that he wanted to develop a young quarterback for the future. Even given my own chronic lack of patience as a young teenager, it seemed like a laudible plan. Nobby had subsequently settled on a promising American rookie named Don Fuell as his starting quarterback for '63. But Lew Hayman apparently had different plans, because before training camp opened he acquired Jackie Parker, the great, versatile, Edmonton Eskimo quarterback. The only problem was that Jackie Parker had reached the peak of his greatness and versatility in 1954, the year he'd run back Hunsinger's Fumble to start the Eskimos on their three-year Grey Cup domination of the Montreal Alouettes. Also, Jackie was a pure college-style "option" quarterback, and Canadian football had long since turned into a pass-oriented game. To my thirteen-year-old eyes, Jackie seemed as poignant in an Argo uniform—with his slender, fragile-looking legs—as my father might have been.

Sandy Stephens was another matter. In fact Sandy was the first individual Argo I ever got truly excited over. Acquired from the Montreal Alouettes half-way through the season—by the time Sandy first donned an Argo uniform, Jackie Parker was playing halfback—Sandy had impressive credentials: he'd been a college All-American playing quarterback for the University of Minnesota, and he was black, which made him somehow more American to an Argo fan than a white player would have been (an idiosyncratic reaction that a much-publicized halfback named George Hughley was also eliciting, and that would shortly burgeon into another Argo syndrome, the Great Black Hope). In addition, Sandy drove a pink Cadillac that was equipped with a portable record-player. The less colourful facts about Sandy—that he had a tendency towards portliness at the age of twenty-two, and had a predilection for throwing high lazy parabolas of passes, *and* that he'd been cut by Montreal—were somehow overlooked. Sandy couldn't miss.

In Sandy's first game with the Argos, he threw two touchdown passes to lead them to a 15-7 win over Hamilton, vindicating my faith and demonstrating impressive enough quarterbacking skills along the way to be called "brilliant" in the *Tely*. In Sandy's second game, in a virtually sold-out CNE Stadium, the Argos lost 50-0 to the Calgary Stampeders, the worst shut-out loss a Double Blue team had ever suffered. Eight games later Sandy was gone and the Argos had ended their season 3 and 11, their smallest number of wins since 1934, when the season was only six games long.

But 1964 dawned with fresh hope. In spite of the dismal record of the year before, no one could deny that the Argos had lost a number of games in '63 they could very easily have won. "Argos worked harder losing at least five games than they would have winning them," was the way Annis Stukus put it, with uncharacteristic pungency. I disagreed. It seemed to me that the team had been struck by impossibly bad luck. Also, Lew Hayman's recruiting for the '64 season had brought in some truly exciting prospects: a quarterback from the Detroit Lions (a tradition in itself for the Argos) named Karl Sweetan; a tiny, swift water-bug of a pass-receiver named Sherman Lewis ("Sherman Lewis is all heart and a mile wide"); and Dave Pivec, a highly touted rookie end from Notre Dame who had dropped out of his junior year for mysterious reasons and was consequently ineligible for the NFL draft. ("Dave Pivec is an NFL tight end, and *we* have him.") On the defensive side the Argos had a "veteran" defensive end (a hold-over from '63) named Ed Harrington, an ex-Mr. Mid-United States who was a classic athletic Jekyll and Hyde. Off the field Ed was a gentle, exceptionally articulate man; on it he had a penchant for breaking people's jaws. In 1964 he broke the jaw of Jim Leo, who unfortunately also played for the Argos. Still, the Argos were awesome enough in appearance that, by the time they'd won their first three exhibition games, they were being widely hailed in the press as a "Super Team" (while disquieting rumbles were reported from around the league to the effect that Toronto had "bought" itself an invincible squad and created an imbalance it would take years to correct). The Argos then lost eleven out of their next fifteen games, finishing the season 4 and 10, with a final day 36-0 defeat at the hands of the Ottawa Rough Riders. Of the three American "sure stars" Lew had flown in, Karl Sweetan played the longest for the team, fashioning a thirteen-game Overnight Visitor career. Dave Pivec was gone after twelve games, as was Sherman Lewis, who was every bit as valiant as he was supposed to be, but even smaller.

In 1965 the Airlift was alive and thriving, but another change was made that was historically more important: Nobby was not rehired as coach. At the time I considered it inevitable. Who was this short, dated hard-rock on the sidelines with the funny name, anyway? I had only the vaguest idea of who Nobby was, or where he was from. I had the traditional sixteen-year-old's view of the past as a place where people had short haircuts and were either hilarious or ineffectual. Nobby I placed on the ineffectual and embarrassing side of the ledger; one of those *Canadian* Americans, an American who had been around for so long he'd become overly familiar and had lost any glamour he might once have had. An American further from the mystique of the Cleveland Browns I couldn't imagine.

To replace Nobby as coach the Argos hired Bob Shaw, an ex-

Saskatchewan head coach who was six feet, four inches tall, and who probably took his football more seriously than any coach the team had had since Frank Clair. Setting the tone for a long line of Argo coaches who would follow him, Bob Shaw repeatedly claimed that he took the challenge of coaching the Argonauts seriously (as if there was another plausible way of taking it).

"Bob Shaw knew that he was flirting with the electric chair when he accepted the job of coaching the Toronto Argonauts," Jim Coleman wrote in the *Telegram*. After the Argos lost their first exhibition game 17-7, to the Edmonton Eskimos, Bob Dennis, one of Shaw's assistants, noted, "I've been with Coach Shaw for five years. He's never had a losing season in those five years, but his teams seldom win exhibition games. Just wait till...the regular season." The regular season brought the Airlift, striking with unprecedented speed. Lamar McHan, the Argos' starting quarterback, lasted two games. He was replaced immediately by Pete Liske, who lasted eleven before departing for Calgary and a career as a passer that would place him in the Canadian Football League record-book in sixteen separate categories, including first place in the most touchdowns thrown during a single season (thus establishing one of the remaining important Argo "themes"—the Argo discard who went on to greatness with another team, the "Dazzling Discard", you might call him). By the season's end, the Argos were 3 and 11 and had had almost twice as many points scored against them as they had scored themselves. Their last loss was a 35-21 defeat at the hands of the Hamilton Tiger-Cats, in a sixty m.p.h. gale. The Tiger-Cats, coached by Ralph Sazio, gained 305 yards on the ground alone. But it was the caption below a photograph of a Hamilton touchdown on the next day's sports page that said it best.

> It looks like a demonstration of the Watusi or the Frug, but it's really Ti-Cat Willie Bethea dancing over teammate John Counts on the goal-line. Ron Howell (30) heads the Argo stag line. For the sad end of another Argo season, see page 19.

It may seem that my description of the Argos' Second Fall so far has been a bit breezy, but the fact is this particular period of Argo history was more painful to me than almost anything else I would go through with the Double Blue. The breeziness is largely defensive. From 1962 to 1966 I spanned the years from age thirteen to seventeen, the most intense years in a fan's life. Approaching an Argo game in the mid-sixties wasn't all that different from approaching sex. There was the same tremendous anticipation, the same giddiness, the same horrible fear of failure. And after-wards—worst of all—there was the same gnawing anguish over opportunities lost. All the "what if's...?" What if the Argos had given Don Fuell a chance? What if her father hadn't turned on the lights in the recreation room? What if Dave Pivec hadn't got hurt? What if your wrist hadn't fallen asleep? What if Sherman Lewis hadn't been so short?

Every summer during the Second Fall the Argos pumped me full of hope, and every fall, at various points during the changing of the leaves, they crushed me. The process was the exact opposite of the occasional merciful periods of fan "hibernation" I would experience over the next fifteen years. A fan's life has a biological rhythm all its own. A fan will have favourite teams within the general shell of his loyalty, and favourite seasons, and seasons that drive him crazy—all acutely memorable—and other periods where he lives semi-comatose inside his skin like a pupa, reading the box-scores with half a mind and waiting for the right individual or crisis to come along and signal the next stage in his life cycle.

In the painful Argo period in question one incident stands out in my mind even more vividly than the rest. It took place at the beginning of the 1966 season, in the first exhibition game the Argos played that year. Bob Shaw, who had been living (like me) with the humiliation of the 1965 3-11 season all winter, had arrived at training camp swearing it wouldn't happen again. To help make sure it didn't Lew Hayman had provided him with a new quarterback, a 22-year-old fresh from the campus of the University of Michigan and already highly thought of, named Wally Gabler. The first game Wally played, the pre-season opener against Hamilton, became instantly famous for a controversial incident, the question of whether or not Hamilton's Angelo Mosca actually spat at Bob Shaw at the end of the game. The Mosca scandal was so notorious it almost completely obscured what had gone on in the first half of the same game: it was possibly the greatest offensive thirty minutes an Argo team had ever played. Wally Gabler completed ten of thirteen passes for 248 yards, and ran seven times for 74 yards. By the end of the half the Argos were leading 34-0. And at the 21-0 mark, in the second quarter, Bob

Shaw burst into tears on the sidelines and had to be comforted by his players. The picture was in all the papers, with the complementary information that the reason Bob Shaw had broken down was that it had been so long in coming, and that the Argos had finally arrived.

I was embarrassed by the incident, and also tremendously impressed. Who could fail to believe a weeping 6′4 professional football coach? Only the Argos. By the end of the season they had won just two more games than in 1965, finishing 5-9 and in last place for the ninth time in the past eleven years. I was seventeen, heading into my second-last year of high school, totally unarmed for the direction the Bounce was about to take — towards a pair of smiling Irish eyes.

6 Leon's Fumble

One warm night in August of 1966, a 6'6 linebacker named Allen Ray Aldridge climbed, spiderlike, onto the shoulders of a burly tackle at one end of Varsity Stadium (Varsity!) and threw his long arms into the blue-black summer sky. The resulting eleven-foot apparition was straight out of a Japanese horror movie, and totally unnerved the human-sized player facing it, who was attempting to kick a field goal. The field goal went wide. In the winners' dressing-room after the game the tactic was discussed with cacophonous wonderment.

The name of the team was the Toronto Rifles. The coach of the team, and the creator of the piggy-back field goal block (which was eventually outlawed in every rule-book in football), was Leotus Cahill.

Leo Cahill was a gremlin. He was a leprechaun. He even looked a bit to me like a leprechaun, a well-fed, plump-faced, boyish refugee from *Finian's Rainbow*, wearing a pair of tinted glasses reminiscent of Annie Sullivan's from *The Miracle Worker*. He was an Irish hustler with a hustler's magical touch for discovery, a consummate PR director who wore his heart on his sleeve, a vulnerable confidence-man full of bluff and *schtick* and contradictions.

In 1966, though, Leo was primarily the coach of the Toronto Rifles. A few years earlier the United Football League, a minor professional league with teams covering the eastern U.S. as far south as Charleston, had decided to expand into the Canadian market, specifically into Montreal. For their name the team chose the nickname of their owner—none other than Sam "The Rifle" Etcheverry himself. For their logo they chose a symbolic compro-

Leo Cahill, the winningest coach in Argo history,
during his first sojourn with the team.

mise (coincidentally containing all the elements of at least one Toronto fan's football psyche): a Canadian maple leaf over an American minuteman's musket, both superimposed on a football. For their head coach they chose Perry Moss's offensive-line assistant coach with the Montreal Alouettes—Leo Cahill. When Montreal, a traditionally terrible football town, failed to support the Rifles, now in the Continental Football League, the team moved to Toronto in 1965. This meant that the Rifles started to play football in the city at about the time that Bob Shaw was insisting he took the challenge of coaching the Argos seriously—and the majority of Argo fans (myself included) were believing him. This, plus the fact that for their first season the Rifles would be playing their home games in a Triple-A baseball park—Maple Leaf Stadium at the foot of Bathurst Street—led most experts to predict a rocky future for the new team.

In fact they couldn't have been more wrong. Leo and the Rifles started slowly, but by the middle of the '65 season they had fans flocking in droves to the dimly lit unlikeliness of Maple Leaf Stadium. The reason was simple. It was embarrassing. Not only did the Rifles win games, they were actually *fun* to watch. Fans in Toronto had forgotten that football could be fun to watch: with the Argos fun was not an operative factor. *Angst* took up most of your time with the Argos, either that or fear, or hope, or acute cynicism. Fun was for baseball, with its merciful hiatuses between innings; or for Sunday trips to Toronto Island, where you could learn how to speak Italian while you ate your lunch. But now, here was a football team you could come to watch with that compulsive thrill of delight in your heart. "Whatever happens tonight," I remember thinking on my way to Rifle games, "I will probably have a good time." Nothing could sabotage a fan at a Rifle game— there were no mine-fields of doom under the turf.

Part of the reason may have been the location of the games— in 1965 Maple Leaf Stadium with its improvised friendliness; in 1966 the perfect enclosed football park: Varsity Stadium itself. But an equal part was the nature of the game on the field. The football the Rifles played was unapologetically *American* football: four downs on a 100-yard field. It was the fulfilled promise of all those Browns' games on Sunday afternoons. During the 1966 season at Varsity the novelty was most dramatic. Down on the field where Joe Krol had kicked and Royal Copeland had run, down where Zeke had made his catch, twenty-two Americans from

Richmond and Rochester were playing a game that up to now had been imprisoned on my television set. Four downs! Aside from being free of doom, the game the Rifles played was expansive, offensive football, football where you had room to breathe, and point, and laugh. Any second I expected the concession vendor to come around with a tray of Hershey bars and a carton of Kents.

Added to the real McCoyness of it — or perhaps knocking the edges *off* it to exactly the right degree — was the Rifles' loony, Cahillesque character. Everything about the Rifles was either vaguely crazy, or vaguely familiar, like an in-joke from your old neighbourhood. From the beginning Leo attracted the discarded, the rebellious, the half and the wholly insane. One Rifle quarterback, mature and unharried himself now, was none other than John Henry Jackson, the black quarterback who had left his Argo failure behind. The other was a pudgy, tobacco-chewing rookie named Tom Wilkinson. The Rifle right defensive end was Tom "the Emperor" Jones, an ex-Ottawa Rough Rider on his way to stardom on the professional wrestling circuit (along with Angelo Mosca, the man who had spat on Bob Shaw). The roster was rounded out by Allen Ray Aldridge, and players with such improbable names as Joe Loudermilk, Crash Craddock, and Dick Limerick. As though this weren't enough, Leo had embellished the team with innovations that no one had ever seen on a football field before anywhere. Besides the piggy-back field goal block, Leo had thought up something called the "Indian blitz", as well as another dozen or so slot and double-wing formations that utilized the sophisticated motion he had learned from coaching the Montreal Alouettes. After a 21-13 win over the Brooklyn Dodgers one night, Andy Robustelli, the New York coach (and ex-New York Giant great), commented: "All that motion. We've never seen anything like that before. What was that anyway?"

I went to at least half a dozen Rifle games, but there is one I remember in particular. It took place not at Varsity but during that first season of '65 at Maple Leaf Stadium, the baseball park which would be torn down in 1968 to make room for a parking lot. In its way Maple Leaf Stadium was as perfect a stadium as Varsity, but not for football. That night the gridiron had been laid out lengthwise between centrefield and home plate, so that the near end-zone was well lit and reasonably visible, while the far one faded into darkness in the depths of centrefield. I don't recall whom the Rifles were playing — it may have been one of the southern teams, with a dying fall in their name, Richmond or Charleston—I only remember that the stands were filled; there didn't seem to be a seat left in the house. And I remember one play. The opposing team had punted from the 50-yard line and the Rifles' return man, for some reason disdaining the touchback, chose to run. He ran towards the sideline at first, while the unrestricted American blocking formed in front of him, and then turned upfield, tightroping along the line while the sound in the stands rose. At about mid-field he suddenly started to fade into the deepening darkness, until finally, around the 20-yard line, he vanished completely, becoming a sort of imagined football force, the molecular essence of a punt return, so that only the up-flung arms of the trailing referee confirmed what we suspected. It was one of the eeriest, most beautiful touchdowns I had ever seen.

It was also much too good a moment to last. In 1967 the Rifles had started a slow fade, and Leo Cahill was hired to coach the Argos.

From the beginning it was a love-hate fan relationship without equal. This happens sometimes with coaches, especially coaches who are fired only to return again—Lou Saban in Buffalo is another example that comes to mind—but with Leo the paradox was on another stratum altogether. For one thing, no one was ever really convinced that Leo could coach football at all. His genius as a recruiter and general manager was undisputed, but the success he had on the field always seemed somehow unsatisfying and suspicious: Leo seemed to be doing it with mirrors.

The problem was uncertainty. Whereas fans could be relatively *sure* Lou Agase couldn't coach, it was harder to know with Leo. By the time he'd reached 1971 (and a certain day in the rain in Vancouver) Leo had compiled a record of forty-seven victories, twenty-seven losses, and two ties, making him the *winningest* coach in Argo history (in terms of total victories), more so than Lew Hayman, Tedder Morris, or Frank Clair. And in the process Leo had brought the average attendance at Argo games from 21,048 in 1966, under Bob Shaw—its lowest level since the move to CNE—up to 33,135 in '71, the season of Joe "the Throw" Theismann and true hope. Even the next year, 1972, when the fans were singing their goodbye *en masse*, there were more than 33,000 of them in the stadium. It was Leo who affected Argo fans in a way which would never be undone: he brought them into the stands for good. This may possibly have been the thing the majority of Argo fans could never forgive Leo for, and the reason they serenaded him farewell the vengeful way they did.

The thing *I* could never forgive Leo for was his annual "Leonine" version of the Tease-cum-Gimmick—the dramatic unveiling, in every exhibition season, of the revolutionary American-tinged innovation, or formation, or player deal, that would invariably arouse in me uneasiness, suspicion, and doomed curiosity. His opening surprise of 1967, his first season, is a case in point. The Tease-cum-Gimmick in this case was the "Numbers Game". As of 1967 the import rules of the CFL allowed for fourteen Americans per team. Ordinarily the imports were divided fairly equally between the offensive and defensive squads to take advantage of their skills, but what Leo proposed to do was to overload the offence with the more talented Americans, putting eight with the offence and only four with the defence. This left three Canadians on offence (tackle spots or short-yardage pass receivers, traditional Canadian positions), but *nine* on defence, a precarious gamble according to the majority of football pundits. "How would all those Canadian boys fend for themselves out there virtually alone?" they asked. Like all of Leo's innovations, though, this one fell brilliantly into place if you considered it not as a football tactic but as a response to the secret longings of the *fans*, a piece of public relations by ESP. Dividing the Argos' Americans equally might have been prudent, but in doing it Leo would have been forcing the fans to admit that a compromise of talent was necessary to be successful in the Canadian Football League (out West this kind of admission had created champions and exciting football for years). If, on the other hand, Leo put all of his Americans on the field at once—on the offence, of course, the glamour squad of accomplishment—the fans could almost pretend, for half the game anyway, that they were watching an American team play Canadian football: the ultimate in dreams. On the other hand, if the defence played with the normal Argo malaise, you could always ascribe it to the Canadians. And if against all odds the Canadians were actually good, the chauvinistic thrill would be unequalled—it would be over-matched Canadian boys *beating* Americans, the way Morley Callaghan always said they could. Leo couldn't lose. As the Argos approached their first exhibition game in 1967, I felt suspicious, skeptical, and fascinated.

The Argos, with Wally Gabler at the helm, beat Winnipeg in that game 42-20. And although the Argos cooled off somewhat as the season progressed, and although the Numbers Game innovation was gone by mid-September (the usual expiration date for Leo's inspirations), by the time the Argos had played their last game they were 5-8 and 1, and in the playoffs for the first time since 1961.

The playoffs! They were gone, granted, just as quickly, 38-22 to the Ottawa Rough Riders and Russ Jackson (a Leo nemesis till he retired in 1969), but a number of important precedents had been set, one of them the similarity of Leo's Argos to the now-defunct Rifles. Some of the more unlikely characters on the '67 Argos Leo had inherited, but others he added himself, forging a team that was radical even for the times, a team that may have been the first hippie-ish (or yippie-ish) professional sporting team anywhere. "What I discovered," Leo would point out, "was that the length of a player's hair doesn't have anything to do with the size of his heart." And also—"Jim Hunt says I should have got a medal just for putting up with the sons of bitches. But we had to do it—we had 13,000 people in the stands." Leo was exaggerating, as usual—but about the low attendance, not about the team. Five of his more visible cast members, Argos I will not forget, were: Mel Profit—a superb, candid tight end from UCLA who looked like a Norse God and who, towards the end of his Argo days, would open a boutique called "Asylum"; Bobby Taylor, an anarchic, long-haired flanker who looked like a cross between Bobby Kuntz and a homicidal muffler mechanic; Dick Thornton, "Tricky Dicky", the flamboyant cornerback/would-be-quarterback from Winnipeg and Chicago who was the first white player anywhere to shave his head (and who might have challenged Leo for his public relations flair); and, for a quiet change, Bill Symons, a handsome, granite-jawed running-back from the British Columbia Lions, a powerful swift *white* halfback who lent the illusion of credibility to the less neat Argos surrounding him; and finally Zenon Andrusyshyn, a soccer-style field-goal kicker (one of the first of that breed) from Oakville, Ontario, via UCLA who had distinguished himself during his college career by wearing a gold kicking shoe, attracting more publicity than any kicker in college ranks had before, and marring that reputation by having two field goals blocked and missing a critical convert in a famous 1970 21-20 loss to USC.

And then there were Leo's quarterbacks for 1967, Wally Gabler (the starter), and Tom Wilkinson (the back-up). By this time Wally, with his sleek, boyish head and vulnerable, collegiate eyes, had established himself as the quintessential "Jewish" Argo (a friend of mine in Bathurst Manor had started a separate Wally Gabler fan club), the Argo more likely to be felled by doom and pathos than any other. Tom Wilkinson — Wilkie — was another matter. With the exception of Charlie Tolar, the Houston Oiler fullback who had been billed as "the Human Bowling Ball", Wilkie was the most improbable-looking football player I had ever seen in my life. In full uniform he resembled someone's short, overweight uncle who had taken a wrong turn on his way to a *bocce* match. Over the next three years Wilkie's quarterbacking would be characterized by a pair of opposing trends that would frustrate me almost as much as Leo did: a consistently high pass-completion average, and a woefully weak arm. What this meant was that while Wilkie completed the majority of his passes, on most of them he was close enough to the prospective receiver to shake his hand. By 1970, his last season with the club, I was convinced that *I* could throw a football farther than Wilkie.

In '67, though, Wilkie was a plump secret weapon, pregnant with exciting possibilities. Leo, true to his dramatic flair, restricted him to spot duty until the opening quarter of the last game of the season, when Wally Gabler made one mistake too many. At that point Leo sent Wilkie out to finish the game, which Wilkie did, completing 15 of 23 for 266 yards and four interceptions (perfect Wilkie statistics in both their triumph and their tragic flaw).

The next year, 1968, was even better. With Wally and Wilkie alternating, the Argos finished in *second* place with a 9 and 5 record, the first winning record they'd had in seven years. It was completely unexpected. It could have been the favourite old Argo record reversed, in fact — 10 and 4 — except for an ill-timed collapse by Wally Gabler again in the last regular-season game, a head-to-head contest with Ottawa for first place. "What can I say?" Wally said after the game, which Ottawa had won 31-9. "I had a bad day. A very, very bad day." Alas, Wally.

Amazingly enough, Leo *started* Wally in the semi-final against Hamilton the next week (Leo always had a special feeling for Wally, from what I could see, maybe because of a perception of their shared mortality). In the first quarter the move did not seem like a stroke of genius. Hamilton jumped out to a 14-0 lead in the first five minutes, at which point Wally threw an interception deep in Argo territory. But then a remarkable thing happened. "Nobody said a word when the offence came off the field," Wally would remember, "but we all knew what the *customers* were saying. 'Same old Argos', that's what they were saying. We couldn't hear them, but we all knew it. And suddenly the mood changed and we got mad." As far as I know, Wally's reference to the silent whispers of the Argo fans is the earliest such remark on record from a player, both the first public acknowledgment of the Bounce and the first expression of guilt towards the people who were forced to watch it. (Also interesting was Wally's use of the word "customers".)

At another time the effects might not have been salutary, but these were Leo's times, when anything was possible. Back on the field the Argos promptly intercepted a Joe Zuger pass, and on the very next play Bill Symons took a handoff from Wally on the Argo 10-yard line, proceeded through an enormous, yawning hole (courtesy of a classic Mel Profit block), hopped daintily over an outstretched ankle (in a manoeuvre I can still see perfectly in my mind's eye), and took off downfield with his paradoxical hunched swiftness—nothing moving but his feet, it seemed—for a hundred-yard touchdown that put the Argos back in the game. With the exception of Leon McQuay's stumble and maybe a rainbow-shaped touchdown pass thrown by Greg Barton under the lights in July of 1970—and maybe also a limp-legged seventy-yard run off a screen play by Dave Raimey in '69—Bill Symons' hundred-yard run may have been the most memorable moment for me of the Leo Cahill years. Ironically, it was so memorable it almost overshadowed the game it was played in, an oasis of great, satisfying football, the kind that wasn't supposed to happen with the Argos, let alone the Argos under Leo. Over the next three quarters the lead changed hands three times, before the Double Blue finally pulled the game out 33-21. Bill Symons ended up rushing 153 yards on eighteen carries, to go with his 1,107 yards for the regular season (which still stands as an EFC record). "People ask me about the game here, do I think we should change the rules," said Ralph Sazio, the Tiger-Cat coach. "Well, I've seen a dozen NFL games this year, and this is better than anything I've seen down there. Maybe they should change *their* rules." Ralph Sazio was right. The game had been a masterpiece—and the Argos had won it.

Two weeks later, though, they were being annihilated again, this time in a two-game total-point series, by Ottawa and Russ Jackson. Jackson was even more bewitching than the year before. "We keep hitting him," said Wilkie, "and he keeps bouncing back. He's not a person." The final score was 47-27, a perfect confirmation (to me) of the flukiness of the Hamilton win, and the fundamental flimsiness of Leo as a coach and Leo's Argos as real football players. Notwithstanding Faloney's Run, it was the greatest blow I had suffered as an Argo fan to date. I watched the first Ottawa game in the basement of a Grade 13 colleague of mine, who was trying to pretend he was studying for a Christmas math exam. (He was toying with the kind of "indifferent" fandom that my father had already perfected.) I sat on a Naugahyde couch, with carved marimba players on the wall and my friend's phony logarithms in my ear, and agonized over the changeability of it all: how could they be so *bad*, when a week before they'd been so phenomenal? It was as though they'd gone right back to the beginning of the season at the speed of light, as though all those wins (nine regular-season, one playoff) were suddenly erased. It was Leo. He was a pathetic excuse for a coach. What did Leo think Russ Jackson and the Rough Riders were going to do — not show up? His offence was embarrassing, a blight. Maybe if he got rid of those sunglasses, he could see it himself.

At the same time I knew that, without Leo, chances were I'd be watching Illio de Paulo and BoBo Brazil take on the Kalmakoff Brothers in a tag-team match from War Memorial Auditorium in Buffalo. As usual, my cynicism was mostly cosmetic.

The next year, 1969, was more of the same, but Leo at least partially rewarded my patience by fielding what was to become over the years my favourite Argo team. If most fans have a tendency to fixate on one particular season's team, the Argos of 1969 were mine. Their allure was based mainly on their backfield, arguably the most exciting Argo duo ever to run the ball. One half of the unit, Bill Symons, Leo had already brought to the team; to complement Bill he now added a veteran running-back from the Winnipeg Blue Bombers, Dave Raimey. A brilliant football player, Dave Raimey was less a modern black halfback than an elusive throwback, a deer-like anomaly with incredibly delicate balance, like the Chicago Bears' great contemporary back Gale Sayers or, for that matter, the Argos' own legendary Uly Curtis. Backs like Dave Raimey and Gale Sayers had all but been rendered extinct in

1969 by the refined violence the modern game of football visited on anyone who stayed on his feet too long. But Dave had somehow survived, and for that season Dave and Bill were perfect, a masterpiece of balance in the backfield, white and black, power and grace, Yin and Yang. Along with two other fan favourites — a gentle giant of a defensive end named Vernon Vanoy and a whippet-like wide receiver with a maddening habit of dropping passes just when his speed had put him fifteen yards in the clear, Jim Thorpe — Symons and Raimey gave the 1969 Argos a quality that sports teams in the coming era of the Super Star would rarely have: a sense of proportion. There were great players on the '69 team, but they all had small, redeeming blemishes in their careers — Dave was a throwback, Bill Symons had been cut by the Green Bay Packers — that prevented any of them from being larger than the team itself. Of all the intangibles that are essential for maximum fan identification, this proportionality may be the most necessary ingredient of all. It lets a fan relax, and watch.

And to the blind, to the guileless — to me — 1969 looked like *the* year. On offence Raimey and Symons were explosive; the defence was spearheaded by Marv Luster, a safety with a mind like a chess Grand Master, and Ed Harrington, who was still being thrown out of games. By the end of the season the Argos had scored more points than any team in the CFL and had finished with a 10-4 record, in second place behind Ottawa, who were 11-3.

By all rights it should have been first — I felt it in my bones. In the first game of the two-game final against Ottawa the Argos proved it. After a terrible first quarter, something clicked. "Something happened out there," Leo would say, with startling honesty for a coach, "but I can't quite put my finger on it." Whatever it was, the Argos went on to win, 22-14, beating Ottawa in a playoff for the first time in more than twenty years. It was a day when Marv Luster prevailed, when Tom Wilkinson went all the way brilliantly, when Russ Jackson was knocked down by an Argo blitz in the second quarter and rose bleeding from the nose. "Jackson bleeds!" the headlines trumpeted (Russ's bleeding nose was actually chronicled in the Monday papers as a huge psychological lift for the Argos). It was also the game after which Leo made the statement he might have been remembered for above all else. "Nothing can beat us now," Leo said, "*except an act of God*." Leo! The next Sunday, on an ice-rink of a field in Ottawa, the Rough Riders and Russ crushed the Argos 32-3, to take the series 46-25.

In that second game the Argos, the highest scoring team in Canada that season, gained twenty-eight total yards on offence, and made just five first downs.

But what I remember from that game is a pure idiosyncrasy — something that could only reside in a fan's memory: *broom-ball shoes*. All week the Argos had apparently been leafing feverishly through the catalogues of athletic shoe companies, trying to come up with some sort of cleats that would provide traction on Ottawa's frozen field — only to get to the stadium and find Russ and the Rough Riders outfitted in high white sneakers, like a platoon of early Elton Johns. The papers on Monday even showed close-ups of the disparity in soles in their pictures of pile-ups: the Rough Riders; the Argos — pathos in footwear. Not only did the broom-ball shoes work — broom-ball was played on ice, after all — but the Rough Riders had only come up with them because of a letter sent by a local sporting-goods-store owner to none other than Frank Clair, now Ottawa's general manager. It was 1950, the Mud Bowl and the University of Toronto's cleats, all over again, but in reverse; it was another Argo inversion of the past. Leo hadn't been defeated by an act of God, but by an act of Frank.

But I wasn't thinking about that at the time. My groaning, and the groaning of most Argo fans, was anticipatory rather than historical. Even the next season, when the Argos slipped to an 8-6 record, with Leo alternating Wilkie and a swarthy, ex-Continental League star named Don Jonas at quarterback, and then lost to the Montreal Alouettes in the first round of the playoffs — even then the mood didn't change. Leo had made the mistake that can be unfortunate for a coach of an ordinary losing team, but fatal for a coach of the Argos: he had made expectation legitimate. I didn't trust Leo, but I was beginning to trust the future. (In fact my distrust of Leo worked to his advantage; if he could get this far with mirrors, went my thinking, what would happen if he stumbled onto something solid?)

One thing was certain. The time was past for retreads and patchwork, for late cuts, even for attractive anachronisms like Dave Raimey. The jinx of the fifties and sixties had been buffered by three years of relative success. Harry Sonshine was a whisper from the past. It had been nineteen years. Who even knew any more who Harry Sonshine was? I was twenty-one years old. Other Argo fans were older. It was time — time for the genuine article, the championship team that would bring the Grey Cup back to where it belonged: Toronto.

There is of course a less poetic way of looking at this. By the end of 1970 the Argos had established themselves as an excellent football team with a tough, even violent defence and a somewhat spotty offence. To fix the offence Leo would have to deal with two problem areas. From Wally to Wilkie, from Tom Dublinski to 1970 for that matter—with the single exception of Tobin Rote—the Argos had suffered from the lack of an inspiring signal caller. Also, both Bill Symons and Dave Raimey were getting old. Leo needed a quarterback; and he needed a runner.

The quarterback Leo acquired "legally", as it turned out. At Notre Dame the year before a cocky, infectious senior named Joe Theismann had captured the imagination of college fans in the U.S.—and consequently in Toronto—with his daring, scattish play, and especially his fortitude, during Notre Dame's volcanic 1970 defeat of the University of Texas. Joe Theismann's talents were indisputable: he could run, he threw passes like laser beams (if anything too much like laser beams for his intended receivers), and he could think. All of the advance word on Joe would eventually be borne out, in my opinion, and would never really be questioned, even after he'd broken his ankle in '72, and defected in '73 to the Washington Redskins.

If Joe had been a little taller and had had a little less of a tendency to throw the ball into crowds of opposing defensive backs, he probably would have been selected in the first round of the 1971 National Football League draft. As it was, he was drafted in the fourth round by the Miami Dolphins, who were counting on him heavily as an eventual successor to their great bespectacled quarterback, Bob Griese. But the Dolphins had figured without Leo. They had also figured without John Bassett, who by 1971 had finally divested himself of his partners (Lew Hayman included) and become the first individual to own the Argos in their history. The first thing he did was to give Leo carte blanche to acquire Joe Theismann. When Leo accomplished the feat, with his blarney working overtime, the announcement was as much of a shock in NFL circles as it was a sensation in Toronto. It was one of the most satisfying, exciting announcements I'd ever heard as an Argo fan: for the first time in the modern era—the first time since Harry Sonshine—a bona fide potential star of the first rank had practically been stolen from the Americans by the Argos. At least by Leo.

The running-back Leo really *did* steal. A twenty-year-old junior at the University of Tampa, Leon McQuay was not yet eligible for the NFL draft, but he was already coveted by a number of NFL teams, especially the New York Giants. Leon had thighs like a weightlifter's, he ran the 100 in 9.3 seconds, and he had spent his short stay at the University of Tampa rewriting practically every rushing record at the school. Leon's talent as a runner was other-worldly — "A coach runs into a player like that once in a lifetime", Leo would recall six years later. "Leon could run sideways faster than most people can run straight ahead." Leo obviously suspected possible complications as well: "I guess there's a bit of a saviour, the social worker, in every coach," he also said at the time. "Here's a boy, after all, who made me promise that I'd go into grocery stores to help him shop, that there were actually *neigh-bourhoods* he could move into in the city." What Leo obviously knew was that, aside from possessing a genius for running with a football, Leon was an introverted black youth with no experience of the world about to enter a snow-white Canadian city whose football team was under a possible curse that Leo himself had barely managed to stay a step ahead of. Leo may even have suspected that Leon would be his cross to bear; maybe, with his blue-eyed gaze, through his tinted glasses darkly, Leo could even see Vancouver in the rain, Leon drifting to the right, seeing the opening and the end-zone. . . .

But at the time of Leon's signing, all I could think of was his speed, and the fact that he was *the* prototypical new black run-ning-back, one of the modern breed of runners who, in an orgy of spiked footballs and high fives and all the other displaced urban ceremonies of manhood that now epitomized black football involvement, had become the most *American* of all American football species. As a result Leon was also the prototype of some-thing else, the seventies version of the Argo Saviour-of-the-Year — no longer the Great White Hope, but the Great Black Hope. Everything about Leon was gratifying to an Argo fan of 1970, including his nickname: X-Ray. It was a perfect name. Highly theatrical, a bit absurd, and syntactically refreshing. As far as I was concerned, its significance was unmistakable: Leon would sift through anything at lightspeed, and never be seen.

If Leo Cahill was a fan in disguise, he was nowhere more fan-like than in his love of excess. As if Leon and Joe Theismann weren't enough, Leo now started adding dazzling ingredients to the 1971 Argos at an amazing pace. One of these was Greg Barton, a back-up quarterback from the Detroit Lions who was thought to have as much potential as any other young quarterback in the NFL. (Where the Argos had never ever had *one*, now they had *two* possible quarterback saviours, a bonanza.) Another ingredient was Jim Stillwagon, a perfectly named tackle from Ohio State who weighed 260 pounds and had the agility of a midget wrestler — and who represented a recruitment coup for Leo, considering NFL interest in "the Wagon", that possibly even outdistanced the signing of Joe. And then there were other additions: George Wells, and Gene Mack, and Tim Anderson — a defensive back from Ohio State who was as coveted in NFL circles as any of the above; and Jim Corrigall, a defensive end Leo had signed the year before out of Kent State, a Canadian with impeccable American credentials.

It's difficult to convey the exact scope of the fan excitement Leo had created by the early summer of 1971, with all his glamorous recruiting coups. A simple comparison may be edifying. In 1970 the Montreal Alouettes had played an exhibition game against the Winnipeg Blue Bombers in front of 5,142 fans; the first game the 1971 Argonauts played was an inter-squad Blue-White game and the attendance was 14,318. Fourteen thousand fans for a *scrimmage*. Greg Barton's Whites beat Joe Theismann and the Blues 21-6, with Theismann throwing four interceptions — the first time it had happened since he had played against the University of Southern California on a muddy field — and Barton finding the three downs "a bit depressing". But both of them had shown flashes of undeniable brilliance, and Leon had been nothing short of electrifying. A week later the Argos overpowered the Alouettes 29-10 in their July night exhibition opener, with Barton throwing an arcing sixty-yard bomb that Leon McQuay essentially out-raced to the end-zone. It was one of those plays you never forget; the night air shimmered with the crisp dazzling efficiency of it; real football had come to the Argos at last. The season of 1971 was on.

It was, when I look back, one of the strangest seasons I had ever seen a sports team play. It was the quintessential Leo Cahill season: frustrating, maddening, yet somehow successful and irresistible. The Argos played in fits and starts, at no point exploding with the potential power that was there in front of the fans on the field. There was no continuity, little sustained artistry. There were only wins. Not that it was a season devoid of comic relief. "I remember on the mornings before our games we'd meet at the Seaway Motel, for pre-game briefings," Mike Eben would say one day. "And without fail Leo would have come up with a last-minute, completely bizarre play he was sure was going to win the game for us. Leo would get out his chalk, and Profit and I would look at each other and try to keep from laughing. I remember one play that involved about three passes behind the line of scrimmage, and then a quick kick. Fortunately for Leo he'd been wise enough to surround himself with a team of experienced ball-players, who knew when to ignore him and just go out on the field and play actual football."

Eben himself was one of those experienced ball-players, a Toronto-born all-star flanker who had spent 1970 on loan to the Edmonton Eskimos, and was back now to play for the Argos and finish his doctorate in German Expressionistic Drama at the University of Toronto. A relatively slight human being (in football terms) with average speed, Mike had a strangely erect way of walking, superb peripheral vision, more remarkable body control, and, outside of Mel Profit, the surest hands on the team — sure enough that Joe Theismann started to direct passes his way with regularity. Joe, from what I could tell during the first half of 1971, was a case of sheer talent making up for a host of sins. He was still throwing rashes of bullet-passes to the opposing team, but he had such a gift for offence, rolling out and running *and* passing — with a characteristic little lateral flare of the ball beside his ear on the wind-up — that it didn't seem to matter. Leon McQuay's peccadilloes were less technical, and more problematic. On September 25th against Calgary the "X-Ray" injured his knee; from that point on he withdrew into a Brandoesque kind of isolation, sitting by himself on the bench, smouldering, laconic, limping back to the huddle, missing practices (with Leo's permission), developing strange secondary injuries I had trouble believing in. In the meantime, he was rushing for 977 yards despite missing three games with injuries — an incredible figure. The Argos won ten games while losing four (*10 and 4 again*), and finished in first place for the first time in a decade.

The Eastern finals of 1971 were a total-point series against the Hamilton Tiger-Cats, the same team and type of series the Argos had played in 1961. Just to make things more excruciating, in the first game in Hamilton Joe Theismann led the Argos to a strangely subdued but impeccable 23-8 win; in '61, with Tobin, the lead had been 25-7. Even considering the Argos' usual penchant for duplicating their own history, this seemed extreme to me. Reading between the lines in the newspaper stories leading up to the second game — particularly between Bob Frewin's lines (back on the Argo beat with the paper that had risen from the rubble of the *Telegram*, the *Toronto Sun*) — I could practically taste the preparations for doom: the preparations, to be exact, for Faloney's Run. It was almost as if some of the writers *wanted* Faloney's Run to happen again, so they could get it over with quickly; either that, or maybe they were suggesting that the 1971 Argos *deserved* Faloney's Run, for not having lived up to their potential. When it came to the Argos, the city's sportswriters had always been enigmatic to me. It was a mystery I wouldn't begin to solve until I became a sportswriter myself half a dozen years later, and a radio host from Winnipeg asked me a critical question: he could understand the fans, he said, but how could the Toronto press turn such a blind eye to history every spring, and award the Grey Cup to the Argos? Weren't journalists supposed to be seasoned and objective? I tried to answer the question in two ways. First I pointed out that all sportswriters were by necessity "homers" to some extent — even if it simply meant paying attention to the home team when none was deserved. (The Catch-22 of sportswriting is that a writer is very much dependent on the goodwill of the home-team players and coaches for information, the life-blood of any journalist. For better or worse, a consistently objective, critical sportswriter would quickly find himself interviewing thin air.) And secondly, I said, there was something about the optimism colouring the springtime football stories in Toronto newspapers that went beyond expediency. In May and June, I'd become convinced, the Toronto writers actually *believed* the Argos could win. Like most of the people composing paragraphs in what the newspaper world calls the "Toy Department", they were closet fans.

This could very well have been the reason why, in anticipating the second Argo-Hamilton playoff game in 1971, the writers couldn't seem to keep Faloney's Run out of their columns and stories. It kept slipping in, parenthetical and foreboding, the central theme to half a dozen larger scenarios of doom.

It didn't happen. In the second game, at CNE, the Argos tied the Tiger-Cats 17-17 on a late field goal by a tiny Scottish field goal kicker named Ivan MacMillan, taking the series 40-25. "The Argonauts," wrote Bob Frewin, "achieved victory over tradition and control over trauma." Jim Coleman described the sound in the Argo locker-room after the game as "terrifying". According to Coleman, Mel Profit, the first Argo to come into the locker room, clumped down the concrete steps like a sleepwalker—then faced the row of dressing-room cubicles, threw back his head, and from a well of frustration five years deep (just *five* years?) bayed, "It's been so long—so damn long!" A few moments later, an old ex-Argo named Joe Wright got up on a chair to remind everybody that no Argonaut team had ever lost a national Grey Cup final. It was the same Joe Wright who had paced with Bill Ross and Ted Punchard that night in Winnipeg so many years ago and listened to Harry Sonshine. According to Jim Coleman, Joe's "heirs", the new Argos, cheered with something more than just politeness.

There was only one small peripheral observation Jim Coleman made that might have tolled in a different way. "Through all this one Argonaut was sitting," Coleman wrote, "very much alone on a bench at the extreme rear of the room. The solitary athlete was Leon McQuay, the brilliantly talented but sombre ball-carrier. At the very height of Joe Wright's magnificent oratory, McQuay arose from his lonely seat and he walked quietly, right out of the room...."

But it was just an aside to the general euphoria of Jim Coleman's column, and reading it, I felt more pity for Leon than anything like foreboding. The important fact was this: nineteen years, eight head coaches, twenty-two quarterbacks, and 294 games after Nobby and Zeke and Frank had stepped onto the field at Varsity Stadium, the Argos were in the Grey Cup.

I watched the Grey Cup of '71 in a suite at the Royal York Hotel, with eleven friends from a third-year psychology course. It was a mistake. The last thing a fan needs, watching a game that his life depends on, is to be surrounded by people whose lives are not similarly on the line. Even a casual word spoken during a commercial time-out of a critical game can grate on a fan's nerves, like the sound of a mosquito to a man going slowly insane in the subtropics. This was probably why in my pre-adolescence I had invariably tried to watch games completely alone, or at least with just my uncle, in surroundings that were subterranean and/or claustrophobic. On the other hand, for the past year or so—

stemming from a night on the subway when I'd been thinking about dying—I'd noticed myself *seeking out* exactly the kind of neutral dilettantes I knew would drive me crazy during games, maybe so that in the event of disaster I could use their indifference to rescue me from the pit. I told myself I was at the Royal York Hotel for the colour television, that is, but I had an instinct I was there for distraction too.

It wasn't just raining in Vancouver on November 28, 1971; it was pouring. Football commentators love to use the word "factor": the rain that day was a factor. By all rights, it shouldn't have mattered: Empire Stadium was the only stadium in Canada equipped with artificial turf, which should have provided excellent traction, wet or not. But for some reason the groundskeepers had disdained the use of a tarpaulin, and even the Astroturf couldn't drain fast enough to keep up with the West Coast deluge. By game-time there was a heavy enough glaze of water sitting on top of the sodden carpet that every time a player fell he would skid at least ten yards before coming to a halt, sending up a spray like a giant squeegee.

If they had tried consciously the Argos couldn't have come up with a more appropriate opponent for the Grey Cup game of '71 than the Western Conference's Calgary Stampeders. Although the Stampeders had played in the Grey Cup just the year before, against Montreal, they could count only one other Grey Cup victory in their history: a 1948 win over Ottawa, whose team was quarterbacked by none other than Frankie Filchock. The 1971 Stampeders included players like Forzani, Linterman, Herm Harrison, Jim Furlong, Basil Bark, Dick Suderman, Jerry Keeling, and Granville (Granny) Liggins. The last, a bald, duskily sweet-looking fire-hydrant of an offensive guard, was one of the main reasons the Stampeders had been touted all week in the press as slight favourites to defeat the young if talented Argos. The other was number 55 for Calgary, their soft-spoken, iron-plated middle linebacker, Wayne Harris. Experience at quarterback was also considered a factor—Jerry Keeling was a veteran, Joe a rookie—as well as the interesting charge that Theismann was a "programmed" quarterback who could not deviate from a series of pre-chosen plays. But most important, it was raining in Vancouver. It was raining, and the traction at the 11-yard line at the south end of Empire Stadium was dissolving like so much spring snow.

The game started with Calgary looking as though they were going to bludgeon the Argos out of Empire Stadium and into the Pacific Ocean. In the first five minutes the Argos fumbled twice and gained minus fourteen yards on the ground. The footing was appalling for both teams, but for some reason the Argos seemed to be having more trouble with it—watching them in the Royal York suite was an exercise for me in classic Argo frustration. Something more than Calgary, more than even the weather, seemed to be pushing them back—an invisible hand. There were other mysteries: on their third possession, with the Argos back to their own 10-yard line, Joe Theismann walked over to the referee with the ball and started remonstrating with him passionately, as though he wanted to return it for flaws. Whatever Joe was asking, the referee looked bemused and slightly troubled. Two plays later the Argos punted, and Jerry Keeling promptly connected with Rudy Linterman on a pass to the Argo 31 (all day long Linterman, a short blond Canadian, would seem perfectly at home in the water, as though he had webbed feet). After running it down to the Argo 15 on two handoffs, Keeling threw again to Herm Harrison, this time for a touchdown.

The second quarter was more of the same. At one point Joe faded from his own 42 and hit Mel Profit with a sodden, 56-yard parabola down to the Calgary 18-yard line—an incredible throw considering the conditions—and the suffocating, congealing feeling in the wet air lifted for a moment. But after the Argos kicked a field goal to make it 7-3 it was back again with a vengeance. For two or three plays the Argos would move the ball, then Joe would be thrown for a huge loss and Zenon Andrusyshyn would have to come out to punt. The only Argo who was enjoying any sort of offensive consistency at all was Leon McQuay, who kept churning out three- and four-yard gains with hard-headed, uncharacteristic reliability. But two four-yard gains only added up to eight, and another Zenon punt.

It was like an entire Leo season condensed to half an hour: it was all fragments; there was nothing like a sustained drive anywhere. Instead, there was a parade of turn-overs in the second quarter that would be called "bizarre" in half a dozen reports of the game, and that the Stampeders participated in equally. In one stretch the teams fumbled three times in the space of twelve plays, the last one coming on a Rudy Linterman run down to the Argo 5-yard line. A quick whistle saved Rudy, but not the Argos. Two plays later Calgary scored its second touchdown, to make the score 14-3, and the half ended.

I hate half-times. They can only delay the inevitable or — more rarely for an Argo fan — tempt you to celebrate too soon. Also, half-time shows operate under an inverse-interest law: the better they are, the more maddening they are. This half-time would have been no different, if one of the dilettantes who was watching the game in the Royal York with me hadn't decided to switch the channel to an NFL game being played in Baltimore, to check out the progress of a bet he had down. As soon as he did I knew — in a surge — why the Argos were losing.

It wasn't the Stampeders the Argos were playing against on this particular afternoon, it wasn't even the weather. It was the Canadian game. It was *three downs*. Three downs just weren't enough to generate any offence on the slippery field. *Ten* downs might not have been enough on this day, considering the rain in Vancouver, but in Baltimore where the weather was only Baltimore-sludgy, I could see the difference plainly. The Baltimore game was no classic — nothing like 1960s Cleveland Browns' games — but at least in Memorial Stadium the players blocked crisply, they ran and tackled with something like confidence, they were masters of their own fate. In Vancouver they had been tentative, slow-motion, futile — it was as if the air were congealing into an opposing denseness around them. Football on this day was an American game; a Canadian perversity was destroying it. It was also destroying the Argos.

The second half began. About a minute into it Joe Theismann broke into another animated conversation with the officials about the football — what he was doing, it turned out, was asking them to place it on a towel before they put it down on the sodden turf, a commmon practice in the U.S. but one that the Grey Cup refs apparently couldn't grasp. ("They just looked at me when I asked them," Joe would report.) A few moments later the Argos punted, a high Zenon kick that a Calgary punt-returner named James Sillye charged — and fumbled, directly into the hands of the Argos' Joe Vijuk. While the hotel room fell incredulously silent with what was happening, Joe Vijuk lateralled the ball to Roger Scales, a *guard*, who lumbered like a water-buffalo thirty-three yards into the Calgary end-zone, etching his name beside Zeke's in Argo immortality and more important, narrowing the Calgary lead to 14-10.

The next nine minutes or so of the 1971 Grey Cup game I rank as the most torturous I can remember watching as an Argo fan. If it hadn't been for what came afterwards it's mainly this barren stretch I would remember. It seemed impossible that the Argos, a big-play team, wouldn't put some points on the board—but the rain and the wet ball and the unknown enemy force were making it impossible. The longer nothing happened, the more I was sure nothing ever would. It was like an actual grey weight settling over the area between my solar plexus and upper thighs, pinning me to the bed. Finally, with three minutes left, Ivan MacMillan managed to kick a single, on a wide field goal, narrowing the score to 14-11. And that seemed to be it; there was almost no time left, and Calgary had the ball. A first down would pretty well end the game. A deep punt into Argo territory would do the same.

And that was the situation when it happened. Jerry Keeling, in a latter-day impersonation of Bernie Faloney, threw a *pass* from well within his own zone. It wasn't a classic throw to begin with; the rain did nothing to help it. Some twenty yards downfield an Argo defensive back, Dick Thornton, went up high, and at the apex of his jump intercepted the ball. In one fell swoop the torpor of the day was shattered. Thornton came down with the ball and started upfield towards the Calgary goal-line. For a moment I was sure he was going to score, but the last man back, Jerry Keeling himself, fought off a block and tackled him on the Calgary 11-yard line: giving the Argos a first down there, giving them a certain tie on the short field goal—which would send the game into overtime— giving them a chance to win it now, with a touchdown.

This time even with the Argos there couldn't be any controversy over strategy. Ivan MacMillan had been kicking with accuracy in post-season play, and with the odds of a successful field goal and overtime so high, it would have been reckless for Joe Theismann to even try passing the ball, doubly so considering the weather conditions. Joe didn't. On first down he called Bill Symons on a straight-ahead run, Symons plunged down to the seven. With second down and six yards to go, the Argos went back into their huddle. They stayed there so long I was positive they were going to be called for taking too much time. At what seemed like the last instant, they broke the huddle, with that little hand-clap from Joe that I had watched a thousand times. They came out over the ball. Joe called the snap signal, turned, and handed it off to number 24 — to Leon McQuay. Leon drifted to his left; it was a wide run, the perfect play, I realized, to put the ball in position for the field goal. What I didn't realize was that Leon had seen Wayne Harris, the Calgary middle-linebacker, coming up on the outside. To the right of Harris, Leon saw a hole. Through the hole, he saw the end-zone.

And in the same way I presumed to wonder about that moment back in 1952, with Nobby's pass in the air and Zeke O'Connor looking up, I'd like to speculate about something now: who *was* Leon McQuay? Who are these athletes who, at arbitrary times during various seasons, have the power to lift our spirits — or, in the case of the Argos, prompt us to think about death on the subway? With Leon the question was doubly pertinent. For a player who had become indelibly labelled in my mind as a malingerer over the course of the season, Leon's demeanour following the 1971 Grey Cup game was shrouded in ambiguity. There were stories in the paper about his "leisurely shower" and his "lackadaisical air", but there was also a picture in the *Star* showing him covering his eyes with his hands, under his multicoloured pieman's hat, possibly weeping, like Bob Shaw. Finally, there was his comment about the play: "It was the first cut I tried to make the whole game. If I make the cut we win the game." This statement may be the key. In the end, Leon, who had tried to convince people he couldn't move all season, was sabotaged by the idea that action was possible. At the one moment when he would have been better off to merge with the sluggishness of the day, Leon chose to be the Leon the fans had always wanted him to be.

Seeing daylight, Leon cut back towards it. He never got there. His left foot, coming down on the slick 10-yard line, shot out from underneath him — giving rise to the unfair charge that he "tripped over the 10-yard line" — and he landed on the Astroturf on both elbows. A Calgary defensive back named Reggie Holmes had reached Leon by now and put a hand on his shoulder, but it wasn't necessary. The ball squibbed out of Leon's grasp, rolling at a tantalizing speed away from where he sat helplessly on the sodden ersatz grass. What Reggie Holmes did was to fall on the fumble, recovering it for Calgary, and stealing the Grey Cup from the Argos.

In the ninety seconds between the time the ball eluded Leon and the time the final gun went off to signal the end of the 1971 Grey

Cup game, Harry Abofs, an Argo punt returner, would earn his own place in the annals of the Bounce by kicking a Calgary punt out of bounds, invoking an obscure rule that called for a change of possession and cost the Argos one more last-ditch attempt at victory. But it was Leon's fumble that would become instant myth, equalling and even surpassing Hunsinger's Fumble in notoriety. And because Leon was Leo's man, it would become Leo's fumble too — or, as Leo would put it: "Leon tripped, and I fell." Half-way through the next season, with Joe Theismann sidelined with a broken ankle and the Argos languishing in last place, the fans would be chanting "Goodbye, Leo" in earnest. By the end of the season John Bassett would have joined in, and Leo would be gone. Leon would not be far behind.

So now I had seen the Argos play in a Grey Cup game, and lose in impossible fashion. I could have done without it. Down on Front Street, outside the Royal York Hotel, the weather was better than in Vancouver, but not much. Grey clouds scudded low over Union Station. The wind from the lake was knife-edged with coming winter. The Bounce had just chewed up Leo's glamorous, star-studded Argos like so much candy floss. It had sunk the unsinkable.

What I never suspected was that it was about to do something even worse.

7 The Immolation of Russ

Half-way through the fall of 1972 I went to Europe. I wasn't alone. It was the tail-end of the great North American student caravan to the Continent, when eastward-bound chartered planes were in danger of falling out of the sky, what with 150 undergraduates jammed into one corner of the fuselage clutching their free drinks; when in the line-up outside the door of the American Express office in Athens' Syntagma Square you were almost sure to run into Fawn Rosenberg of Scarsdale, or Mendel Schnitzer of Bathurst Manor. It was a particularly good time to be a Canadian in Europe; at least it was a good time not to be an American. Vietnam and the Nixonian vibrations of what was to be Watergate had made the Maple Leaf flag a hotter item than ever with young Americans wanting to "pass" as Canadians. (With the prerequisite Maple Leaf, of course, there was no doubt an American student *could* pass — who knew what a Canadian looked like?)

One thing I've never been absolutely sure of is whether I may not have chosen to cross the Atlantic precisely when I did to avoid seeing the end of the 1972 Argo season. The disappointment of it certainly warranted drastic measures. Notwithstanding Leon's fumble, and the Grey Cup game of '71 as a whole, the Argos had come into the 1972 season as a team with sterling prospects. They were young, talented, and already tempered by the fire of post-season play. By the unanimous consent of the experts — as well as their '71 Grey Cup opponents, the champion Stampeders — they were considered *the* team of the future in Canadian football. Their legitimacy was so unquestioned it had even overflowed onto Leo, who at the end of 1971 had been chosen by his peers

Russ Jackson, the greatest quarterback in the history
of Canadian football, was a bust as coach of the Argos.

throughout the league as the CFL's Coach of the Year.

But in all sports—particularly football—there is a critical factor that tends to intrude at the least opportune moment: the mortality of athletes. In the first game of the regular 1972 season, Joe Theismann broke his ankle. The blow was particularly devastating because of the emphasis placed on a quarterback's mobility in the Canadian game; Joe's replacement, Greg Barton, quickly proved himself to be as mobile as a quarterback cast in bronze. And although Greg could still throw the ball prodigious distances —he had once held a contest with Joe to see who could hit the roof of the covered stands at CNE Stadium with a pass—accuracy turned out to be not his long suit. To replace Greg the Argos brought back none other than Wally Gabler, the "Unknown Argo", a move that to me was in itself an admission of defeat. As if the problems at quarterback weren't enough, the Argos were also playing without Leon McQuay (for a change) and Tim Anderson, their brilliant rookie defensive back.

The point is that injuries—a rash of them—probably had at least as much to do with the startling Argo nosedive in 1972 as poor play or bad luck. But unfortunately injuries are one of those sports phenomena that no fan really believes in. A fan will nod understandingly when he reads about a manager saying, "Now, if we can only stay healthy..." but usually he considers statements like this just part of the background noise that makes sport sport. Fair or not, to a fan the sporting world is a kind of fifth dimension where the ordinary laws of nature do not apply, and hypocrisies abound. A fan is allowed to grow old, but an athlete isn't. What an athlete is expected to do is to perfectly anticipate the season when his reflexes are due to desert him, and to fade gracefully from the scene before that season begins, and not embarrass himself with unseemly self-delusions about playing one more year. And while an individual player may be allowed to be injured—nothing less than *torn* ligaments (not *strained*, which has an ersatz ring) or actual fractures qualify—teams are expected to weather wounds without blinking. When they don't, a frustration often grows among a team's followers that can vent itself at arbitrary moments —the waning days of the '72 season for one, when the fans at CNE Stadium began chanting their most famous chorus, "Goodbye, Leo," directed at 1971's Coach of the Year. A friend of mine who was there later told me it reminded him of the dirge-like hymns Welsh fans sing at rugby games.

116

I read about the last game of the '72 season in the library of Canada House in London, not a hundred yards from Trafalgar Square. The ceiling of the Canada House library was stratospheric; the tables were long and polished. I sat at one of them, with a week-old *Globe and Mail* spread in front of me, and I pored over reports of the game in question, a 26-16 loss to the Hamilton Tiger-Cats that dropped the Argos to a 3-11 record (matching their worst ever). It was a game during which Joe Theismann, back again to take over from Wally Gabler, had four passes intercepted by the same man, Al Brenner (also a record), a game during which Leo Cahill spent most of the time, according to the *Globe* reports, baiting the Tiger-Cats' rookie quarterback, an incredibly poised black graduate of Toledo University named Chuck Ealey.

But the thing that leapt up at me most strikingly from the *Globe*'s refined typeface, even more than Leo's bush-league antics, was the attendance figure: 35,217. Virtual capacity at CNE—for the season-end game of a *3-11* team. Outside in Trafalgar Square, newsboys were hawking tabloids with news of Richard Nixon's second-term victory over George McGovern, but in my mind's eye all I could see were the people in the covered stands, looking down as Lewis Porter of the Ti-Cats ran ninety-eight yards for a touchdown on a kick-off return to sink the Argos. Homesickness is not exactly the correct word; it was more a fan's moment of truth, my coming closer to an idea of who I was (a Toronto boy to the core) by suspecting who I wasn't (a carefree globe-trotter). By the spring of '73 I was back home, working in a sporting-goods store near the foot of Yonge Street, thinking about writing a novel, and watching the Argos.

It was a perfect time for an Argo fan to return. The 1973 season saw the strange fan psychology Leo had nurtured blossom into a novel kind of glory: the worse the team did, the steadier the attendance held. It even rose slightly towards the end of the season. This was in spite of the fact that, having fired Leo (who had been general-managing as well), John Bassett had hired as his new general manager the former Tiger-Cat defensive legend, the John Wayne of Canadian football: John Barrow. I didn't have to guess at John Bassett's motives. It was an obvious attempt to import a little Hamilton steel-town toughness forty miles down the Queen Elizabeth Way into CNE Stadium—something that the

Argos would try again, and that would almost never work. The problem was the inevitable stylistic clash between the Argos—a wealthy team built on dreams—and the Tiger-Cats—ostensibly a working-man's organization dedicated to puncturing dreams (usually the Argos' own, in the last game of the season). The Hamilton "lunch bucket" image was a bit too pat to be completely accurate, but as an irritant for rivalry it was ideal. To Tiger-Cat fans the Argos were pampered and supercilious. To me the Tiger-Cats were soulless and neanderthal. The fact that nearly fifty per cent of the players on both teams were Americans from places like Savannah and Los Angeles, and consequently interchangeable, was only a minor stumbling-block to the feud. Under all the pageantry and hyperbole professional sport is about neighbour-hoods—my neighbourhood and yours—and the difference of opinion that makes a ball game. In the early days of the semi-professional leagues, when large numbers of players actually came from the towns they represented, this kind of chauvinism was natural for spectators. Nowadays, with the increased mobility of players, it gives rise to illogical and sometimes bizarre allegi-ances. And so you get the New York Rangers being feted for their Broadway glamour although half the players grew up in small Ontario towns, and the Montreal Expos being hailed as Canada's team without a single Canadian on their roster, and a Toronto football fan developing an immediate antipathy towards a group of complete strangers wearing yellow and black Hamilton Tiger-Cat sweaters (which, like Chicago Bear sweaters, tended to look too tight in a thuggish way and which had the same small, primi-tive numbers on the back).

John Barrow's first move in the capacity of Argo general manager was to hire John Rauch as head coach. A Philadelphia-born ex-quarterback who'd played his college ball at the Univer-sity of Georgia, Rauch came to Toronto with what appeared to be impeccable coaching credentials. He had spent over a decade in American pro ball, mostly with the Oakland Raiders, beginning as a backfield coach in 1963 and finishing as head coach of the Oakland team that had journeyed to Miami to play the Green Bay Packers in the second Super Bowl ever held. The catch was, the Oakland Raiders of the John Rauch era belonged to the pre-merger *American* Football League, as opposed to the NFL. Despite the terrible shock Joe Namath had in store for the Baltimore Colts in 1968, and the one Len Dawson and Hank Stram had for Bud

Grant and the Minnesota Vikings in 1969, the AFL in my opinion never managed to shake its fly-by-night circus image. There were too many players named Lance in the AFL; one more year, I got the feeling, and they'd be playing with a tri-coloured football.

For another thing, as unfair as it may seem, to me there was always something John Erlichmann-like about John Rauch, some pale, humourless, dessicated essence of soul, a bit offensive and completely un-Argoish. When he wasn't fading into the wood-work, he was calling Leo, who wasn't there to defend himself, "Cahill". "Cahill obviously offered him a lot of money because he was a Toronto boy," he would say, or "Cahill had his way of doing things, I have mine." No matter how erratic or overly romantic or even alien Leo might have been, he still deserved to be called Leo.

Not that I wasn't willing to give John Rauch the benefit of the doubt. With the kind of welcome the Argos had planned for him, he needed it. On the second day of training camp Leon McQuay welcomed John Rauch to Toronto by getting into a fight on the sidelines with the team's equipment man, Randy Beatty. Ten days later, the Argos lost their first exhibition game of the season 21-7 to the Tiger-Cats, generating a total offence of fifty-five yards in the first half. But somehow the new head coach overcame both these auguries, pulled the team together, and led them through a surprisingly successful but weirdly uninspired season. John Rauch was an instant soporific, it occurred to me later; all by himself he could create those periods of semi-hibernation during which a fan was reduced to reading the trotting results. Still, under Rauch in '73 the Argos finished with a winning record, 7-5-2, and a berth in the playoffs once again.

The playoff game that the Double Blue subsequently played against the Montreal Alouettes was an instant Argo classic. Filled with mistakes and fitful, abortive offence, it ended in a 10-10 tie and went into overtime. That was when it became famous for its birds. As the overtime began, a group of seagulls banked in from the south-west corner of the stadium and started circling lazily overhead. Seagulls were not new to CNE Stadium, but something — maybe a combination of the terrible play on the field, and the autumn drift in the air — drew a large percentage of the 35,000 pairs of eyes up into the chill November sky. The fans watched the gulls wheel — with some of them placing scatological bets, some just surrendering to the Zen of it — while down on the field the Argos blew a field goal and Montreal scored a touchdown to take the game 32-10. In the Monday papers the gull-watching received as much ink as the score, as a supposed indication of the new brand of gross indifference and cynicism Argo fans had perfected. But to me the gull-watching doesn't seem like indifference —but the *opposite*. Indifference would have been staying away from the Montreal game altogether. Coming to a game and then watching seagulls was an entirely new mode of fan behaviour, a complex attempt to reconcile love and impending disaster, while trying to keep your dignity intact at the same time.

It was immediately following the last game—and the last seagull—of 1973 that John Bassett, the Argos' owner, gave Joe Theismann (who had recovered from his broken ankle) his blessing to sound out offers from the National Football League, in particular the Miami Dolphins, who still owned his NFL rights. One reason John Bassett may have had for being so understanding to Joe was that he had a family interest in the south himself. Shortly after giving Joe his head, in the winter of 1973, John Bassett sold the Argos; at about the same time his son, John Jr., purchased a Toronto franchise in the newly formed World Football League, an American-based league that was courageous enough to think it could compete with the sleek behemoth the NFL had become. John Bassett Jr. would call his team the Toronto Northmen, hire one Leo Cahill to run it, and lure from the roster of the Miami Dolphins no less than Larry Csonka and Jim Kiick, the backfield combination that had carried that team to Super Bowl victories in 1972 and '73, and Paul Warfield, the elegant, impeccable ex-*Cleveland Brown* flanker who had been Bob Griese's favourite receiver. For political reasons the new team would leave Toronto without playing a single game, but in the planning stages it would kindle a growing excitement among starstruck Toronto football fans that would outstrip even the Rifles' effect. It would also create an undercurrent of ambivalence about what that excitement might mean: the end of the Argos....

But for the moment let's consider owners in general—owners as they relate to fans. To my mind the perfect owner is unobtrusive without being insipid, awed without being obsequious, unstylish without being a boor, ironic without being cynical. He should also be perfectly willing to accept his own essential lack of colour. My personal model for the ideal owner would be Art Modell, the chief executive of the Browns during my Cleveland-watching heyday, whose 1960s public profile could not have been lower.

The modern antithesis to Art Modell would be George Steinbrenner conducting a fist-fight in an elevator. And George Steinbrenner is only a symptom of his times. One of the greatest shortcomings of modern professional sport is its growing preoccupation with all those things — not just owners going two rounds in elevators, but players' unions and million-dollar salaries — that have nothing at all to do with the central idea of fandom. Over the past decade and a half, the game itself has gradually come to be seen as far too childish an obsession for an adult — while mature considerations like Pete Rose's tax lawyer and Guy Lafleur's skill with an automobile have moved to stage centre. But if the worldly approach can help a fan avoid embarrassment, it also has a tendency to rob him of the passion that made him a fan in the first place. Fandom removed from the childish core of sport — the fortune of the home team — is no fandom at all. This is something the fans of a losing team can never forget — one of the few perks. They may be light-years from the spine-tingling giddiness of the big win, but at least their gaze is constantly focused on that distant possibility.

But back to owners. The man John Bassett sold the Argos to in the winter of 1974 was an ambitious, self-made entrepreneur named Bill Hodgson. Bill Hodgson had made his mark in the world by building up an impressive hotel chain, with drive and apparent clear-sightedness. This alone would not have made him unique among owners in general, or even Argo owners. But Bill Hodgson was different in another way. To date the Argos had had a general manager who was fatally infatuated with the team (Harry Sonshine), and a coach who had his soul in the stands as well (Leo Cahill) — but they had never had a fan for an owner.

It wasn't glaringly evident from the beginning, Bill's fandom, even to another fan like myself. The '74 season started off as usual. The Argos had three quarterbacks in camp: Mike Rae, Buddy Carter, and someone with the fabulous name of Sonny Sixkiller, who, it was said, couldn't miss (Wally Gabler had finally faded for the last time from CNE Stadium). They also had not just one but *two* great black hopes: Ed Shuttlesworth, a highly touted hope from Michigan, and Doyle Orange, a less great hope from South Mississippi. The promise for '74, it was generally agreed, was unprecedented. I was one of those who agreed. By the first game of the season Sonny Sixkiller was gone, discharged into the land of Arnie Galiffa without even having fired a shot in regular-season combat, and Ed Shuttlesworth was proving to be possessed of all the moves of a catatonic. Doyle Orange was a surprise – in terms of character Doyle would prove to be a kind of black Dick Shatto, a runner who would gain over a thousand yards in 1975 so surreptitiously, without disturbing the general terribleness of the team, that you wouldn't even know he was there. In fact Doyle was there, only the Argos weren't. By early September they were 3 and 4 and getting worse. Home-game attendance, meanwhile, was holding rock-steady at the 33,000 mark, the highest in the league. What were the people doing in the stands? What were we waiting for?

It was in the eighth game of the season, against Montreal, that a species of answer was provided. It was also in this game that the Bounce finally caught up to John Rauch. Late in the fourth quarter, with Montreal leading by 14-0, the Argos put together a drive and moved down to the Alouette 5-yard line. Two passes (the Argos' staple from inside the 10-yard line) went incomplete, and now, faced with a decision, John Rauch sent in a play – at least, he sent in a reserve halfback named Ernie Carnegie with a play. Ernie Carnegie relayed the play to quarterback Mike Rae in the huddle, and the Argos came out over the ball. Mike Rae took the snap from centre and handed off to Ernie Carnegie, who started running laterally with little nervous steps, holding the ball up like a loaf of bread and looking into the end-zone. It was obviously a halfback option. There was only one problem: Ernie Carnegie had never run the ball for the Argos up to this point, much less passed it; Ernie was a player out of a hat, a cipher. When Ernie did finally throw the ball it had no spin at all – it looked like Garo Yepremian's infamous crippled knuckleball in the 1972 Miami-Washington Super Bowl. It went up and came down, covering about seven yards and ending up in the hands of a Montreal defensive back.

Up in his private owner's box Bill Hodgson's fandom – the papers later reported – burst over him. He waited until the final gun sounded, then raced downstairs into the Argos' locker-room and fired John Rauch on the spot. It was a fan's dream – instant cause and effect. "That guy should be fired," a fan will say, after a particularly ill-conceived play. And now he was! But Bill Hodgson had a plan. For the remainder of the season he elevated Joe Moss, John Rauch's offensive-line coach, to head-coach duties. Under Moss the Argos won two, lost six, and tied one, finishing the season in last place and out of the playoffs for the twelfth time in the last twenty-two years. But it wasn't Joe Moss Bill Hodgson had in mind. A week after the season ended, he announced the hiring of Russ Jackson to coach the Argos.

Even considering the half-decade or so that's passed, it's impossible not to remember the sheer thrill, the feeling of vindication, that swept over me (and, I'm willing to wager, a vast majority of Argo fans) when Russ Jackson's signing was announced. Not to mention the good will. In looking for a parallel, this is as close as I can get: imagine that the New York Yankees have been plucked from New York and transported to Peoria, Illinois, and that Peoria's greatest local athlete of the last half-century, the unblemished, toothy, all-Peorian boy — now a high-school principal — has been chosen to coach them to a World Series victory. Imagine how Peoria would feel.

At the time of his signing, Russ Jackson was the indisputable, radiant, archetypal All-Canadian Boy grown to manhood. There had never been anyone in the modern era as All-Canadian as Russ, and there has been no one since. This includes Bobby Orr (even the night in 1976 when he kissed Karen Magnussen at centre-ice after dazzling the Russian National Hockey Team at Maple Leaf Gardens) and Wayne Gretzky (scoring five goals against anyone). What Bobby Orr and Wayne Gretzky both lack is the gloss of history: they're both too modern. Russ by contrast always managed to convey a rugged, innocent, campus old-fashionedness. No small part of this was due to the Hollywood coloration of his career. Russ had started in three sports at McMaster University in Hamilton, turned down a Rhodes scholarship, and then joined the Ottawa Rough Riders, where he had been, for more than a decade, the single greatest consistently dominant player in Canadian football.

Up until his retirement in 1969 at the age of thirty-three the rest of the Canadian Football League had been helpless against his quarterbacking genius. Three times in those twelve years he had led the Rough Riders to Grey Cup Championships — in '60, '68 and '69 (just before he retired). He had been selected as the league's most valuable player three times, and the most outstanding Canadian player four times. In 1969 he won the Jeff Russel Trophy as the player who combined a sense of fair play with a high calibre of performance. As a quarterback he was immensely durable, unusually powerful, and highly intelligent. He could run like a halfback, throw like a catapult, and think like a computer with military training.

Russ's last game I will never forget. It was the Grey Cup of 1969, against Saskatchewan. A group of NFL scouts had made a highly publicized trip to the game in Montreal to examine a fleet Ottawa wide receiver named Margene Adkins. What they saw instead was Russ. During the game he played more brilliantly than ever, if that was possible, picking up the Saskatchewan blitz with some sixth sense (Russ was murder against a blitz), dumping little passes into the gaps left in the defence, teaming up with a stocky lawyer/halfback named Ron Stewart to win the game. And then there was the locker-room interview after the game, the one I would have given anything for the American scouts to have seen. Russ sat on a bench patiently answering questions, holding his left shoulder which, he told the interviewer, he'd dislocated some time in the first half. He called it "the shoulder", referring to it with modesty, as though it was a pet that was receiving far too much attention. And all the time Russ was smiling his incredibly toothy caricature of a smile, his head altogether too up-front and whole-some, too large in the jaw and small in the crown, the hair too moulded to the skull, the nose and ears too large to belong to anyone but an original.

He was an absolutely *unique* football player. This point can't be overemphasized. No one who ever saw him execute his boot-leg, with that haughty military manner — what, me with the ball? Go back to your barracks, son — no one who ever saw him throw a pitch-out could deny it. Russ played quarterback as no one else ever had. Johnny Unitas might not have looked like Frank Ryan when he retreated into the pocket, but at least there were common elements in their styles. Russ did *everything* differently. He rein-vented quarterbacking the way Barbra Streisand reinvented sing-ing. He may even have reinvented the huddle. Instead of a circle Russ favoured a double phalanx formation in front of him, the first line hunched, the second standing up — what made it more unusual was that Russ stood straight up too, with his hands on his hips, looking his team directly in the eye. Then — the truly myste-rious part — seconds before the breakup he would extend his right hand and rest two or three fingers firmly on the centre's helmet. What was it? A healing? Knighthood? Years later a theory would arise that it was just the snap-count — one finger meant the first "hut", two the second, etc. — but I kept holding out for a more Magian interpretation.

Once the huddle was over, Russ's approach to the line of scrimmage was equally singular. Most pro quarterbacks will amble up, even sidle up, and then settle in behind the centre, scanning the defence and drinking in the scene before they call the signals, or audible off. Russ on the other hand always stopped a foot behind centre to do his reconnoitring, standing rigid, his arms at his sides, his honest prow of a nose looking common but noble — like the nose of a foot soldier who had risen to the rank of general in one of Marcus Aurelius's legions — then suddenly he stepped up with knife-edged precision, bowed his legs powerfully, and barked the signals all in one crisp surge, either drawing the opposing team off-side, or freezing them in place, while he rolled out and threw a forty-yard pass on a line to Whit Tucker.

I hated him, of course. What Argo fan didn't? Our antipathy was born of all those playoffs in the late 1960s when Russ had razed the Argos, by dint of his running and passing and broom-ball shoes and — most of all — his brain. It was Russ's brain that made the prospect of his coaching the Argos so tremendously satisfying. As it happened, the Argos had had a master defensive tactician in those days too, their safety and captain of the defence Marv Luster. Marv's tactical battles with Russ had been like intricate chess games, filled with feints and fake double-coverages and automatics at the line. But Marv had almost always lost. Ninety per cent of the time, no matter how Marv tried to disguise it, Russ knew whether it would be zone or man-to-man or double coverage on the tight end. By the end of most Ottawa games in those days, Marv would have a spooked look, like the head of a Secret Service trying to figure out who was leaking information to the enemy.

I had a fantasy about Russ, hinging on the Cleveland Browns. In 1970 a teammate of his at Ottawa, a large, punishing back named Bo Scott, had left the Rough Riders to try his luck in the NFL, and had caught on with the Browns as a running-mate for the great Leroy Kelly. In the process Bo had undergone a change that affected most CFL players who went to the States, one that was obvious the first Sunday I happened to stumble across a Browns' game that year on television: he had shrunk to approximately fifty per cent of his original size. Something — the camera angle, the narrowness of the field, the largeness of the crowd, or Leroy

Kelly and the other Browns—had robbed Bo of half his heft.

But if Russ was transplanted to the Browns, I told myself, he would not shrink; I firmly believed he was the one CFL player who would resist the reducing-ray of Municipal Stadium. I had a vision of him trotting out onto the field, with his nose, his posture, and his high-school shoulder-pads (the same pair he wore for his entire professional career), lining up behind the Browns' centre and proceeding to stun the 70,000 fans into silence and revolutionize America's concept of football with one Jacksonian four-down sequence. My fantasy had some foundation in the real football world: after another ex-Rough Rider, Vic Washington, had joined the San Francisco Forty-Niners in the sixties, he had commented more than once that Russ was as good a quarterback as any he had seen in the NFL. But my faith went further. I believed that Russ was not only as good as any quarterback in America, but better. I thought Russ Jackson was the greatest quarterback anywhere. In a way I still think so. I certainly thought so in the winter of '74-'75, surrounded by sporting goods, and trying to imagine Russ as coach of the Argos.

Russ' first season with the Argos, 1975, was like the first season of a new U.S. president—a period of grace. Both the fans and the press were careful, accommodating, extremely understanding of small clumsinesses and poor timing. It was that good will again: it was surreal. At lunch hours I spread the newspapers out in front of me in the ski-shop and marvelled. Here were newspapermen toughened to leathery skepticism, fans who had been reduced to watching seagulls, now overflowing with the milk of human kindness.

Considering the state of the team that year, kindness was certainly called for from the public, with Russ or without. In 1975 the Argos had to deal with a woeful and unprecedented lack of talent. Leon was long gone, along with Mel Profit, the most talented victim of the CFL Numbers Game ever; so was Bobby Taylor and, on the defensive side, Marv Luster and Dick Thornton (who had followed Leo on his travels). The three quarterbacks in camp, the players I assumed Russ could best work his personal magic on, were not exactly household words: Mike Rae, Bill Bynum, and Rick Worley. Outside of Doyle Orange, the team really had no explosive offensive threat at all—how could even Russ defeat three downs under those conditions?

To Russ's credit, he didn't try. For most of 1975 he seemed satisfied to look good on the sidelines, and to sound mysterious. As far as looking good went, Russ's favourite pose was a blend of military watchfulness and understated confidence: he stood comfortably erect, with just the *hint* of a sway back, one powerful forearm held horizontally across his midriff, the hand attached to the arm cupping his opposite elbow, his other hand holding one earphone to his ear. As far as mystery went, Russ turned out to have the knack of talking for several sentences without saying anything at all. This was more than fine with me. If winning was simple, I reasoned, the Argos would have started doing it a long time ago. "Of course, we'd like to win," Russ said in the papers before one exhibition game, "because you like to get into the winning habit, but that's not our prime concern. We have certain things to do in this game and if we do them I'll be satisfied, even if we don't win." Four years and three coaches later this kind of statement would sound suspiciously like the peculiar Argo version of double-talk, but with Russ it had the ring of pure promise. This was the man who had turned intelligence into an offensive weapon, after all, the man who had made believers of Americans on a daily basis, as easily as an ordinary fan made toast.

All things considered, the Argos didn't do too badly in the fall of '75. They struggled, losing two games for every one they won, but in the weak East they were still in contention coming down to the final few games, battling the Hamilton Tiger-Cats for the final playoff spot. There were occasional problems, things like Mike Rae complaining that he was having trouble establishing a "rapport" with Russ—a dubious claim, considering Russ's motivational qualities as a player—but no one took them too seriously. The autumn of '75 was an Argo fan's holiday, a brief season in the sun, a time to lean back in the open stands and lock your fingers behind your head and enjoy life. In retrospect it was more like a baseball season with a chronically terrible team, than a season with the Argos; what omens there were didn't seem like omens at all, but like the zany, salubrious occurrences baseball is filled with. That fall, for instance, a French comedy called *Cousin, Cousine* opened at the Towne Cinema on Bloor Street. *Cousin, Cousine* was about a man and a woman who became cousins by marriage, discovered that their spouses were conducting an affair, and decided to fight fire with fire by having one of their own. Halfway through the film there was a scene where the initially cuckolding now-cuckolded husband (played by actor Guy Marchand) came down a staircase on his way to the supper table. As he came into view on the staircase, a murmur of disbelief rose from the first-night audience at the Towne Cinema. When he reached the bottom of the steps the crowd reaction grew louder, including scattered *no*'s and *it can't be*'s. And then Guy Marchand turned around, and the theatre erupted; people actually stood up and pointed, cackling; the girl I was with—who would shortly become my wife—kept tugging at my arm, asking me what was so funny. Stitched across the shoulders of the navy blue jersey was the name "Theismann". Below that was a large "7".

Guy was wearing an Argo sweater.

The one omen no self-respecting Argo fan probably had any business missing came on the last day of the 1975 season, also the occasion of one of the most exasperating, incredible finishes in Argo history. Going into the final game, against (once more) the Tiger-Cats, the Argos were leading Hamilton by one game in the standings with a 5-9-1 record. The Argos had a 2-1 lead in the three head-to-head games the teams had played to this point, and a 15-point lead in total points scored in the three games, which meant that Hamilton could win the last game by as much as 15 points and the Argos would still beat them out for the final playoff spot. (In the event of a tie in total points scored against each other, third place would be decided by total points over the entire schedule, where the Argos were also superior.) All the Argos had to do, that is, was avoid losing by more than 15 points. They lost by 16, 26-10, losing the total-point aggregate by the margin of 96-95. Two of Hamilton's touchdowns in the game came as the direct result of blocked punts, exactly the number the Tiger-Cats had blocked one week before at CNE Stadium in a loss to the Argos. Worse, with five minutes left in the game the Argos were still ahead by two points on the total-point aggregate, when Zenon Andrusyshyn fumbled a low snap from centre on a punt attempt, decided he didn't have time to kick the ball or pass, and ran the ball out of bounds short of a first down instead, stopping the clock for the Ti-Cats. These fugue-like lapses of consciousness—to most of the people watching, he appeared to have plenty of time to get the kick-off—would plague Zenon during his career as often as his bouts of inconsistency. A minute later, Ian Sunter kicked the field goal for Hamilton that made the critical difference. "How do they do it?" Trent Frayne quoted Argo alumnus Don Durno ('48-'51) in his Monday column following the game. "How can any team, I mean *any* team, allow four blocked kicks in two games? You know who they remind me of? They remind me of the little guy in L'il Abner who walks around under a cloud. Wherever he goes, the rain finds him and falls on him."

Russ' explanation didn't improve matters. "We worked on punts all week," he was quoted as saying. "It should never have happened. I thought we had a better ball club."

How could I have overlooked that? There is a possible defence — another story printed on the same page as the one containing Russ's quote. Originating in Los Angeles and entitled "Too Late, A.D.", it informed the Toronto public that within forty-eight hours Anthony Davis would sign an Argo contract for the coming season of 1976.

Everything that Russ Jackson was on the Canadian-Hero side of the ledger when he came to the Argos, Anthony Davis was on the page reserved for Great Black Hopes. The easiest way of explaining Anthony's intrinsic glamour in the spring of 1976 would be to say that compared to him, Leon McQuay had been an unknown. Anthony's credentials were far more impressive than Leon's, his profile was much higher, and his moves on the field were more famous. "I've made just one request of A.D.," a beaming Bill Hodgson said just after signing Anthony. "I've asked him when he scores his first touchdown against Montreal to turn around and cross the goal-line backwards." The "backwards" touchdown Bill Hodgson was alluding to belonged to Johnny Rodgers, the Alouettes' own former college star (and Heisman Trophy-winner) who had electrified the CFL in the previous season with his gaudy and sometimes condescending play (including running the last few yards of certain touchdowns with his back to the end-zone). I thought that in mocking the quality of the opposition Johnny Rodgers was also belittling the fans, but there was no denying his effectiveness. And there was every reason to believe that the bigger, more powerful A.D. would be every bit as dominant for the Argos.

It would take a separate chapter to list all of Anthony's pre-Argo accomplishments on the gridiron; just a few of them will give you the idea. Where Leon McQuay had set his college records at the University of Tampa, Anthony had broken no fewer than six of O. J. Simpson's rushing marks at the University of Southern California, including nine Pacific Coast and four NCAA records. Where Leon had been seduced by Leo into skipping his senior year at college, Anthony had stayed for his and, on one fairy-tale afternoon against Notre Dame in 1974, scored *six* touchdowns in little more than thirty minutes. Where Leon had fallen into the Argos' clutches without demur, Anthony had resisted two supposedly irresistible offers, one from the New York Jets (who had taken him in the NFL draft) and the other from the Montreal Alouettes (who had plans to join Anthony to Johnny Rodgers in a backfield made in heaven). Instead Anthony had signed for more money with the Southern California Sun of the doomed World Football League, where he had led the league in rushing, over proven NFL running-backs like Larry Csonka and Jim Kiick. The label "superstar" is overblown and over-used in contemporary sport, but A.D. was the first modern import to arrive in Toronto with that word being bandied about freely.

He was also the first person in this story that I interviewed face to face. In fact, Anthony was the first celebrity I'd ever interviewed in my life. One afternoon in the winter of '75-'76 a shaggy-haired man came into the shop looking for a set of mountain-climbing crampons for his son. He turned out to be a magazine editor, and a month later I found myself transformed into an instant sports journalist, sitting in the lobby of the Skyline Hotel at 9:30 in the morning and talking to Anthony Davis.

It was one of the strangest conversations I've ever had — possibly because for the first forty-five minutes I couldn't seem to consider A.D. from any level but that of the rawest fan. The lobby of the Skyline, where Bill Hodgson had moved the Argo offices, was dim, lush with broadloom and hushed conversations. Anthony came into the lobby so soundlessly he was barely a pitchout away from me when I detected him. His apparel was my first surprise: he was wearing no beads or leather ten-gallon hat, but a three-piece navy pin-stripe suit and a watch fob. No sooner had he sat down than he started to talk about his modelling aspirations, and the two vintage Rolls-Royce Silver Clouds in his garage back in Los Angeles, and the Hollywood thriller he'd just finished with Charlton Heston, set in the L.A. Coliseum. After a few moments it occurred to me that in Anthony I was dealing with a new kind of "corporate" superstar, who took his outside interests as seriously as the newspapers did. To me he looked something like a sullen,

baby-faced hit-man, but he obviously regarded himself as a con-
glomerate; he had no sense of self-irony. He also seemed immune
to surprise: every time I asked him something, he would nod
slowly as if he'd been expecting that question all along; then he'd
look out into the lobby with a glint of restlessness and, circling one
large square hand around the other as if he were sculpting air,
he'd launch an extremely thoughtful answer along one of two or
three philosophical flight paths he'd apparently selected before
coming downstairs. Gradually, as the haze of sitting next to a
human being of such extraordinary physical potential wore off, I
started to realize something else: A.D. was as full of himself as
anybody I'd ever met in my life. I began to suspect it seriously
after twenty minutes or so, when I asked him a sloppy metaphysi-
cal question, like something out of a Woody Allen movie, about
whether or not there was a core of Anthony Davis that was not
defined by football—a piece of pure, distilled Anthony Davis.

There was a digestive pause. Then Anthony said, "No, not
one piece in particular. That's because I'm versatile. You have to
be versatile in these times. You know it, you're a writer. I play
football. It's the same thing, man. That's why I have my modelling
and my acting and my cars. Even my sewing."

Claiming celebrity for yourself is one thing. Insisting on it for
your sewing is enough to make even a fan uneasy.

Still, sewing or not, A.D. was the goods. Specifically, he was exactly
the offensive weapon Russ Jackson had lacked in his first year
with the Argos. There were other promising lights studding the
Argos' hope for the '76 season: Matthew Reed, a statuesque black
quarterback also from the defunct WFL; a superb defensive tackle
named Ecomet Burley; holdover rookie of the year from 1975
Sam Cvijanovich; not to mention cornerback Wonderful Monds.
But A.D. was the key. He was the perfect complement to Russ's
Canadian genius, the American who would set it free.

And along with Russ, A.D. was the prime cause of the amazing shattering of attendance records that went on at CNE in the
summer of '76. By the end of May, before the Argos had even
stepped onto the field, over 32,000 *season's* tickets had been sold,
with expectations of another 6,000 to come. On August 11, for a
game against Ottawa, the Argos drew 50,212 fans, an increase of
approximately 15,000 people over the previous record. A week
later, against Hamilton, they drew 49,724. Granted, CNE Stadium

had been enlarged that summer in preparation for the arrival of the Blue Jays and major-league baseball in 1977, but — besides the fact that the designers had somehow managed to expand the stadium without in any way diminishing the distracting open-endedness of the field — the extra seats they'd installed, especially the bank along the third-base line behind the western end-zone, were, almost without exception, terrible for watching football. Twenty-four years after the team had last won a championship, people were paying triple the price to watch the Argos through binoculars. If there is a better definition of the word "hope", I have yet to run across it.

The stands were full, the nights were warm, the pressure was intense — and all eyes were on Russ and Anthony. How could they miss? In the first pre-season game, A.D. seemed merely to be toying with his talent and the opposition, but such was the quicksilver of even the few moves he did put on that no one even noticed. In the next game the Argos had to come back from a two-touchdown deficit to tie Calgary 25-25, but Anthony scored on a 63-yard pass and run from Chuck Ealey that "brought the crowd of 37,343 to their feet as he spiked the ball." *Sun* columnist Jim Coleman, obviously disturbed by the Argo offence in general, nevertheless described A.D.'s run in glowing terms. "When Bold Anthony caught a pass and sped 35 yards for his touchdown against Calgary, it was the first occasion on which I've ever seen a halfback leave a trail of smoke arising from the scorched artificial turf of a football stadium." The only description that would make more of an impression on me was an account of another A.D. touchdown by flanker Mike Eben: "There was one play of A.D.'s I recall, a dive play going towards the Flyer. I guess he just wanted to do it. It was a simple dive play, bear in mind, but the timing was superb. A.D. hit the hole, and we just watched; it was so fast the other twenty-three guys didn't know what to do. Two little wiggles and he was in the end-zone, thirty yards away. He scored before the crowd had a chance to gasp. It was against Montreal, I think, near the beginning of the season."

The game Mike Eben cited was played on August 4 at CNE Stadium, against the Alouettes; the Argos won 23-10, giving them a 2-1 record on the season. A week later they lost 27-16 to Ottawa and were 2-2; three weeks later Montreal shut them out 23-3 in Montreal, and they were 3-3. They hit the .500 mark again on September 18 in Calgary, but then slipped below it once more and didn't get back to it until their second-last game of the season, October 30, against B.C.

If this roller-coaster pattern does not exactly strike you as the product of a settled season, you've grasped a fundamental truth about the 1976 Argos. As a team they were more frustrating to watch than any Argo club before them. Where the Argos had gone through moments and even entire games before in a fog, they had never, in my experience, played an entire season that seemed to make no sense. 1976 was the first full irrational year I lived through with the Argos; and the irrationality swung on the two principals, Russ and A.D. themselves.

The second-last game of the season, against the B.C. Lions, was a microcosm of the entire year. Coincidentally it was also the first game of any sort I'd ever watched from a press box. It was also the first Argo game I had a decent seat for in the entire 1976 season — my customary procedure of arriving at the CNE ticketless and trying to face down the last scalper as the kickoff approached had left me in the new Siberia of the end-zone every time. By 1976 I could afford to buy reserve seats, but I was still labouring under the elitist delusion that no true fan ever did. But my article about Anthony Davis had been published by this point, and I was more or less an official sportswriter, which meant that I was invited to sit in the long, draughty room wedged into the slice of roof over the covered side at CNE Stadium, while patient boys walked back and forth behind the desks with boxes of cheese sandwiches and a cluster of non-sportswriting freeloaders to my left tried not to look guilty about being there.

The Argo-B.C. game that day can be summed up by citing one particular play. Near the beginning of the second quarter, with B.C. leading 16-7, the Argos scrimmaged from their own 35-yard line. On first down Matthew Reed, who was playing quarterback, took the snap from centre and threw a pitch-out to his right to Anthony Davis. The ball was a little low and to the outside, but perfectly catchable for an octogenarian, let alone A.D. But A.D. dropped the ball, and it took a horribly familiar bounce back *towards* him, making him straighten up stiff-legged like a matador about to execute a Veronica — until a B.C. lineman cut him down with unintentional mercy and fell on the ball.

In all fairness, A.D.'s fumble could have been put down to lack of practice — it was the first ball that had come his way that day. In the remaining forty-five minutes he ran with it exactly four more times, and had it thrown to him once, statistics which were in no way atypical. By the B.C. game A.D. had carried the ball only 103 times in the regular season, for an average of a little over six carries per game. At USC, when he was setting his records, he had carried the ball an average of thirty times per game. Moreover, those 103 carries had netted Anthony 414 yards, which made him only the fifth-best rusher in the East, wedged between Matthew Reed and Chuck Ealey, both of whom happened to be Argo quarterbacks.

Why wasn't A.D. getting the ball? To answer that you have to swivel back to the more mysterious half of the equation: Russ Jackson. It was Russ, as head coach, who was self-admittedly responsible for not using Anthony more — but either great discretion or an inability to talk in anything but riddles was keeping him from telling anybody why. My suspicion, based on years of admiration, was that Russ was too proud to complain, and that the entire story would eventually be told and vindicate him. And it did, emerging in tantalizing pieces once the season was over. Anthony's presumption about his sewing turned out to be characteristic. He was a walking grab-bag of antisocial paradox, spoiled and insecure, uncertain and swell-headed. Compared to A.D.'s brand of sullenness, Leon McQuay's had been cloaked in majesty. To make matters worse, A.D. had been pampered during training camp (on the orders of Bill Hodgson himself), and granted preferential treatment as the season wore on. He had watched the first training-camp practice, held in a downpour, from the comfort of a van parked beside the field — "We'd look over and see A.D.'s little face peeking out through the window," Mike Eben would remember — and during the regular season he regularly refused to "run the defence" with the other offensive starters (simulate the upcoming opposition's offence so the defensive team could get used to it). He also had a habit of not knowing the play-book — in a game in Saskatchewan he had refused to run a sweep because he didn't know the play, a lapse that infuriated Joe Moss, the offensive assistant coach, to the point where he almost took a swing at A.D. as he came off the field.

But no truthful evaluation of the Argos of '76 under Russ Jackson can end there. If A.D.'s not getting the ball wasn't enough to sink Russ, who *did* get the ball was. As the season progressed, Russ's offence gradually evolved — or *de*volved — into something that can best be called . . . *linear*. In fact it wasn't really an offence at all; it was a junior-high aberration, a sort of *Reader's Digest* version of the *Golem of Prague* — or the quarterback sneak. If it was planned — which I wanted to believe — it was the most brilliant piece of awkwardness ever devised. Basically it consisted of the Argos' quarterback, Matthew Reed, taking the ball from centre, retreating a few uncertain steps — nowhere deep enough to be situated in anything like a "pocket" — waiting for a few players to bounce off him, and then heading downfield in large deliberate strides, at something like a walk. What made it spookier was that Matthew didn't seem to be sure where he was; he had the preoccupation of Boris Karloff on an old Saturday afternoon *Shock Theatre*.

It was a horrible sort of offence — but then Russ was a horrible sort of coach. It was as though he was trying out a kind of neo-reductionism, reducing football to the purity of one play — Russ Jackson, who had always had a couple of dozen up his sleeve. Either that, or he had picked up a Canadian fatalism he'd never had as a player: if all you had were three downs you were doomed anyway, so why not just have your quarterback run around in the backfield for a while and see if anything happened?

The amazing thing was that, even with Russ's offence and A.D.'s tantrums, by the last game of the season the Argos were in a position to reach the playoffs again. Once again the game was in Hamilton and once again the winner would take third place, the third year in a row that a sudden-death last game would decide the team's fate.

On eight of the first ten Argo plays from scrimmage, Matthew Reed carried the ball himself. As Trent Frayne later reported in the *Sun*, "Sometimes he'd throw it, sometimes he'd run with it, sometimes he'd get smeared with it. Maybe it could be called the Quarterback Option: do something with it or get killed." At half-time Mel Profit, who was serving a stint as a radio broadcaster, walked through the press box and made his deathless statement, one that would live at least as long as Leo's "act of God". "Jackson's offence," said Mel, "is the only one I've ever seen that could be inscribed on the head of a pin." In the entire game the corps of Argo runners touched the ball exactly seven times. A.D. handled it once.

Two months after the season, after A.D. had applied for his release and fled to Tampa Bay and his former college coach at

USC, John McKay (with whom he wouldn't do much better), after I had just started to recover and think about next year, Bill Hodgson fired Russ. From all the newspaper reports he did it with the greatest reluctance, and afterwards added an extraordinary, and as far as I know unprecedented, postscript by personally inviting Russ and his family down to Florida to use his private vacation home. It was the final exhibit needed to prove Bill Hodgson's fandom. If I had had a summer home, chances are I would have invited Russ to use it myself. Reading about the offer (which Russ accepted), I felt what I was sure the majority of Argo fans did—commiseration, apology, and an awareness of the fickleness of the universe. But mostly sadness, a blanket of it, settling over the sporting spirit of a city. The general mood was like that of the last scene of *West Side Story*, where the Sharks and the Jets wordlessly regard the bodies of Tony and Maria.

But none of this outpouring of compassion for Russ from the fans could mask the single burning question: How could Russ Jackson, genius of three downs, the walking play-book, have become so lost in the space of a year? How could a mind brilliant enough to pick holes in opposing defences for twelve years be the same mind that conceived a pin-sized offence, an offence that would later inspire Anthony Davis to claim that he had received better coaching in the Pop Ivy League?

As always the temptation is to blame the Bounce—and there was no dearth of people who did just that at the conclusion of the '76 season. But another theory that started to surface that fall as the Grey Cup approached (Ottawa vs. Saskatchewan) stemmed from a harder fact most experts had managed to gloss over in the excitement of the early months of '75. Prior to coming to the Argos, Russ had never coached a game of professional football in his life. As a chief strategist he was completely inexperienced. Given that inexperience, his brilliance as a player may have been irrelevant. Geniuses do not as a rule make the best teachers. The legendary Russian ballet star Nijinsky was notoriously unsuccessful in getting other dancers to be convincing fauns in the afternoon, just as the great Boston Celtic centre Bill Russell made a fair-to-middling basketball coach at best. The gifts of the gifted tend to be instinctive and not transferable. And so it was with Russ. If he had been just an excellent quarterback, things might have been different. But how could he convey virtuosity to a team of merely mortal Argos? It was another Double Blue paradox: the very thing that had made me so sure he couldn't fail may have doomed Russ, and the team (and A.D.), to a frustrating last-place season, the Argos' fourth in the last five seasons, their thirteenth in the last twenty-one.

As a theory it came dangerously close to being plausible, and I made a note to try to work it into an article some day. As soon as the grief wore off.

8 Leo Redux

It's axiomatic in professional sport that there are always more coaches than jobs available, and that as a consequence whenever a coach is fired half a dozen applicants immediately line up for his job. Remarkably enough, this phenomenon has always seemed *more* pronounced, not less, with the Argos. For some reason large numbers of otherwise sane American football experts have been anxious to "take a seat in the electric chair" (in Jim Coleman's phrase) and accept a head coaching position with the Double Blue. Economic pressure isn't an adequate explanation on its own; another reason, I think, is that the tenor of Argo doom is impossible to communicate accurately. The vast majority of men who come to coach the Argos have no idea what they're getting into.

In the off-season of '76-'77, though, after Bill Hodgson fired Russ, the pattern seemed to be breaking down. As winter deepened the list of legitimate coaches appearing in the newspapers grew shorter instead of longer. But then a new name was added to the short list, a name that I immediately discounted on the grounds of wild improbability. By this time I was working as a regular sports columnist, driving out to interview welterweight boxing contenders who raised horses and Grand Prix horse-jumpers who were famous for their pugnacity; but if I knew about anything, I thought, it was the Argos. This latest rumour had all the earmarks of just more Argo parlour talk, a little casual craziness to pass the time. It couldn't possibly happen. One of the weakest elements of my sports-writing, it turned out, was my talent as a prognosticator. In December of 1976, with time running out on preparations for the upcoming season, Leo Cahill was rehired as coach of the Argos.

Terry Metcalf, the only "Great Black Hope" to perform effectively with the Argos.

But what a vastly altered Leo he was! A decade earlier, in 1967, Leo had come from the Rifles in cross-town triumph, swaggering in from football's boondocks with Allen Ray Aldridge and the Indian blitz. Now he came muted and subdued, wanting another chance at the Argo job so much that he actually backed out of a contract he'd signed the day before with the British Columbia Lions. Rehiring a coach who's been fired once before is always an uncomfortable psychological process, but rehiring Leo, who'd been serenaded sayonara by 45,000 people, had the mark of something else: an attempt to grapple with Time. In the rehiring of Leo I thought I detected the first conscious Argo effort to go back in time, back along the history of the Double Blue to the glory days of Leo's previous team (up to Leon's Fumble), and maybe even farther back, through the mists, to the afternoon of November 29, 1952. (I was approaching thirty in 1977, without having written another *For Whom the Bell Tolls*, so naturally I was a bit obsessed with Time myself.) Dick Shatto, the Argo general manager, had a different idea. "Leo was hired in panic," he would recall. "I was on holidays and Hodgson kept calling me every day saying we had to have a coach."

Leo had made his way back to the Argos via a circuituous route. After his first firing from the team in 1972, he had been hired by John Bassett Jr. to manage the city's new team in the new World Football League, the Northmen (the squad that had boasted the Dolphin trio, Csonka, Kiick, and Warfield). When the Northmen were exiled from Toronto, thanks to a skittish Canadian government afraid of American football imperialism, Leo had followed them to Memphis, overseen their transformation into, logically, the Southmen — and promptly led them to the WFL Championship. It was only when the WFL and the Southmen collapsed under him that Leo had finally returned to Toronto and taken a job as sports director at a local radio station. Since then he had risen at five in the morning, haunting the city (one of my favourite Leo images), exiled from football completely, unless you count an incident that took place towards the end of the 1976 season. At half-time of the British Columbia-Argo game of October 30 — the same game during which I sat in the press box and watched Anthony Davis fumble — a novelty game was played for charity involving something called an Earth Ball, a fifteen-foot-high inflated white plastic sphere that was supposed to be pushed across the goal-line by one of the two teams. In fact the Earth Ball was as unwieldy as a planet; the players leaping on its slick surface — ex-Argos and media members — might have been ants. And the most ant-like, the least likely, was Leo.

It was in the spring of '77 that I did my first interview with Leo, at the Argo training camp at the campus of York University, north of the city. It was a blustery day, chilly for June. Standing on the sidelines of a practice field, wearing a turquoise shell and a baseball cap, Leo was a revelation: he wasn't P. T. Barnum any more — he was William Faulkner. He talked about mortality and doom, and pride coming before a fall, and how he'd always hated the sound of the wind roaring in his helmet. He told a wistful, Faulknerian story about the cornfields back in Illinois, the dust rising off the gravel road that ran between them, an old "Beau Bridges" who used to drive him and two or three of his friends down to the river, which was a perfect place for mystical moments. He talked about watching the man who speared up waste paper after the Argo practices ("What does he care about the Argos?"). He talked about the fans in Toronto and their strange ambivalence, about how people would come up to him during his exile and say, "We sang 'Goodbye, Leo', but we didn't really want you to go." Then he looked at me and squinted. "Jay Teitel. That's a good name. You could have made All-Conference with a name like that. I'm not kidding, I've seen them make it just on their names. Bart Starr. Jay Teitel."

It was one of the high points in my life as a fan.

Along with the rehiring of Leo, Bill Hodgson had another surprise that spring of '77, a stern new irreversible moratorium on the signing of big-name big-money American stars. No longer would Leo be loosed on the recruiting trail. This time around, also, Leo would be only a coach; above him in the Argo hierarchy were the two men Bill Hodgson had put in place with Russ Jackson in '76: Dick Shatto, the former Argo star who had dropped Nobby Wirkowski's last pass, and who was now managing director of the team; and J. I. Albrecht, the vaunted "Super-Scout" from Montreal (and Texas), whom Bill Hodgson had hired as something called "Manager of Football Operations" (what other central areas of concern are there on a football team, I've always wondered). Dick Shatto's appointment was something I'd been genuinely excited about. If he had been a bit translucent as an active player, he had still succeeded in playing twelve years for the Argos with dignity and skill, and with a low-key brand of efficiency that seemed tailor-made for general-managership. Leo Cahill notwithstanding, flamboyance among recruiters and builders of professional sport is rarely related to lasting success. Dynasties in pro sport tend to be built by networks of quiet egos, some of them verging on obscurity. The two most successful hockey "administrators" of the past decade and a half, Sam Pollock of the Montreal Canadiens and Bill Torrey of the New York Islanders, are tied first by their extreme modesty. How many fans even know what Bill Torrey looks like? For that matter, while the most casual baseball fan can tell you who managed the Cincinnati Reds to two successive World Series victories in the mid-seventies—Sparky Anderson—how many fans can give you the name of the man responsible for putting that powerhouse together, Cincinnati president and general manager Bob Howsam? Red Auerbach, the stubby dynamo who general-managed the Boston Celtics into basketball record-books, could be cited as an exception to the rule, along with the Toronto Maple Leafs' own Punch Imlach during the sixties, and even Vince Lombardi, the legendary creator of the Green Bay Packer dynasty of the same era, and Leo himself—but for most of their careers all these men also coached the teams in question, which made a certain amount of publicity unavoidable. For executives who are not involved directly on the field of play, exhibitionism is almost invariably disastrous. (Harold Ballard isn't nearly as unattractive as George Steinbrenner, but he's still managed to rape the tradition of the Toronto Maple Leafs with his fumbling just as George has gutted the Yankees with his ego.) Measured against this standard of modesty, Dick Shatto seemed like a perfect managing director—whatever that was—for the Argos.

J. I. Albrecht seemed perfect for different reasons. With twenty-eight years in football behind him, J. I. had a reputation as a walking encyclopedia of prospective football talent on the continent (and even beyond). Most recently, J. I. had helped build the Montreal Alouette team that had won the Grey Cup in 1970, the only team to pose a serious threat to the supremacy of the West for the next decade. If my heart was with Dick Shatto, my head was with J. I. Unfortunately, the Argo veterans, it turned out, weren't as enthusiastic. They reacted to J. I.'s habit of sitting in the stands during practice in a business suit, taking notes, by nicknaming him "The Lizard", and flicking their tongues out at him in passing. I heard this story a few years later from Mike Eben, the 1976 all-star flanker who was cut before the end of the '77 training camp. According to Eben, J. I. was like an ancient creature from another era who kept reminding you that your time was running out. It was an evocative description, but as a fan in the summer of 1977 I have to admit I was on J. I.'s side. Time *was* running out for the Argos. It had been twenty-five years, fourteen in the basement.

The only problem was that, for the first time since I'd started watching the Argos, I couldn't see anywhere for the team to go. According to Al Sokol in the *Star*, the Argos were only a "quarterback away from being a solid contender" that summer of '77, but that was a bit like saying that Toronto was only a Colosseum away from being Rome. Notwithstanding Joe Theismann for one season and Tobin Rote for two, the Argos had been a quarterback away from contention for two and a half decades. Where would one come from now? Neither of the two quarterbacks left over from '76 looked promising: Matthew Reed or Chuck Ealey (the ex-Hamilton rookie sensation whom Leo had taunted, and who had come to the Argos from the Winnipeg Blue Bombers in 1975, still searching for his first year's magic touch). For a while there were rumours that the Argos were about to trade for Sonny Wade, the mercurial Montreal veteran who had almost started an Alouette-Argo war in 1970 by stepping on Argo defensive half-back Jimmy Dye after an interception. But the Montreal quarterback the Argos ultimately did get was George Mira, a 35-year-old ex-NFL quarterback with dark, wounded eyes, and a talent for getting injured. To make room for Mira (who would last six games) the Argos cut Mark Cahill (no relation), a quarterback who was twelve years younger and had shown great promise but who, according to Leo, wasn't "ready yet. Time," he added, "is not on our side."

Besides the temporal pressure, and the problem of being an Argo coach in his second incarnation, Leo had a number of strange peripheral occurrences to deal with that summer. The weirdest of these took place just before the Argos' last exhibition game against the Ottawa Rough Riders, when a freak lightning storm cropped up in the vicinity of the lake and the CNE. Bill Hodgson, worried about the fans as well as the players, had the game postponed at the last moment. It wasn't the first time unusual weather had descended on CNE Stadium: there had been the Grey Cup Fog Bowl of 1962 between Hamilton and Winnipeg, begun on a Saturday and finished on Sunday; there was the perennial seasonal downpour or hurricane for the last game against Hamilton; and there was always the wind. But the lightning stayed in my mind; I saw it as part of a painting: *The Argo*, by Salvador Dali; the stands empty, a lone Argonaut kneeling on the 55-yard line to tie his shoelace, and the jagged "Z" of gold knifing down towards his helmet.

The other anomaly was more typical. Just before the Ottawa game, John Harvey, the superb running-back who had shown up A.D. the year before, disappeared. Given permission to take a day off to visit his ailing father, John took two weeks and ended up in Austin, Texas. Disappearing had become something of a pattern with the Argos during the seventies, a variation on the Missing Person — the Missing Halfback or Tailback or Cornerback. Backs of various descriptions had a habit of vanishing from camp, then resurfacing like bedouin, haggard from crossing the desert, with strange stories shrouded in an Arabic kind of ambiguity. What was different about John Harvey's disappearance was that by the time he made it back to Toronto, the Argos didn't want him. Their new policy concerning pampered stars was unshakable. The Argos, Dick Shatto pointed out, had after all just passed on Johnny Rodgers (who had become a bit too arrogant even for the Alouettes) when Montreal had made him available on waivers. "Never," said Dick, "will the Anthony Davis situation be repeated. I blame the management, the coaching staff, and the player in that situation. The talent was there." I half wondered why Dick hadn't implicated the ushers too.

Considering the constraints placed on him and the talent he inherited, the 1977 season has to be regarded as Leo Cahill's crowning achievement with the Argos. It was a masterpiece of public relations. With no stars in sight, no one for a long-suffering spectator to watch (except maybe Leo himself), more fans came out to see the Argos in '77 than ever before, more than would for at least the next four years, an incredible average of 46,881. It's possible that this was just a function of the Argo fan-curve, which since the early seventies had operated as a phenomenon independent of the Argos' success — but it's also possible that it was Leo. At a press conference at the Hotel Toronto the night of the lightning-delay, Leo coined one more new phrase. "The Argos," he said, "are the sleeping giants of the Canadian Football League." The *Sleeping Giants*. After seven games of the regular '77 season the

Sleeping Giants were 2 and 5. But in their eighth game they managed to beat the undefeated Montreal Alouettes 20-14. Over the rest of the season they owned the Alouettes, beating them twice more. They also beat Hamilton, *43-2*, and ended up in third place. (It would have been second but for a 14-4 defeat at the hands of the Ottawa Rough Riders.) Finishing 6-10, they had failed to compile a winning record — but they were in the playoffs for the first time since '73. Along the way, they had also uncovered a gem of a defensive player, Eric Harris, a rookie cornerback from Memphis State who with some prodding from Leo had chosen to sign with the Argos before the NFL draft was held, even though he was bound to have gone in the first round. Eric was refreshing to me for more than just his obvious talent in the defensive backfield. A week before the Argos' playoff game against Ottawa, he taped up a sign over his locker that read, "Second isn't good enough."

After a while, you would think, defeat would begin to pall. If it's variety that keeps a human being on his toes, and the lack of it that puts him to sleep, then unending defeat should be just as monotonous as unending success, maybe more so. But human beings do not work this way — especially those who happen to be the fans of losing teams. To most people, the opening line of Ford Madox Ford's *The Good Soldier* — "This is the saddest story I ever heard" — would be rendered forgettable by the substitution of the word "happiest" for "saddest". Disaster is riveting; too much happiness an ultimate bore. Given this truism, as an Argo fan I spent a lot of time being riveted. Moreover, to an Argo fan each impossible defeat has a certain flavour, a unique ambience that distinguishes it from all the others. No matter how small the catastrophe, I'm willing to wager, there is an Argo fan somewhere who remembers it in detail.

The Ottawa playoff game of 1977 was a case in point: it had nearly every Argo syndrome crammed into the space of sixty minutes: the Tease, the Swoon, the American-Canadian rule tension, the Overnight Visitor, the Missing Person, the Last-Minute Impossibility — even a kind of modified Airlift. The Argos started the game abysmally, got worse, and by the middle of the third quarter were trailing Ottawa 21-8. At that point they suddenly threw up a defensive wall that was valiance itself, shutting down Ottawa's great end Tony Gabriel completely and starting to come back themselves (the Tease). All day Leo had been alternating his two quarterbacks, Chuck Ealey and a newcomer named Clint Longley (the Overnight Visitor), using some arcane formula no one could plumb. With 4:13 left in the game, and Clint Longley in, the Argos scored on a ten-yard pass to Leon McQuay—yes, *Leon*, whom Leo had brought back from oblivion (the Missing Person). An exchange of interceptions later Leo sent Chuck Ealey in, and Chuck promptly moved the Argos to the Ottawa 4-yard line, with forty-three seconds left. It was a perfect spot for Leo to call a time-out to discuss the choice of play. The only problem was that the Canadian game, harking back to its "flow game" ancestor, rugby, didn't include time-outs (the American game, on the other hand, has enough of them to turn the last two minutes of a close game into an extra game unto itself, during which the hurry-up passing offence of the trailing team tends to be so effective that you find yourself wondering whether the first fifty-eight minutes haven't been fixed). Consequently, what Leo did was to order Neil Lumsden, his fullback, to fake an injury to stop the clock. The Catch-22 to this strategy was that Lumsden would now have to sit out one play, in a situation that begged for a power running play. Still, Mark Bragagnolo was on the field, as well as Chuck, who could run himself. With two downs to make four yards, Leo had no choice but to call for a run. The crowd held its breath; Chuck Ealey got the play from Leo, brought the team out over the ball, dropped back to pass, was hit by an Ottawa end named Mike Fanucci, and fumbled the ball into another Rough Rider's hands.

The most painful thing was that, for once, Leo had been right. For once, that is, Leo had called the right play; Mike Fanucci later revealed that Ottawa hadn't been expecting a pass after all; they were playing the run. Unfortunately on a one-in-a-thousand chance the Argos had gotten their blocking assignments confused, with two men knocking down Mike Raines; nobody took Fanucci, who had a clear path to Ealey. To complete the Bounce, it was Raines, lying prone on the ground where the Argos had knocked him, who had the ball fall into his hands after Fanucci had jarred it loose—and who clutched it to his bosom, while the Argos were left clutching the end of another losing season.

At the close of the '76 season Bill Hodgson, the fan in the owner's chair, still controlled the Argos. In the winter of '77, less than twelve months after announcing his categorical refusal to sign American stars, Bill dispatched J. I. Albrecht to St. Louis,

146

where J. I. entered into negotiations with a football player named Terry Metcalf.

And now hope, *real* hope, rose in the hearts of the faithful.

If you find yourself feeling a certain sense of *déjà vu* at this point, an awareness of the growing cyclical quality of the story, you're catching on to something crucial: you're feeling exactly what every Argo fan has felt at one point or another in his spectating career. It's a quirk of losing teams that while they're almost never boring, they're just as seldom original. They wax and wane between the same two poles of hope and disappointment, once a year asking a fan to get excited about a particular coach or player, and to exercise a selective amnesia about ninety per cent of the past. In this sense fans of a losing team resemble recently delivered mothers—if they could recall accurately what they'd just experienced, they'd probably never go through it again. But fans, like mothers, forget. Particularly Argo fans.

The reason for the magnitude of the hope that Terry Metcalf aroused after so many other hopes had failed to pan out was simple: credentials. Up to the spring of '77, almost all the Saviours-of-the-Year that the Argos had recruited to try to counter the Bounce had had flaws in their football résumés, deficiencies that had grown smaller with the arrival of each successive Hope, but that had never disappeared completely. Leon McQuay had had a tremendous reputation at a medium-sized American college, but no pro experience at all. Ed Shuttlesworth had had major college credentials, but still none as a pro. Anthony Davis had had the most stellar collegiate reputation of the three, but his professional credentials with the World Football League were questionable (and turned out to be fatally misleading). But Terry Metcalf came to the Argos as a proven professional in the prime of his career, a star in that league of leagues, the league that had swallowed Sunday afternoons and Monday nights like a mechanical monster, the NFL. Even pedantic fans who pointed out Terry's tendency to fumble could not deny his NFL imprimatur, his unarguable status as a pro.

In fact Terry was strictly a pro—nothing existed in his background to adulterate it. His college career—at Everett Junior College in his home state of Washington, and Long Beach State—had been notable mainly for its lack of glamour. It would probably have proved a dead end if, in his senior year, Long Beach State

147

hadn't played a game against San Diego State, whose coach was a histrionic football maverick named Don Coryell. When Don Coryell was made head coach of the St. Louis Cardinals in the NFL he convinced the Cardinal management to make Terry their third-round draft choice.

It was here that the legend began to grow. In his first play from scrimmage as an NFL pro, Terry — all five feet, ten inches and 185 pounds of him — ran fifty yards against the Philadelphia Eagles. By the end of the season, having run back punts and kickoffs, and having played only sporadically on regular offence, he had compiled just over 1,000 yards in total offence. The next year (1974, while Bill Hodgson was racing downstairs to fire John Rauch) his total yardage was up to 2,058, and his versatility had become awesome: he led the Cardinals in rushing, receptions, touchdowns, and both punt and kickoff returns. And the following year (1975, when Russ was folding his arms on the sidelines) Terry set a combined net-offensive-yardage record for the NFL, compiling 2,439 over a schedule of fourteen games. He was, possibly, the most exciting player in football. O. J. Simpson and Walter Payton may have rushed for more yards, but besides lacking Terry's versatility — Terry had practically resurrected the category of total yards single-handed — they were a step behind in the pure dance of football, the ability to transmit the movements of their bodies to the nape of a fan's neck. Watching Terry *lose* yards was exciting. Watching him fumble — which he admittedly did on occasion — was exciting. Watching Terry *practise* was reportedly exciting. "He's a genius," Wayne Morris, Terry's articulate running-mate at St. Louis had been quoted as saying. "That's the point. He's a genius with his feet. He's the most exciting player to watch in the NFL. He's more exciting than O. J. or Walter Payton. Jim Hart, our quarterback, watches him after he hands off to him, just out of amazement. Terry does things in a game that I wouldn't try in practice. You watch. You watch him up there in practice. You'll see where his nickname, Sweet Feet, comes from. His feet are sweet."

I went to see Terry and his sweet feet on the second day of practice of the Argo training camp that summer of '78, at the University of Guelph. It was a year practically to the day since the windy afternoon I'd talked to Leo at York University. The weather by contrast was balmy and bucolic in Guelph, with the sweet smell of hay in the air. A makeshift section of bleachers that had been set up along one sideline of the practice-field was already filled with people — Argo fans — even though the practice was being held on a weekday a good fifty miles from Toronto. Most of the people seemed to be watching number 21, who was sitting in hurdler's position going through the warm-up exercises beside a painfully unsupple Granny Liggins.

The calisthenics ended and the agility drills started. The opening one had the players running around the perimeter of a ten-foot-long rectangle with scissored cross-over steps. Chuck Ealey was first up, and performed with enthusiasm and precision; Chuck had always been a good runner. And then it was Terry's turn, and suddenly everyone on the field seemed to be without grace. It was a remarkable moment. Negotiating the little rectangle, Terry looked like the offspring of a flamenco dancer and a basketball guard. After each delicate cross-over he would spring into the air and hang there, with a kind of magical pause, as if he had all the time in the world to come down and make his mark. If I had had to categorize him as a football type at that moment, I would have placed him in the genus of lethal small black halfbacks or receivers — those miniature NFL jet-fighters whose jerseys hang loosely on their torsos and on their slender arms, while inside their helmets you see mainly their eyes. The difference is that where most of these small fast men tend to simmer with a kind of menace, Terry practised football on the Guelph field with a high, raucous irreverence. His funkiness was a boppy throwback — speaking of Time — back past disco and soul and Motown, to swing and the confectionary lyrics of yesteryear, Jelly Roll, Sugar Pie, *Sweet Feet*.

And then the practice was over and I was walking beside Terry as he headed back to get a shower, noting the two diamond studs in one of his ears — "One is just different, two is special" — and trying to figure out a way to ask him artfully what he thought of Toronto. It wasn't a unique impulse. The one thing no fan (or journalist) ever tires of hearing about is a new star's reaction to the fan's home town. This is neighbourhood chauvinism rearing its head again, but in the case of a Toronto fan it's complicated further by the peculiar character of the city, and the fact that most of the new stars arriving to play football are Americans. No Torontonian can resist listening to an American's response to Toronto — or Canada, for that matter. To be a football fan in Toronto is to run the risk of a sycophantism that would make

Rosencrantz and Guildenstern look like twin pillars of conviction. In my early interviews with new American Argos I was extremely self-conscious about this tendency, and bent over backwards to compensate for it by sounding worldly. I didn't abandon the sophisticated approach until I realized I had something to tell the U.S. newcomers (who usually flew in with skimpy advance information, if any) that was twice as important as anything they could tell me: what the Argos really were.

As of 1978 I hadn't come that far, so walking beside Terry I mainly listened, intrigued, while he discussed things he considered obvious: for one thing, that as far as he was concerned the "best" did not always play in the NFL; for another, that the linebackers in the Argo camp were generally quicker than most of the ones he'd played against in St. Louis. He also talked candidly about the circumstances of his leaving St. Louis for the Argos, which had been headline news in sports pages on both sides of the border (since the days of Harry Sonshine, no established NFL star in the prime of his career had defected to the CFL). He discussed his growing disenchantment with the cheapness of the St. Louis organization, and their misrepresentation of his motives, and the ugliness of the Cardinal fans. Coming to the Argos was something of an opportunity for vindication to him, he admitted, a chance to clear himself of false charges and prove his detractors wrong. (It could have been a modified version of the Frankie Filchock story, I thought. In sport as in life, there are a limited number of motives.)

"I don't know about the pressure in Toronto," he said at one point, "but you talk about pressure, I played under more of it last year in St. Louis than I ever felt in my life. Nothing could be worse than the fans in St. Louis. But I don't want to talk about St. Louis. I don't want to think about it. I just want to go back once. I hope we win the Grey Cup, man, and I go down there when they're playing a game, and I hope they're losing bad. And then, I'll tell you, that'll be *sweet*."

Who could blame a fan for thinking it would be, too?

The 1978 season opened with two promising omens besides Terry. One of these was the signing of M. L. Harris, the "Human Hammer", who had played out his option with Hamilton the year before (on defence) and who with the Argos would be the perfect Canadian Football League slotback, tall, powerful, glue-fingered, and as professional and courageous as Terry. The other was the strange reticence of the press during July and most of August. Possibly 1978 was the season the accumulative skepticism of twenty-six years finally caught up to the fifth estate. Either that, or Terry's credentials were so unquestionable that the writers were afraid to mention them — maybe out of fear of provoking the jinx.

It was this reticence that created an unusual vacuum of reporting after the second Argo home exhibition game of the season, the second time Terry stepped onto the turf at CNE Stadium and the first time he got to carry the ball more than sporadically. If the press was subdued, though, the fans weren't: the attendance for the game, against the Tiger-Cats, was 31,120. And Terry was brilliant. He ran for 147 yards on thirteen carries, and looked so vivaciously unstoppable doing it that he didn't appear to need blocking at all. One thing that impressed me about Terry was the way he celebrated every good run or first down, slapping backs, giving skin, bouncing up after tackles like a jack-in-the-box. What impressed me the most was the way he reacted to his first fumble as an Argo: with the Tiger-Cats ahead by two points in the fourth quarter, Terry lost the ball to squelch an Argo drive at the Hamilton 50. He came off the field visibly upset. The next time the Argos got the ball he took an ordinary off-tackle handoff and slashed into the defensive backfield, twisting, turning, half-losing his balance more than once, only to regain it, going forty-three yards into the end-zone for the touchdown that won the game 16-11. "I was worried about that fumble," he said after the game, "just when we were going so good. I couldn't wait to get back on the field so I could get it back for the people." My schizophrenia as a journalist-fan was elicited neatly by this quote. As a professional sportswriter I knew I should be feeling skeptical about the sentimentality of Terry's statement; as a fan I felt undying gratitude.

Terry continued to be exciting in the remaining two exhibition games — the Argos finished 2-2 on the pre-season — and in the season opener against Hamilton he was more than that, dazzling the crowd while he gained over 298 yards on the ground and in the air, and leading the Argos to a 34-22 rout of the Hamilton Tiger-Cats. The next week, in Montreal, against the Grey Cup champion Alouettes, he was held in check in the yardage column, but stayed a bright nugget of spirit nonetheless, as the Argos lost a heartbreaker 30-23. After an equally tight win over Ottawa, 20-

16, eight days later, the Argos hosted the Alouettes at the CNE and exacted revenge, beating them 16-11. The facts seemed indisputable. Four games into the season the Argos were 3 and 1 and tied for first place. They were winning close games, with an offence led by Chuck Ealey and two rookie quarterbacks, Rodney Allison and Alvin White, and with a defence that had lost one of its kingpins, Ray Nettles, to Hamilton in the off-season. In a little more than a quarter of a season Terry Metcalf — not to mention Leo — seemed to have inculcated in the Argos the trick of success. In the little hiatus after the Argos' fourth game of 1978 the city actually *felt* different.

Which meant, of course, that it was a time for something to happen. The Argos, on the brink of their fifth game of 1978, were about to embark on the most fragmented, desolate twelve-game stretch in their history.

The standard reason given in months to come for what happened would be the coaching-staff-fiasco theory. It was centred on the fact that Leo Cahill had prepared for the '78 season by first firing the popular defensive coach Lamar Leachman (on the grounds that his meetings were too long), then hiring Del Wight, an insecure ex-Winnipeg coach, to replace him, then adding another Winnipeg coach named Bud Riley to his staff to coach the offence — ordinarily Leo's personal domain — thus creating three armed camps: Leo in one; Wight and Riley in the second; and Chuck Dickerson (offensive line) and Jim Rountree (defensive backfield), both holdovers from the year before, in the third. Ordinary cliques of resentment are almost always guaranteed to pull a football team apart; Leo's internecine masterpiece was an invention Robert Oppenheimer might have envied. The dissension theory was a complete, rational, expert argument, logical to the last detail. I didn't believe it for a second.

The thing was, it was too *sudden*. Other Argo teams had shown early promise and then gradually turned terrible, but this was a new pattern: the establishment over a number of games of a mesa of respectability, then a sudden vertiginal plunge to hopelessness, practically overnight.

What happened to the Argos, and Terry, was this: on August 8, six days after beating Montreal, the Argos lost to Ottawa 37-18. A week later they were beaten 40-3 by Edmonton at CNE. A week after that it was 31-10 at Saskatchewan's Taylor Field. On the first weekend in September Hamilton — a terrible team — beat them

19-16; and on September 10, in one of the worst displays of football ever seen anywhere — there were seven turn-overs in the fourth quarter alone — the Argos lost to the Alouettes 27-2. Over a period of five games they had been outscored 154-49, and gone from a 3-1 record to 3 and 6.

The decline steepened, but it's only fitting that we pause here briefly, at the Montreal game, because when it was over Bill Hodgson fired Leo Cahill. It was probably a superfluous act; Leo had been gone long before this game, maybe even before this season, as far back as that sodden day in Vancouver and Leon's immortal fumble. Still, it was no small distinction to be fired twice from the same job, especially when the second time was in the Bill Hodgson style, swift and ambivalent. "I don't blame Leo entirely for the spectacle on the field today," said Hodgson, "but he was the boss. If you follow that logic, I should be the next candidate." Leo, for his part, was finally the old Leo, if only in leaving. After expressing his disappointment at the negativeness of the city's reporting, and pointing out that "the guy who stops me on the street tomorrow and tells me what a raw deal I got is the same fan who was singing 'Goodbye, Leo', in the stands," Leo noted, "I bear no grudges. If I knew what went wrong this season, I would have corrected it. I have a Master's degree and a little intelligence, I just couldn't put my finger on it...." A Master's degree? Where had it come from? Why hadn't Leo mentioned it before? What was it *in*? I had interviewed him in depth twice, and this was the first I'd heard of it. But then that was Leo — one of the most naturally engaging chameleons I would ever come across in professional sport. A journalist can usually count on one hand the number of "celebrities" who appeal to him on a professional and personal level equally; Leo was one for me. There were ex-Argos who would eventually claim that Leo was often less than fair and more than erratic, but to my mind he was always redeemed by his interest in, and fatalism about, the world around him. Later, it struck me that Leo would have been perfectly at home in Robert Altman's film *Nashville*. He loved sayings, Leo, and heroes, and versatility. His favourite movie star was James Cagney, in *White Heat* or *Yankee Doodle Dandy*. He was a coaching Everyman, a football version of J. D. Salinger's Zooey Glass, the black-haired, blue-eyed Irish-Illinois good old boy who died in your arms at the roulette table at Monte Carlo.

And this was also Leo, at the time of his parting: statistically the winningest Argo coach in history (in terms of total wins), and also the losingest. Leo Cahill, '66-'72, '77-'78, fifty-nine wins, fifty-nine losses, one tie.

After Leo was fired anything that was still intact in the Argo season fell apart with the speed of light. Bud Riley was named head coach, and immediately washed his hands of the offence — including offensive-line coach Chuck Dickerson, who ended up using a "room down the hall" as his office. "Just this week," Dickerson said at one point, "I discovered by the process of osmosis or ESP or something that I was no longer coaching the special teams for kicking situations." This was just before the B.C. Lions game, which the Argos lost 31-15 to go 4 and 12 on the season, a game during which Alvin White had a scuffle with his defensive back Billy Hardee when he tried to send him off the field after the Argo bench had sent him on. "It was a weird experience, playing against such a mixed-up team," said Larry Watkins, a veteran lineman with the Lions. "Sometimes you felt sorry for them and sometimes you felt like laughing." (In the *Star* Jim Proudfoot observed that the 40,120 fans had spent large segments of the game chanting, "We're number nine!" and at one point, when the attendance was announced, booed themselves — a first to my knowledge.) Part of the reason for the players' confusion may have been the Airlift, which was under way by now on a larger scale than at any time since the early sixties. So many players were being shipped in and out that according to Jim Corrigall (in a full-page intimate interview in the *Star* with Peter Gzowski, entitled "An Argo Speaks Out") there were usually half a dozen players on the field whose names he didn't know. "The players in the clubhouse remind me of pieces in a puzzle — just fragments — that no one can put together," said Corrigall.

But the story of the season, for a fan, came down not to Leo or the war-zone he left behind but to Terry Metcalf. The specific image that lingers is a newspaper photo: Terry caught in mid-air, at an angle oblique to the ground, his feet higher than his head, his body twisted in a corkscrew of defiance as he looks for yardage — and finds only gravity. Terry gaining thirty-two yards on ten carries. Terry gaining twenty-nine yards on eleven carries. The figures were relentless, and relentlessly awful to read. One of the by-products of the internal strife and the subsequent collapse of the '78 Argos had been the resurrection of another Argo classic, a personal nemesis of mine — the breakdown of the offensive line.

If the Argos had found competent quarterbacks rare over the years, offensive lines that could block had been rarer still. As usual with the Argos, there was an apparently logical explanation for the failure. It was traditional in the CFL for teams to mass their American imports in the "skill positions", the backfields — both offensive and defensive — and to a lesser extent on the defensive line; the one area that was usually dominated by Canadians was the offensive line. But the Argos, who had never really deviated from Harry Sonshine's path and were still expending all their attention on the more glamorous Americans, had never come up with capable enough Canadians to do the job. As usual with the Argos, again, the validity of this explanation was undercut by a loose end: even when the Argos decided to employ Americans on the offensive line — Leo had tried it by recruiting Ron Mikolajczyk and Noah Jackson from Leon McQuay's Alma Mater, the University of Tampa, in 1972 — they were less than successful. Whatever the correct explanation was, in the long line of Argo refrains that generally started to surface after the first quarter of the season this was the one that came closest to causing me to give up the team altogether: no blocking. "Considering the lack of blocking on the play, Mel, it's amazing that Fuell even got the pass off." "Yes, Dave, what we're seeing tonight with the Argos is a complete breakdown of the offensive line." And now the breakdown burst on Terry with a vengeance. By the end of the season the man who had set records in the NFL had rushed for a total of 691 yards on 141 carries, an average of 4.9 yards an attempt. Subtracting the 143 yards gained in the opener against Hamilton, Terry's average per carry was *4.3*.

The humbling thing is, they were probably 4.3 of the most brilliant yards he had ever run in his life. One of the uncanny things professional running-backs do as a matter of course — even ones not as original or instinctive as Terry Metcalf — is to *spin* at the moment of impact with a tackler: to rotate 360 swift degrees and then continue to search for daylight, as opposed to simply falling forward or lying down, the responses of an ordinary human being. In the last half of the 1978 Toronto Argonaut season Terry Metcalf put on a display of spinning that was like nothing I had ever seen before, or have since. He rotated and drove and rebounded and scatted sideways and bounced and spun again. He slashed and slipped and twisted. There were times when he resembled one of the small silver balls in a pin-ball machine. And all this while up ahead of him the Argo line was behaving as though it was really trying to back through Time, back beyond 1952, to the days when blocking was illegal in Canada.

The last game the Argos played in the 1978 season was against the Hamilton Tiger-Cats, in Hamilton's Ivor Wynne Stadium (which by now had come to be known, predictably, as Never-Wynne Stadium). Incredibly, the Tiger-Cats had been almost as bad on the year as the Argos, and for the fourth time in five years the final game would decide the remaining playoff spot. Incredibly, too—or maybe predictably—the game once again came down to the last play, after the Argos connected on an eighty-yard pass to a flanker named Ken Clarke, giving them a first down on the Hamilton 5-yard line, with 13 seconds left. A touchdown with a two-point conversion would have won the game. The fans at Ivor Wynne held their breath; sitting beside a radio in Toronto I did the same; Alvin White threw three incomplete passes from five yards out, and the season was over.

But the relevant statistic from that last game was not the score, but this: thirty-two yards on twelve carries. That was the number of yards Terry Metcalf gained during the game, and the number of carries it took him; tough, painful yards, on carries that were exercises in grim, solitary genius. The loneliness of it must have been frightening.

There comes a time, for a fan of a losing team, when a curious sort of extra-identification starts to take place. At this point you cease to be merely depressed by a team's deportment, and start to feel responsible for it, to the outside world. What makes being a football fan in Toronto unique is that the outside world includes not only fans from other cities, or non-fan friends and family in the city, but also the American players who happen to come across the border to play for the Argos.

I had managed to avoid this with Anthony Davis, probably because I didn't trust him. But with Terry it was different. Listening to the last game of the season on the radio—the last game of the twenty-sixth year without a Grey Cup—I was touched by the final remaining Argo legacy, the last thing I ever thought I would have to feel as the fan of a doomed team: guilt.

9 Vince's Boys

On December 31, 1967, the Green Bay Pack-
ers defeated the Dallas Cowboys 21-17 in an NFL Championship
game that, with a few notable exceptions — the 73-0 Chicago Bear
rout of the Washington Redskins in 1940 for one — may have been
as significant as any football game ever played in America. The '67
NFL Championship certainly produced the most famous piece of
slow-motion footage the sport has known: the exquisite head-on
camera shot of Bart Starr's quarterback plunge behind Jerry
Kramer's block into the frozen Dallas end-zone to win the game
with sixteen seconds showing on the clock. In a way it was the
artistic culmination of all those earlier slow-motion clips that had
mesmerized me on *Countdown to Kickoff*: Bart squeezing between
Jerry and the centre, descending as inevitably as gravity, bouncing
gently on the rock-hard turf of the end-zone; and Chuck Mercein
arriving a second later, floating over Bart with his hands held high
in victory.

The more I've thought about that play, the more I've come to
realize that it could also serve as a perfect watershed between the
two eras in American football that I was exposed to as a fan: the
reign of the Cleveland Browns and, for want of a better represent-
ative, that of Howard Cosell. NFL football up to the late sixties was
for me a game played on real grass, with an ostensible show of
sportsmanship, by men who battered each other into submission
in a fairly straightforward way. Compared to the CFL, the American pro league of the day retained the glamorous sheen that had
seduced Harry Sonshine, but it was still an "organic" sport, with a
certain sense of proportion — as opposed to a mega-sport that
aspired to control the overall drift of American life on certain

Forrest Gregg dons the Double Blue. Whatever Gregg
learned from Vince Lombardi was no match for the
Argo Bounce.

afternoons and evenings of the week. Its acknowledgement of weather was a key factor. In the era of the Browns, uniforms tended to be as muddy by the end of NFL games as they were by the conclusion of sixty minutes at CNE Stadium. In fact, part of the specialness of NFL Championship games derived from the generally poor late December weather they were played in (paralleling the inclement Grey Cups in the CFL). Although the harsh conditions bothered me as much as anybody—it seemed ludicrous in a way for a showpiece game to be reduced to a spectacle of stumbling inefficiency by glare ice, or mud, or 60 m.p.h. winds—on a deeper level I think I knew that at least the threat of those conditions was what championship games were all about. Champions were meant to be able to overcome more than just their opponents, the same way that sport at its most dramatic and meaningful was always more than just a matter of skill. Football's reaction to bad weather also pointed up its basic difference from another truly American sport: baseball. Part of baseball's circadian rhythm was (and is) the rain-out. Baseball regularly suspended play because of the elements; football never did. Baseball had charm, football heroism. (There are people who believe that a continent dotted by covered stadiums will make cancellations obsolete even in baseball—a horrible thought—but nature has her ways of adapting. In fifty years the rain-out may very well have become the *black*-out, giving fans the edifying experience of walking out of a stadium where a game's just been called because of darkness, into a clear and cloudless day.)

But somewhere in the vicinity of that championship game in 1967, American professional football underwent a change. It became a game played mainly on artificial surfaces, with an ostensible lack of sportsmanship (spiking the football was a prime example) by players whose egos and talents were being exploited in a subtle way that could leave a fan feeling more and more uneasy, even while he was marvelling at the scalpel-edge precision of the play on the field. As the level of skill approached the incredible in the NFL during the seventies, the level of "humanity" dropped to a point where it was all but indiscernible. Seamless packaging became the sought-after ideal; the vagaries of natural weather were frowned on, a fan got the feeling, not just because the unfettered display of skill in the league was so important, but because there was now a stigma attached to pro players looking bedraggled or, worse, pathetic, on anything but a neat, green gridiron. At the same time, a number of phenomena were flowering in the context of NFL ball that have never had a particularly salutary effect on the spirit of sport: technology— particularly television, with its instant replays; sex—the blatant, Dallas-Cowboy-cheerleader kind; and money—not just the new astronomical salaries, but gambling on NFL games, a distracting sport in itself. And hyperbole—Howard Cosell and his momentous monotone are too easy as targets; a more succinct illustration would be Ed McMahon, Johnny Carson's sidekick, in the Rose Bowl parking lot prior to the start of "Super Bowl XI" claiming, "This has got to be one of the great events of the century."

In an elegant little twist, the 1967 NFL Championship game, which can be seen as the division between the old and new eras of football, happened to pit against each other the two teams—the Dallas Cowboys and the Green Bay Packers—who were most emblematic of the split. The Cowboys were the new NFL, with their silver uniforms and supercilious air, and their coach in the grey flannel suit, Tom Landry (over the years I've found no team harder to cheer for than the Dallas Cowboys). The Green Bay Packers on the other hand were firmly rooted in the sixties, as *the* tough, clutch, superb professional team that had dominated the decade. In the eight years leading up to 1967 the Packers had appeared in six NFL championship games and the first two Super Bowls, winning five of them, including the three-season stretch that ended with 1967, their latest championship to date. Coached by the great Vince Lombardi, they were the NFL team I had come to fear and hate most at the time, in the same way I had feared and hated Russ Jackson and the Ottawa Rough Riders. As much as I idolized the Browns, I knew the Packers would win. I can think of only one other football team that was historically as successful in pressure situations as the Packers of the sixties—the Toronto Argonauts up to 1952.

And so it might have been ironically appropriate that the 1967 Packers were the team the Argos "looked to" to help in the off-season of 1978-79. Specifically, the Argos went to them for a coach. As outlandish as it seems, I've always been half-convinced that if Vince Lombardi himself had been available, the Argos would have somehow brought him to Toronto. (Every man has his price, and the Argos had a perverse way of finding it.) But Vince had died in 1970, and the Argos ended up hiring two of his former players to coach the team instead, two players who had starred in the 1967 championship game, and who were tied not only by the matching excellence of their Green Bay careers, but by the arboreal poetry of their names: Forrest Gregg and Willie Wood.

Forrest Gregg was the half of the sylvan duet (his nickname with the Packers was "Trees") the Argos recruited directly. Immediately following the horrible ignominy of the last game in Hamilton the year before, Bill Hodgson had gone into retreat again to his Florida residence. By the time he emerged, he'd decided to sell the team — to Carling O'Keefe Breweries. Once more the Argos would be owned by a group, although one a bit more powerful and less eccentric than the Argonaut Rowing Club. One of Carling O'Keefe's first executive decisions was to elevate Lew Hayman, now seventy years old, from the dubious status of "executive consultant" to the rank of Argo president, and to assign him the task of finding a new coach. The promotion was a warmly received, widely popular one — which was proof of Lew's uncanny genius for laurel-sitting. The last successful Argo team Lew had had a hand in assembling had been the 1960-61 Argos of Tobin Rote. The last Grey Cup team Lew had coached had been the Montreal Alouettes in 1949. The last Grey Cup-winning Toronto team Lew had coached had been the Argos of 1938. Despite the optimism of the press, I wouldn't have been surprised if Lew had hired a late seventies version of Lou Agase to coach the Argos, someone long on style but short on credentials himself. Instead, Lew chose Forrest Gregg.

By anyone's standards it was a master managerial move. Forrest's playing record alone was impressive. During a sixteen-season career as an offensive tackle and guard in the NFL (fourteen with the Packers) Forrest had played on all five of their NFL Championship teams, had been chosen to eight Pro Bowl All-Star teams, and had twice been named the NFL's best offensive lineman. In his entire pro playing career he had *never* missed a game, and had been called by Vince Lombardi himself (in his book *Run to Daylight*) "the finest player I ever coached". To complete his résumé, Forrest was also a proven NFL coach, a man who had won Coach of the Year honours in 1976 for his resurrection of another team brought low by adversity, none other than the Cleveland Browns. In 1976 he had taken a Browns team that had been 3-11 the year before to a 9-5 record. He had subsequently been fired by the Browns in 1977 after a mysterious controversy with manage-

162

ment and a 6-8 season, but for an Argo fan the point had been made. Forrest was not simply an American version of Russ Jackson, a brilliant ex-player with no coaching experience; he was an American Russ Jackson *with* coaching credentials. What inspired me personally about Forrest was the position he had played for the Packers—offensive lineman. No matter what else I might have to worry about with the Argos of 1979, I thought, at least I wouldn't have to suffer through another breakdown of the offensive line.

I interviewed Forrest about a month before the '79 season started, in his office under the stands at CNE Stadium. (The new editor of *Toronto Life* that year was a closet fan himself, and it took only a minimum of fast-dancing to convince him that the annual Argo Saviour made an ideal, thematically continuous subject for the fall issue.) Forrest's office was spartan, with white-painted concrete block walls and rudimentary furniture. On the wall opposite the desk was a photograph of Forrest with his team at the 1977 North-South Senior Bowl—a game Forrest's team, the North, had won over Don Shula's South—and on the coffee table below lay a leather-bound edition of *Vince Lombardi's Football*. Forrest sat behind his desk, prodding its surface with the eraser end of a pencil, now and then bowing it absent-mindedly to the breaking point. He talked about how much he liked Toronto, for its safeness and the subway—he'd never been on one before in his life—and about how he was looking forward to buying a house in Oakville and moving his family here for good. After that he talked about his impressions of the Canadian game and its differences from the one he had grown up with: as far as he could see, with the three downs a team started at second and ten, so obviously there had to be a lot more passing. Then he talked about the Argo personnel; his knowledge seemed exhaustive. He was especially delighted to have Terry Metcalf with the team.

And finally he talked about the play—the 1967 Championship-winning Bart Starr plunge. It was remarkable, he said, but he'd been asked more about that play since he'd come to town than he ever had been anywhere else. Not wanting to be the odd man out, I asked about it myself, and he got up to illustrate the play more graphically on the blackboard beside his desk—reminding me again exactly how large 6′5 and 270 pounds was. His description of the play was essentially the same as the one I'd read in Jerry Kramer's book, his 1967 Green Bay Packer diary,

Instant Replay. As such it differed substantially from a version I'd read in a later book, *The Jocks*, by Leonard Shecter, a *New York Post* columnist who had had his fill of legendary bombast. According to Forrest, and Jerry Kramer, the Packers, with no time-outs left and time for only one more play, disdained the sure field goal that would have tied the game 20-20 (sending it into overtime) and went for the touchdown. According to Shecter the Packers actually thought they had time for another play—the field goal—in the event that Bart Starr's plunge was stopped; that was the source of their daring. (Besides being the kind of revelation no one really needs, Leonard Shecter's explanation demonstrated the danger of a fan reading too much into slow motion, no matter how exquisite.)

Finished with the play, Forrest dropped his chalk into the little blackboard tray and wiped his hands. I took the opportunity to ask the question I'd been waiting to ask for a while, the staple for any Toronto fan or journalist: what did he know about the Argos' history? Before Forrest answered, he frowned and paused, very seriously. His expression was actually a bit overbearing, but I was too interested in what he was going to say to pay it too much attention.

"I'm very aware of the situation here," he said. "I've been told about it. I may be mistaken, correct me if I'm wrong, but I get the feeling that there's some loyalty here, with the fans, but there's also doubt—more than doubt, actually. Cynicism. And I also have a feeling, from reading what's been written here in the press, that as soon as we win a couple of games everyone's going to be as high as kites. Just the way I get the feeling that they're very negative right now. Very negative. It's almost like they're waiting for the football club to fail. Almost as though—" he lowered his voice at this point, as though what he was going to say next was a bit embarrassing, "they *want* us to fail."

And there it was. Out of the mouth of a Green Bay Packer.

As least there was the core of one of the most perverse and intriguing questions you can ask about the relationship between losing teams and their fans. Is there something about the Argos—and all losing teams—that gives people more of a stake in seeing them continue to lose, than in having them break the curse and start to win? Can a group of fans be so spiritually impoverished that they come to regard any change in the status quo, even a digression from disaster, as a threat? More, can a group of such fans, through some sort of telepathic voodoo at the ball park, be responsible for a team's decline?

To some extent the answer to this second question has to be "yes". "I'm convinced," Bob Frewin would say in the spring of 1982, "that one of the reasons the Argos never improved was the lack of pressure *on* them to improve. How much inducement is there to build a team that wins, if the fans fill the stadium for one that loses?" In this sense, Argo fans have been responsible for the team's problems all along — simply by continuing to show up. The solution would be for them to grow so disenchanted and apathetic that they eventually stayed away *en masse*. In a short time the Argos would be shivering in the cold draught of reality, and putting a winning team on the field.

Except that then there would be no one left in the stands to watch them.

Buried in all this, I have a feeling, is a contradiction of human life that philosophers have been wrestling with for centuries.

The team that Forrest inherited for the season of '79 was essentially the same one that had doomed Leo, a team distinguished primarily by its lack of distinction. Its notable holdovers included Terry Metcalf, Ecomet Burley (an erratic but hugely talented defensive lineman), Jim Corrigall, Peter Muller (the tight end I had always admired unconditionally for his stoicism), and Eric Harris (who was eyeing the NFL and no longer putting up optimistic signs over his locker). The team would have included Ed George, the All-Canadian guard who was a free agent and had made overtures to the Argos himself, but Forrest and the Argos had neglected to sign him, with Forrest providing a matter-of-fact if slightly mysterious explanation: "The media all assumed that we blew the Ed George situation, that it was another Argonaut failure. But it wasn't like that at all. He just didn't fit into our plans. Essentially, we didn't *want* Ed George." There was the odd query from the press, but the general tone of the fans and press was one of faith. I was as guilty of it as anyone — I assumed that Forrest's arcane master plan was being put together, and that the overall sense of it would be revealed in due course.

When it came to quarterbacks, Forrest passed up a chance to sign Tom Clements, the talented Ottawa signal-caller who was on his way to the NFL's Kansas City Chiefs, and chose instead a reserve quarterback coming *from* the Chiefs, Tony Adams. For a running-back, to help ease the pressure on Terry Metcalf, he selected a small-college recruit named Mike McArthur, who alienated me immediately by appearing in a photo in the *Star* with his feet up on a bench in the CNE stands eating pizza, and talking in the accompanying article about his plans to take the NFL by storm as soon as his year with the Argos was over. This was a pattern that had recently emerged with American rookies: the blatant characterization of the Argos (and the CFL) as a foreign half-way house on the road to their native big-leagues. The attitude seemed not only graceless, but unprofessional. It was a direct insult to a fan (which with the Argos was more than superfluous). For any fan to enjoy watching a game, he has to believe that the players playing in it care about its outcome at least as much as he does. Although this may not always be the case in the modern world of pro sport, the illusion of it is still critical. Up until the 1970s, most players — Argos or not — fulfilled their part of the bargain as a matter of course; but towards the end of the decade, with so much of the unwritten contract between athletes and fans being shredded to confetti, the notion of a player feeling grateful simply for getting a chance to play was apparently going out of fashion too. The only consolation I would think of was that the Argo rookies who spoke so blithely about the NFL rarely made it through six games with the Argos — and that was a Pyrrhic victory at best.

Forrest's other significant addition to the Argos was the man he chose as his defensive backfield coach, a former Green Bay teammate of his, Willie Wood. At the time the appointment was of only passing interest. Willie's profile was extremely low in the summer of '79 — he was a shy man who seemed to speak thoughtfully and sometimes even sadly, and with complete candour. His coaching credentials were not quite as extensive as Forrest's — his only head-coaching job had been with the Philadelphia Bell of the defunct World Football League — but from the beginning I found it far easier to feel a fan's affection towards Willie than towards Forrest Gregg. None of the ambivalence that eventually accrued to Forrest would touch Willie. He was a modest man and, notwithstanding his later troubles, people would love him for it. He had also led the NFL in punt returns in 1961 and in interceptions in '62, and had been selected to eight Pro-Bowl teams as a defensive halfback, so there was every reason to believe that he would provide the defensive complement to Forrest's offensive expertise.

166

And so the Argos entered the season of 1979.

The pre-season was an enigma. The Argos split their exhibition games, two wins, two losses, and Forrest seemed less concerned about the outcome of the four games than any coach since Bob Shaw. If anything he worried more about the wins than about the losses. But this was pure Vince Lombardi in style; a staple of the Green Bay legend was that players would come out of Vince's film sessions following a lopsided Packer victory wondering which team had actually won.

Also enigmatic was a controversial incident that took place in pre-season, just before the last exhibition game against the Roughriders in Ottawa. Forrest had brought the Argos out onto the field first for the team calisthenics, and he chose the left end of Lansdowne Park, which turned out to be the traditional Rough Rider end. "It's an old NFL trick," said George Brancato, the annoyed Ottawa coach. "You take the other team's end before they come out to try to intimidate them." Forrest, for his part, claimed it was an honest mistake. "In the NFL a team always warms up in the end to the left of its bench." Having made the mistake, though, he refused to move. "We won't be intimidated by any team." George Brancato, equally unwilling to be intimidated, had Gerry Organ kick his practice punts into the Argo calisthenics circle. The entire exercise, while a little silly, had the feel of a secret NFL dominance rite. This wasn't Leo Cahill, I reminded myself, sending linebackers out piggy-back to block field goals.

The first game of the regular season, against Montreal, was played at CNE Stadium in a rainstorm, with 42,000 fans in the stands. The Argos lost 11-9—a lacrosse score. The offence netted 105 yards on the ground, with Terry Metcalf gaining 37 of them on ten carries. Tony Adams was less than awe-inspiring. Half-way through the game a low moaning sound, like the lowing of cattle, was heard from the drenched open stands.

Still, I was sure that it wasn't the true opener, that Forrest was still biding his time, acquiring the feel of three downs, trying to inculcate the notion of execution into the Argos' skulls. "The trouble was," said Forrest after the game, "we excited no person with our running." Exactly, I thought. Running, the staple of the classic, conservative, Green Bay game plan.

I felt the same sense of restraint listening on the radio to the Argos' next game, an 18-11 win over Hamilton, in Hamilton. It was a pretty terrible victory; "Argos Win Battle Of Inept", ran the headline in the *Sun* the next day. But there were finally signs of Forrest's influence. Terry Metcalf, who fumbled three times (his nine the year before had been the second highest in the league) also picked up ninety-three yards on fifteen carries; Mike McArthur, pausing on his way to the NFL, ran thirteen times for fifty-seven more yards. In spite of the running game's success, the win disturbed Forrest twice as much as the loss to Montreal. "We have to play better," he said. "We must learn that doing two or three things well is better than all the gimmicks you can dream up. You don't forget something very quickly when you've gone over it a thousand times." A thousand times! When Forrest said that, I saw the Green Bay sweep, with Jerry Kramer and Fuzzy Thurston leading Jim Taylor around the end, with everybody in the *world* — the Browns' outside linebacker and me in my recreation room and a laid-off machinist in Topeka, Kansas — knowing the sweep was coming, but all of us helpless to stop it because of that infallible, machine-like execution.

It was the third game of the '79 season, against Ottawa, that I felt would be the turning point for the team, the night when Forrest would go into the locker-room just before the game, close the door behind him, and emerge five minutes later with a team of Argos transformed for ever. One of the reasons I thought this might happen was the promised presence in the stands that night of an "indirect" celebrity more important to an Argo fan — or maybe to any football fan — than a host of presidents and movie stars. After Vince Lombardi's death, Forrest and Barbara Gregg had stayed in close contact with his widow, Marie, and Forrest had invited her to be his guest for the Ottawa-Argo game of July 24. Marie Lombardi at CNE. I had a vision of her sitting in the covered stands — probably behind a pillar but nevertheless there — looking out at the unfamiliar open end-zones, the broad field, the unusually plump ball. If anything could bring the latent pride of the Argos to the surface, it would be the name Lombardi. There was also Marie's personal endorsement of the Argos' new coach, which had appeared in the papers that day. "In my books Forrest Gregg is a winner. I've followed his career, and he seems to be a lot like my husband in his strength of character and his approach to the game of football." Fans tend to take things personally. Without having ever met Marie Lombardi — even to interview her — I felt an obligation to her, and to Forrest Gregg, who it seemed to me was operating under pressurized conditions. I hoped the Argos would win, naturally. Barring that, I wanted the game to be at the very least well played. After eighteen years with the Argos, it didn't seem like a great deal to ask.

The Argos lost 31-2. In the process they gained one hundred yards more than the Rough Riders in total offensive yardage, and ended up scoring two single points. In the papers the next day there was a picture of Marie Lombardi, a nice-looking matron wearing a white dress covered with tiny stars and crescent moons, like a female Merlin, squinting painfully at the field. "Phooey," ran the caption, "That would seem to be the reaction of Marie Lombardi, wife of the late Vince, as she watches the Argos in action." To this day I find myself hoping that the photographer had just caught Marie in the middle of a sneeze.

The connection is improbable, but the ignominy of the Ottawa loss in front of Marie Lombardi seemed to energize the Argos. Exactly a week later, in Ottawa this time, they beat the Rough Riders 18-16. "It would have been easy for this team to quit," said Forrest. "When you get beat 31-2 it can take the heart out of a team. But these players are not the old Argos. The old Argos would have quit." It turned out to be a favourite phrase with Forrest, the "old Argos". Ordinarily only Canadian veterans with the team, or Americans who had been around at least half a dozen years, talked about the Old Argos. Over the 1979 season, however, Forrest referred to them — usually to dispute the idea of an Argo jinx, as in "These aren't the old Argos" — so often I started to get the feeling that maybe he'd been there, scouting for the Packers (who were known to prepare for *any* eventuality), watching Leon's Fumble and Faloney's Run and the string of all those heart-breaking season-ending games against Hamilton. But of course he hadn't been, which led me to wonder what he did see in his mind's eye when he talked about the "old Argos". How far back did Forrest's old Argos go? Did he have any idea who the truly old Argos had been, a team that in reputation could have challenged the Green Bay Packers? How responsible for their fate did he think the old Argos were? And how presumptuous was Forrest being in referring to them so casually?

But now the Argos were on a streak. In their fifth game of the season they shut out the Tiger-Cats 25-0 — with Terry averaging six yards a carry (despite throwing up at half-time). On one run, only a five-yarder, he executed three distinct spins in the space of the same number of seconds, running sideways, backwards, his legs never stopping — the pin-ball trick again, but with results. It was the Terry of St. Louis returned — Sweet Feet. Taking off on the confectionary theme, Al Sokol of the *Star* named Terry and Mike McArthur the M & M men, and called them the best thing to happen to the Toronto running game "since Anthony Davis left". A week later at the CNE the Argos beat the Saskatchewan Roughriders convincingly, a victory which gave them a 4-2 record, and first place in the east.

And here let us pause for a moment.

The point we've stopped at happens to be the pinnacle of a classic representation of the Tease. It is precisely the point at which an Argo fan would be closer to sheer euphoria than at any other point during the season. Coincidentally, the best description I ever heard of the Tease was provided to me by another Argo fan who was recalling exactly this point of the 1979 season. He was English-born, a handsome, creative, vibrant man of forty, the president of a publishing firm. We met at a bar mitzvah. Within ten minutes he had confessed gloomily that he'd been a season-ticket holder for eleven years, that he was waiting to get closer to the 25-yard line, and that his son, whom he's been taking to the games all along, was finally coming to appreciate the Argos too. His eyes glazed over for a moment — he hadn't been drinking — "That time under Forrest Gregg when they teamed up Metcalf with Mike McArthur. That was our year. Those two were dynamite together; we couldn't be stopped. If they keyed on one, the other would take off. Going into the Edmonton game, remember, we were 4 and 2? The Cup was looming." He held up his hand in illustration, seeing things beyond even my imagination. "It was just *looming*."

On August 28, in Edmonton, in the game my book-publisher colleague was referring to, the Argos lost to the Eskimos 28-13. Still, the game seemed to prove they "belonged". Although Mike McArthur was lost in the first few minutes (fulfilling the destiny of rookies who talked publicly about the NFL), and the Eskimos scored a slew of points early, the team hung in to the end. "This is a much more disciplined team," said Dave Fennel, a member of the Eskimos' vaunted defensive line. "They didn't panic early the way the old Argos would have." (Forrest's affinity for the phrase seemed to be catching.)

On September 4 the Argos lost 28-25 to the Montreal Alouettes, bringing them to 4-4, a game that was noteworthy for the dozen-odd turn-overs the Argos committed and the fact that the Alouette's new middle linebacker, a recruit named Tom Cousineau, rescued a wounded seagull from the Argo 35-yard line. "When I came here I would have been happy with 4-4 half-way through the first season," said Forrest, "But not now. We're a better team than that. These aren't the old Argos."

And on September 22 the Argos played a game against the British Columbia Lions in Empire Stadium, site of Leon's fumble. I remember this game in particular because it was the eve of my thirtieth birthday, and I stayed up late to watch the game alone on television. Western games on late-night TV had always had a certain unreal aura for me. Because of the time difference they came on at a lost, solitary hour when no football game was meant to be played; the primacy of offence in the Western Conference made the experience that much more unusual. It happened at least twice a season: I'd be flipping from Johnny Carson to an old William Bendix movie and there it would be, a football game at 12:15, the Stampeders playing the Lions, or the Lions and the Eskimos, crazy shoot-outs with scores like 45-39 or 36-35, with black running-backs from the ghettos of Cleveland or the clay-lands of Georgia gambolling like cowboys, and footballs filling the air. Even when the wind-chill factor was minus ninety and players like George Reed and Jim Furlong resembled mastodons breathing vapour into the black night air, the offence was uncanny. It was as though, somewhere west of Thunder Bay, three downs became a perfectly workable matrix for offensive football, as opposed to the strait-jacket it was starting to seem to be in the East, particu-larly with the Argos. I wondered about the difference, until I took a trip to Regina to do a story on the Roughriders and Western football in general. What I found there, among fans and manage-ment alike, was a complete lack of the self-consciousness over the minor-league status of the CFL that was so prevalent in Toronto and Montreal; and a parallel dearth of awe at big-league Ameri-can ball. It was a matter of exposure; cable TV had been installed in the province of Saskatchewan just a few weeks before my arrival, giving the fans their first regular exposure to NFL games. There was no anxiety in Regina over whether the Roughriders were major-league—they were the only game in town. Fans came *up* from North Dakota to watch the Riders play. In terms of peace of mind, the football atmosphere was probably very close to what it had been like in Toronto in 1952. What this meant for the

Western coaches and strategists was that they were allowed to accept the Canadian game for what it was, and to exploit its peculiarities—three downs and the import quota both—instead of trying to ignore them and force the northern brand of football to be something it wasn't. The result was a Conference of increasingly dominant teams, playing games characterized by efficient, terrifically exciting offence.

And this night was no exception. While my youth ticked away, a Samoan quarterback named Joe Paopao completed twenty-one out of twenty-four passes on the screen in front of me, for an astounding completion percentage of .875, the second-best night a quarterback had ever enjoyed in Canadian football (second only to a 19 for 21, .905 performance in 1974 by Edmonton's Tom Wilkinson, who the Argos had decided was over the hill in 1971). The only problem was that Joe Paopao played for B.C. The Lions won the game—leaving the Argos with a record of 4 and 6, and leaving me with the thought that I was almost exactly contemporaneous with the Argos' three-decade slide.

And leaving Forrest with his stoicism. Never had a coach stood so firm in the face of facts; never had a coach denied the Bounce so thunderously, or had it laugh so cruelly in his face. Forrest seemed to have two rules: nobody would intimidate his team, and the supernatural did not exist. When the Argos lost 17-16 the next week, in the last minute of the game (their fifth loss in a row), Forrest was adamant. "Gregg Doesn't Believe Argonauts Under a Curse", ran a headline in the *Star*. "Superstition, the breaks, have nothing to do with it," said Forrest. "The team that does the best job of executing will win. We'll simply have to play better." The next week, on Thanksgiving in Hamilton this time, the Argos lost 42-3 to the Tiger-Cats. The Argos had 163 yards total offence, the Tiger-Cats 622. *622?* "We just came up with a very poor ball game," said Forrest. "We were really stinko." "It was unbelievable," said centre Doug Redl. "I have nothing to say," said Paul Bennett, "but don't quote me on that." "As long as the Argos are in this league," said Harold Ballard, new owner of the Tiger-Cats, "we'll make the playoffs." It was after this game that the Argos were pelted with refuse thrown by some Hamilton fans as the team was leaving the field, and Forrest exploded. "They're animals!" he said to the press. "Little snot-nosed jerks who are afraid to play football and get their enjoyment out of throwing missiles at people who do!" He was loyal, Forrest; he was craggy; he was—even now, it's not easy to write this—*pathetic*.

The *Argonaut Media Guide* would later say that the Argos of '79, Forrest's team, had "peaked too early." It was an interesting way of putting it. In fact after being 4-2 on August 15, the Argos won exactly one game for the rest of the season, finishing 5 and 11 and in last place for the fifth time in the past six years. In its shape the collapse was almost identical to the fall of '78, the year before, with Leo and his internecine warfare. Except that Forrest wasn't Leo; Forrest as a coach was worse than Leo at his most abysmal; Forrest was worse than Lou Agase.

He was worse than Russ. Ultimately the comparison, no matter how painful, has to be drawn, and it turns out to be as telling a measure of Forrest as there is. The critical area of contrast was offence. Neither Forrest's Argo offence nor Russ's enjoyed much success, but they were widely divergent stylistically. What Russ's offence had was a certain homogeneity. While it was conceived in chaos, it was at least consistent—it looked chaotic. But under Forrest the Argo offence looked superb. It was balanced, it was intelligent, it was professional. The guards pulled on cue, the backs got the ball the proper number of times, the prerequisite plays were all there: the draw, the screen, even the sweep. There was a heady crispness about the plays, a streamlined sense of purpose reminiscent of the Packers. But there was something wrong about the plays as a whole. It was as though they were a perfect set of plays set into the wrong game. Not just an ill-conceived game plan, but the wrong game altogether. It was as though the Argos were playing Winnipeg, on October 4, but Forrest was still playing the Dallas Cowboys in December, 1967.

Later it dawned on me that I had missed a glaring hint myself during my interview with Forrest in his office under the CNE. At one point I had asked him what he thought was the critical difference between the Canadian and American games, and he had replied, "To my way of thinking, with the three downs, *you're just starting at second down and ten*. So naturally...." But there was nothing natural about it. Thinking that three downs was just the American game with the first down removed, the American game penalized, was exactly the wrong way of looking at it. Second down and ten in a world of four downs was light years away from first and ten with just three downs. The former implied that you had blundered your way out of a down, or been found unworthy of a down, *temporarily*, that around the corner the extra down was waiting to be picked up. The latter was immutable; three downs was the given, and it would never change. Is it any wonder that the

173

Argos seemed a bit out of sync with reality during the fall of '79? It was a season of second and tens, a season when every time the offence went out on the field they were trying to impersonate the Green Bay Packers a quarter of the way through an offensive series.

In the end Forrest managed to do what no Argo coach had done for a decade: he turned the last game of the season, an away game against Ottawa, into a true nothing game. There was nothing the Argos could do, that is, to alter their fate; there was no golden opportunity they could squander.

But the habits of a quarter century are difficult to break. By the end of the fourth quarter the Argos were trailing 16-6, and had looked worse getting there than any Argo team I had suffered through before them, worse than Bob Shaw's Argos, or Nobby's, or (I was willing to bet) Hampton Pool's. With less than a minute left, Ottawa intercepted a pass deep in Argo territory; they promptly sent in their reserve quarterback, Charlie Weatherbie, and on the last play of the game Charlie threw a touchdown pass to Jeff Avery, a meaningless and—considering the circumstances—classless score. Forrest was livid. "That was unnecessary," he fumed. George Brancato was phlegmatic. "What am I supposed to do, go in and knock down the guy's pass? It was only his fourth play; I guess he wanted to impress me. Besides, what the hell difference does it make whether you lose 23-6 or 16-6 or 84-6? A loss is a loss." Forrest was undoubtedly right—the Rough Riders didn't need to pad their point total to get into the playoffs, and one of the prime unwritten commandments of team sport is that you never intentionally humiliate a beaten opponent—but George was probably recalling Forrest's psychological ploy of usurping Ottawa's end of the field in the pre-season, and trying a little late gamesmanship of his own in revenge. Besides, Forrest's tone was so high-faluting compared to George's that it was hard for me to sympathize with him. Here the Argos were, waxing terrible, and here was Forrest, protégé of Vince Lombardi, ranting about courtesy.

By the end of the last Argo game of 1979, I had come to one unshakeable conclusion. I was sure that Forrest Gregg's size-14 feet were made of clay, that his year at Cleveland had been a fluke. If there was one unassailable truth in the universe it was this: Forrest Gregg was a terrible football coach.

He was also peripatetic. Two months after the end of the '79 season, Forrest, who had given his bond to live in Oakville and save the Argos, signed a contract to coach the Cincinnati Bengals of the National Football League. The speed of his defection was as dazzling as it was disillusioning. Suddenly Toronto was once more an obscure football outpost on a distant northern horizon.

And suddenly Forrest had all the old Lombardi magic back. Home again, in the simple land of logic and four downs, he was nothing short of a mastermind. In 1980, with a team strengthened by M. L. Harris (the Human Hammer, whom Forrest had purloined from the Argos) but also decimated by key injuries, he led the Bengals, 4 and 12 the previous two seasons, to a 6-10 record in the tough Central Division of the NFL. The next year, with quarterback Ken Anderson back and an unlikely-looking antelope named Chris Collinsworth catching passes at wide receiver, Forrest's Bengals began to win. By the season's end they were 12 and 4 and had finished in first place in the American Conference. On a lethally cold day in December, even colder than the day of the '67 Dallas-Green Bay game and Bart Starr's plunge, the Bengals put on a display of gritty Clutch execution that was straight out of the pre-'67 Packers era. Even the Argos of *1950* might have been impressed. When the game was over the Bengals had defeated the San Diego Chargers convincingly and earned a berth in the Super Bowl.

There were generally two responses available to an Argo fan when something like this happened. The first was a kind of provincial pride—we shaped him, went the refrain, and now look where he is. The second was put most adeptly into words by none other than Harold Ballard, the coarse custodian of loss who had a way with a blunt phrase. "We can say goodbye to Forrest Gregg," Harold said. "He may have been great in Cleveland, but he's nothing here."

It was no *doppelgänger* we saw charging across the frozen field in Cincinnati, his fist held aloft. The Forrest who led his team to the NFL Championship game was the same Forrest who had misguided the Argos. It had come down to a battle between the myths—the magic of Vince Lombardi and the "old" NFL versus the curse of the Argo Bounce—and it had been no contest. Under Forrest the Argos had finished 5-11, in last place for the fifth time in the past six years and the fifteenth time in the past twenty-four. As of the end of 1979, they had also gone through the entire hierarchy of possible American Saviours, including one Canadian. There was even a certain peacefulness to it; it seemed to me, as I said goodbye to my twenties, that the Argos had reached a natural nadir, that we were all beginning a fresh new decade.

In the fan's dictionary of terms, this is known as hubris.

10 The First Touchdown

If I was exposed to one cliché more than any other during the period I wrote about sports, it was that things in the world of professional athletics take time. Draft choices take time to "come around", rookie quarterbacks take time to mature, championship teams take time to build. More often than not I heard these opinions voiced in utilitarian administrative offices, by chunky general managers who wore checked sports jackets and put their feet up on the desk, but you can find them just as easily on the sports pages every day. A willingness to wait is revered everywhere in pro sport; haste is widely damned. Considering the evidence, the prejudice is probably a valid one; as a journalist I was forced to acknowledge the wisdom of it more than once. But as a fan it always bothered me at least as much as the excuse of injuries. This is one possible reason why losing teams are popular: whether it's a case of cause or effect — or eventually both — they are rarely patient.

And this may be why it was so surprising when the Argos appointed Willie Wood, Forrest Gregg's assistant, to coach the team for the 1980 season. The Argos had promoted assistants before — Bud Riley in 1978, Joe Moss in '74, Steve Owen in '59 — but the promotions had almost always been on an interim basis, for the remainder of the season that had seen the firing of the original coach. The Argos had generally been too impatient with the entire "old" regime to let any ex-assistant coach continue into the next season. Assistant coaches also tended to lack charisma and drama, two qualities the Argos had been known to look for following particularly crushing disappointments.

Given all this, the choice of Willie in January of 1980 was a

Argos triumphant, 1981. The bench is euphoric after Cedric Minter's winning touchdown after eleven consecutive losses.

strangely subdued one, a welcome departure from the pattern. I saw it as a confirmation of the idea that the team had "bottomed out", and was ready to enter the eighties with a sober, controlled approach to building a winner. As fatuous as Forrest had been, Willie was unassuming. He was affable, courteous, and refreshingly humble — probably the most likeable coach the Argos had had since Leo Cahill. Willie had a big round moon of a face, sometimes smiling, sometimes lugubrious, but always accessible. To have found Willie anything but sympathetic, to have wished him anything but well, a fan would have to have been a monster.

The monsters were the Argos. After jumping out to a 3-1 record in the first four games of the season — an even more classic Tease than '79 — they lost their next five games in a row, and nine of the next twelve, the last loss coming in Hamilton to the Tiger-Cats. Once again it was a game that could have put them into the playoffs, and once again the Argos chose the worst possible moment to collapse; they failed to score a single offensive touchdown in the game, going down 23-16, finishing the season with a 6-10 record and in last place.

If there was a bright spot to 1980, it was the presence of Willie himself, and his unflagging honesty. The only Argo coach I could think of who had been as honest was, again, Leo Cahill — but Leo had somehow managed to be honest without being altogether forthright. Willie was both. When the Argos won their home opener 18-11 over the Alouettes, he did nothing to hide his astonishment, especially at the play of the second-year quarterback, Mark Jackson. "Up here you have to have a quarterback who plays well," said Willie (an astute statement for its apparent obviousness). "I thought Mark was in the groove, and polished." When the Argos won two out of their next three games, Willie stayed surprised. Under a headline in the *Star* reading, "Even Coach Amazed By Argos", Willie was quoted: "There's no way I figured we'd be 3 and 1 at this point. We're still a pretty hit-and-miss team." It may have been my prejudice, or some residual antipathy to Forrest Gregg, but it seemed to me that even in trying to refute the Bounce and the question of a hex in general, Willie never lost his appealing, humanitarian outlook. "I keep referring to this thing as a demon of the past," he said. "It's something that hangs over them...." And later, after losing to Hamilton again on Thanksgiving, 23-2: "We can't seem to get any excitement on offence. There seems to be a certain numbness of offence, which is extremely disappointing...."

Willie's understated personality—and the lack of grand designs in the Argo universe as a whole—are the only two things I can cite to account for the feeling of modified optimism that sprang up around the Argos as they approached the 1981 season. I was particularly surprised that I was feeling it. The idea of actually abandoning the team was still heresy, but I'd been convinced that the Forrest Gregg fiasco would keep me cynical for at least one full season. Possibly the notion of rooting for the Argos without the weight of impossible expectations was too appealing to pass up.

Then again, the optimism may have been a matter of viewpoint. There were always two ways of looking at a past Argo season. The Argos had finished last in 1980, granted, but their record, 6 and 10, had been an improvement on 1979, when they were 5 and 11 under Forrest. A similar increment in 1981 would leave them at 7 and 9, a mark that, considering the overwhelming dominance of the Western teams, was almost guaranteed to put them into the playoffs in the East. And once they reached the playoffs, where chance played such a large role, the unprecedented (in my experience at least) could actually happen. It was possible. The Cup could loom.

What I didn't expect was that the truly unprecedented would happen, including one play that circled back to touch the Argo legend at its beginnings, providing a perfect climax to an amazing sports story and shaking my fandom to its very foundations.

As a team, the Argos of 1981 were almost as modest as Willie himself. In fact, in their lack of bombast and fanfare the 1981 Argos were more intrinsically appealing to me than any Argo team since the 1969 Dave Raimey-Bill Symons edition; like the Argos, none of the '81 players was bigger than the team as a whole. The sole exception might have been Bruce Clark, a huge defensive end from Penn State who had been chosen in the first round of the NFL draft by the Green Bay Packers only to be lured away by a more lucrative Argo contract. But Bruce, for all his big-league size and menace, was a lineman, decidedly a second-class saviour as far as Argo tradition went. The glamour position with the Argos was still running-back, and after the 1980 season Terry Metcalf, with the consent of the team, had finally left the Argos and taken his spinning wizardry back to the NFL, specifically to the Washington Redskins and Joe Theismann.

The running-back Willie Wood had recruited to replace

Terry, Cedric Minter, fit perfectly into the unpretentious 1981 Argo mould. I had a chance to experience Cedric's lack of pretension first hand, because he was the new Argo I interviewed that summer. The interview was unusual for me because of its venue — my car. Cedric had come to town early to find an apartment for himself and his new wife, and I ended up asked him questions while we drove through Mississauga, the highrise-laden suburb on the western edge of the city that had become home to most of Toronto's professional athletes. The actual story, I quickly realized, was less the list of questions I was asking than Mississauga — or at least the ordeal of adjustment Cedric was undergoing, the same one that faced dozens of homesick 21-year-old athletes in cities across the continent every summer. Cedric's background had made the process of acclimatization to Toronto doubly disorienting so far. A native of Boise, Idaho, he had set several records at his home-town university, Boise State, a school whose football stadium held a scant 22,000 spectators, and whose student population was virtually all white. Besides Cedric, there had been only one other black player on the Boise State team. The first day of practice at CNE Stadium had been a culture shock for him, not just because of the size of the park (and the city surrounding it), but also because of the Argos' racial mix. "There were more black players on the field than I've ever played with in my life," Cedric pointed out, "unless of course we were playing Grambling, and that's an all-black school." To try to ease the disorientation of that first day, he had spent the afternoon watching a baseball game at CNE between the Blue Jays and the Chicago White Sox, the first major-league game he'd seen in person in his life.

As a quarterback for 1981 the Argos had Condredge Holloway, the talented scrambling signal-caller who had come to them from the Ottawa Rough Riders in an off-season trade. Condredge had always been murder against the Argos, but in itself that obviously wasn't an unqualified reference. Two things nagged at me about Condredge, despite his considerable gifts: one, he was notoriously injury-prone (possibly because of his small size and sometimes imprudent courage when he was scrambling); and two, ever since Tom Clements, the other quarterback in Ottawa's two-quarterback system, had left the Rough Riders, Condredge had lost a certain finishing touch — what you could call the football equivalent of boxing's knockout punch. From the opponent's 20-yard line to the goal-line, Condredge was no longer nearly as effective as he had been while Clements was in the line-up. How serious this malady could be in a quarterback was something I knew only too well from watching the Argos. I harboured a suspicion that Condredge was a natural symbiotic, a player fated in his sports life to be happiest as half of a larger whole. There was also the matter of his appearance — in the full-face close-ups in the newspapers Condredge looked alarmingly young; he had the beaming eyes of an eight-year-old in a Jell-O commercial. But, as with Cedric Minter and Willie Wood, there was something immensely likeable about his vulnerability.

To round out the muted roster of '81 the Argos had a pair of players who had been surprises in the 1980 season: Dave Newman, a slight, white slotback from Kirksville, Missouri, who had been noticed inadvertently by an Argo scout at one of the more obscure college-bowl games, and who as a rookie had somehow, with less than blinding speed, managed to score more touchdowns (ten) than any other receiver in the country in 1980; and Bob Gaddis, a wide receiver *with* speed who had been tutored by Lynn Swann of the Pittsburgh Steelers before reaching the Argos via Montreal and Hamilton. Bob Gaddis's migration to the Argos had all the earmarks of another classic Argo phenomenon, the "Second Coming" (the discarded player who returns to haunt the team by scoring touchdowns in devastating bunches) — but in reverse. The Alouettes had considered Bob expendable after 1979 because they'd acquired Fred "Stickum" Belitnikoff, the recently retired Oakland Raider great who had made a career out of moving at hypnotically slow speeds; as for Hamilton, they had considered Bob's ability to hang onto a pass questionable. Over the course of the 1980 season Fred Belitnikoff caught all of thirty-eight passes for 420 yards for the Alouettes before loping back into retirement, while with the Argos Bob Gaddis managed to hang onto sixty-eight for 1,112 yards, the top figure for all Eastern Conference receivers and enough to earn him the Argo nomination for the year's Schenley Award for Most Outstanding Player.

Besides his banner year in 1980, Bob Gaddis enjoyed one other distinction. He was one of only six players on the 1981 pre-season Toronto roster of forty-seven who had been alive when the Argos had won their last championship, in the fall of 1952.

The Argos split their first two exhibition games of 1981, against Ottawa and Hamilton, and then lost their next two, for a 1-3 pre-season record. It was less than disconcerting to me. Pre-season with a normal team is deceptive, but with the Argos it had always been positively illusory. There were times when I could have sworn that the actual physical appearance of certain Argos had changed in the week or so between the last exhibition game and the first regular-season game. Success was always the more dangerous quality in the pre-season with the Argos. It was when they went 3 and 1 that you had to worry.

Besides, there was a drama unfolding in another part of the league in the summer of '81 that was extraordinary enough to distract anyone from the Argos' results. During the winter Nelson Skalbania, a Vancouver entrepreneur with a head as sleek as a mink's, had purchased the Montreal Alouettes from their stubby, long-suffering owner, Sam Berger. Since the days of the infamous Sam Etcheverry non-trade in 1960, attendance had been a problem in Montreal, even in the Grey Cup years (scandalous as that seemed to Argo fans). In an attempt to turn things around overnight, Nelson had opened his wallet and signed three established NFL stars: James Scott, a receiver with the Chicago Bears; Billy "White Shoes" Johnson, another fleet fighter-jet late of the Houston Oilers; and, most celebrated of all, Vince Ferragamo, the handsome med-student quarterback who had come off the bench in 1979 to lead the Los Angeles Rams to the Super Bowl and a near upset of the highly favoured Pittsburgh Steelers, and who was generally considered to be *the* NFL quarterback of the future. As if that weren't enough, Nelson had also recruited a halfback named David Overstreet, a first-round draft choice of the Miami Dolphins whose only visible flaw was a Metcalfian tendency to fumble. Aside from Harry Sonshine's own wholesale talent-hunt in 1955, and maybe the signing of Billy Vessels by the Edmonton Eskimos in '53, it was the single most stunning Canadian raid on big-name American football players in history.

The publicity surrounding the Alouettes was so overwhelming that the Argos' opening game of the regular season arrived before I'd had a chance to mentally prepare myself for it. The same thing seems to have held true for a lot of fans: the official attendance at the game was the smallest opening-day crowd the Argos had drawn since the expansion of the stadium. The opposition on opening night was the Saskatchewan Roughriders, a team that had slumped to an abysmal 2 and 14 record in 1980 (the worst in Canada) but that under their new head coach, ex-quarterback star Ronny Lancaster, was expected to improve dramatically in '81. The Argos led the game 18-16 going into the last five minutes of the fourth quarter, when Cedric Minter fumbled on his own 25-yard line. Saskatchewan recovered, kicked a field goal, and won 19-18.

It was a fairly standard Argo loss; what was unusual was how genuinely promising the team had looked while losing. Aside from Cedric's unfortunate fumble, he had been brilliant all night — albeit in a quiet, workman-like way — while the team as a whole had simmered for most of the game, threatening to explode at any moment. A real football team seemed to be lurking under the cloak of that opening loss. I had felt almost as much for Cedric when he fumbled as I had watching him look up at apartment complexes in Mississauga. I felt a more detached pity for Condredge Holloway, who had suffered a gash on his index finger in the first half (a typically unusual Condredge injury) and who insisted on taking full blame for the Argo loss. "I stunk," Condredge said in the papers the next day. "I guess that happens in professional sports, but I don't know why it had to happen in the first game of the season with a new team." (This penitential bent of Condredge's would develop into a full-blown pathology by the middle of the season, at which point it would become a bit oppressive.)

The second Argo game of the season pitted the Boatmen against Montreal in Olympic Stadium. In their own opener in Vancouver the Alouettes, with their phalanx of high-priced Americans, had been prohibitive favourites, but had somehow managed to lose stunningly to the Lions, 48-8; Vince Ferragamo, the man who was going to take Montreal to the Grey Cup, completed just thirteen of thirty passes, with two interceptions. It was an unmitigated disaster. Knowing the Argos, who tended to be infected even by mitigated disasters and to respond with more inventive versions of their own, I was anticipating the worst.

It turned out to be one of the most exciting games I'd ever seen them play. At half-time they were ahead 21-1, and had moved the ball with a crisp, controlled ease. Cedric Minter had already gained over fifty yards rushing, and Condredge Holloway was playing like an intellectual water-bug, sprinting out, running bootlegs and play-action passes, and disassembling my natural symbiotic theory in the space of thirty minutes. On the other side of the field Vince Ferragamo looked uncomfortable and unsynchronized with the game, like a Tony Curtis character from a late fifties college football film who had found himself in the wrong movie.

Then the second half started, and Vince lost some of his discomfort and began to connect on a series of sharp, short passes, releasing the ball with tantalizing quickness. The Argos for their part continued to move the ball at will when they got it, but now they were treating the Alouettes' 20-yard line like the Berlin Wall; they seemed stricken once again by the lack of a knockout punch I thought I'd detected in Condredge. It didn't help that Zenon Andrusyshyn, reacting to the All-or-None law of consistency that had dogged him throughout his career, missed four field goals. With fifteen seconds left in the game David Overstreet dove over the goal-line from one yard out to tie the score. The convert made it 23-22 for the Alouettes. The Argos were 0 and 2, but they had lost those two games by the absolute minimum margin, two points, and they had looked better doing it than any Argo team I could remember since Leo Cahill's 1971 Grey Cup contestants. Their potential was a tangible thing; they seemed to be on the brink of a football self-discovery.

On the morning of the next Argo game, July 16, against B.C., a *Globe and Mail* writer named Al Strachan made one of the most disturbing observations I had ever read in reference to the Argos, or any losing team for that matter. It went beyond strategy to anti-strategy. "Curiously enough," wrote Al Strachan, "it would probably be better for Toronto Argonauts if they lose tonight's game against British Columbia Lions by a fairly substantial margin rather than by a close score." His reasoning was that if the Argos lost another game by a hair's breadth, they might be so damaged psychologically that they would take a number of games to recover; a lop-sided score, on the other hand, could be shrugged off as inevitable, and put cleanly out of the team's mind. The possibility that the Argos might *win* the game was apparently so remote to Al Strachan as to be laughable. Even for Toronto it was an incredible piece of pragmatism. It violated every instinct of faith and hope a fan felt as a matter of course. I wondered how Al Strachan had come to have a soul so devoid of love and light.

That night the Argos lost to the Lions 32-29, with Condredge Holloway overthrowing a wide open David Newman at the goal-line with less than a minute to play. The ball sailed into the hands of the Lions' rover, Tony Proudfoot, and Condredge ripped his helmet off and hurled it onto the artificial turf, strewing its innards across the field. The Argos had lost their first three games by a total of five points.

The next week, on July 25, the Argos lost to Hamilton 57-13. The fifty-seven points Hamilton scored broke the record of points scored against an Argo team set by Ottawa in 1957 in their 55-14 win over Hampton Pool's Argos. It was one of the worst losses an Argo team had ever suffered. Al Strachan was a genius.

Five days later, back at the CNE on July 30, the Argos lost 21-18 to the Winnipeg Blue Bombers. They had led 10-7 going into the fourth quarter, then collapsed abysmally.

Eight days after that, on August 7, the Argos lost in Ottawa to the Rough Riders, 38-11. It was their sixth consecutive loss of the season.

And it was the Ottawa game that turned the tumblers—at least it was at that point I realized what might be happening. The Argos had finally embarked on the one form of catastrophe that had eluded them all through the years. They were headed for the ultimate streak: the perfect season.

It wasn't generally acknowledged until the Edmonton loss, or maybe the subsequent loss, to Saskatchewan again, in the last week of August. There was a marked dearth of reference to it in the newspapers, as though a kind of reverse no-hitter was in progress and no one wanted to say anything for fear of causing it to actually happen. I felt something different: a mixture of resignation and relief.

It wasn't (as Forrest Gregg had claimed in his office that morning in 1979) that I wanted the Argos to lose. It was just that there comes a time in the life of a doomed fan when any sort of perfection has a strong appeal. After nineteen years of disappointment with the Argos there was something tremendously therapeutic about the notion of a "perfect" season, a season without a single win to adulterate the purity of loss. It was the true absolute bottom, the ultimate purge. If it was perverse, it would also satisfy my hunger for historical significance.

In short, the prospect of a winless season was enough to arouse in a fan a wild ambivalence.

The Argos, on the other hand, weren't ambivalent at all: they were panicking, plain and simple. After the Winnipeg loss Lew Hayman—now seventy-three—announced that he had hired a man to replace him as president: Ralph Sazio, the ex-president of the Hamilton Tiger-Cats. The move caused an immediate scandal, with Ti-Cat owner Harold Ballard claiming that the Argos had tampered with Sazio, and also that Sazio had been ethically guilty of breaking his contract, even though he didn't have one. "Sazio is a wealthy man," Harold was quoted as saying with indignation. "It would have been an insult to ask him to sign a contract." It was perfect Harold thinking: parochial, a bit vulgar, and touched with a warped humanistic logic all its own.

And then there was the logic of Willie. It's difficult to imagine any coach in any professional sport delivering a series of quotes, day in and day out, that were stranger than Willie's for the season of '81. As the Argos moved farther into the streak, and closer to the half-way point of the season, Willie gradually lapsed into a state of self-contradiction that bordered on Tibetan mysticism. It was as though Sam Goldwyn had spent a month eating lunch with the Dalai Lama and then signed to coach the Argos. Willie was as polite as ever, and as modest; he was just making less sense. "Despite the six turn-overs, inept offensive display and the execution breakdowns," Willie said after the Argos' first loss, "there was plenty to be enthusiastic about." Asked to do a quick personality sketch of himself, Willie was quoted: "The guy is a man of many moods. He responds to people fairly evenly. Sometimes, he may be a little impulsive, but he's always trying to be fair. Sometimes, he can really be tough." Besides the streak, Willie's mystification was one of the two most obvious anomalies of 1981 to a fan as the season moved towards its anything-but-obvious summit.

The situation in Montreal was the other. After their last-second victory over the Argos, the Alouettes had reverted to their first-game form and had started to lose, at first mildly, then with growing facility. They lost in succession to Ottawa by two points, to Edmonton by sixteen, to Saskatchewan by twenty, to Winnipeg by fifty-six. Even by Argo standards it was a collapse of major proportions. Most of the blame was placed on Nelson Skalbania's American saviours, in particular Vince Ferragamo. Vince's intellectual inability to absorb the Canadian game was mentioned more than once. "I don't really like the three-down system," Vince said in the papers, "I'd prefer another down." As an Argo fan I knew exactly how he felt, but somehow I couldn't help thinking that we were approaching the problem from different directions. In the middle of September an article by Earl McRae was published in *Today Magazine* entitled "Waiting for Vinnie", and subtitled "Vince Ferragamo: he's gorgeous, but is he smart?" Earl McRae never came out and said it, but every other line in the article implied that Vince was not merely dumb but possessed of an Olympian vacuousness. The article also made it obvious that the Alouette coach, Joe Scannella, who characterized Vince as "so bright it's scary", had succumbed to some kind of spell. But there had been signs of that even before Earl McRae's article appeared. "How can I not start Vinnie?" Scannella had said at one point. "How do you disgrace a guy who is making that kind of money?" Joe declined to disgrace Vinnie, and the Alouettes kept losing.

It only occurred to me later that the important issue may not have been Vinnie at all, but the Alouettes' collapse in general. What the Alouettes were trying to do, consciously or not, was to usurp the Argos. All the ingredients were there: the interfering owner dazzled by American glamour, the Great Black Hope (three of them), the Great White Hope, the inexplicable collapse and the recriminations—everything but the tradition.

It was after the Argos' tenth consecutive loss, to Ottawa once more, that Willie Wood was fired. It was more merciful than sad—in my opinion Willie had been doomed after number eight against Saskatchewan, when he said he thought the team was "digressing". With the winless season beckoning, the last link to the Green Bay Packers and Vince Lombardi cleaned out his desk and faded silently away. In his farewell pictures in the newspapers, Willie looked like a mournful giant panda. One more legend was gone.

To replace Willie as coach, Ralph Sazio appointed general manager Tommy Hudspeth, whose previous head-coaching experience consisted of an interim job with the Detroit Lions from 1975 to 1977. Tommy Hudspeth's first official act was to publicly chastise players for being Good-Time Charlies who were overly concerned with the partying life. It was a completely unprecedented theory for the Argos' problems: a life of sin! The next thing Hudspeth did was to note that a lot of Argos had gotten into the habit of walking off the field with their heads bowed; from now on, he said, they would "walk proud". Then he asked Bruce Clark, 250 pounds, to switch from the defensive line to linebacker. Bruce switched, the players walked proud, and on September 19 they were annihilated 45-14 by the B.C. Lions.

And then the Argos won a game.

I remember the details exactly, because I was caught in a

mammoth Sunday afternoon traffic jam on the Queen Elizabeth Way on my way to the stadium and I ended up listening to the entire first half on the radio. By the end of it the Stampeders were leading 20-11 and appeared to have the game under control. But shortly after I took my seat in the western end-zone, Calgary collapsed completely, scoring only one unconverted touchdown in the entire second half. I was convinced the Stampeders might have won the game even then, if Tommy Hudspeth hadn't chosen to replace Dan Manucci, Ralph Sazio's first candidate for Argo quarterback saviour status (from the Buffalo Bills — quarterback number 24 since 1970) with Condredge Holloway, with 3:21 left in the game, and the Argos behind by four points, and on their own 27-yard line. Condredge was brilliant; for once he had nothing to apologize for. He scrambled and passed the Argos eighty-two yards to the Calgary 1-yard line where, with a mere fourteen seconds left on the clock, Cedric Minter dove over for the winning touchdown.

And that was it. The streak had been stopped in its tracks, shattered. One and eleven was awful, but not transcendent. And in fact that might have been it, the meaningful end of the 1981 season, if it hadn't been for another game that was played the day before the Argos' victory, one time-zone to the west. In that game Vince Ferragamo and the Montreal Alouettes lost to the Edmonton Eskimos by a score of 62-11. The loss left the Alouettes with a 1-10 record, with a game in hand on the Argos. Over the next fifteen days the Alouettes split two games with the Calgary Stampeders, while the Argos, possibly hurt by a long fourteen-day layoff after the euphoria of finally winning, lost to Winnipeg 43-12. That left them with a 1 and 12 record, to the Alouettes' 2 and 11.

Twenty-six years before, in 1955, the Big Four had adopted a rule permitting the top three teams of the four in the conference, as opposed to the top two, to continue on into post-season play. Anticipating the general drift of pro sport by at least a decade, the league had made the change to avoid the inevitable loss of fan interest in losing cities as the playoffs approached. It was a philosophy that would always seem self-destructive to me, whether it was being put into practice in hockey, or contemplated in baseball. Whatever fans you gained in a numerical sense in a particular city, you lost emotionally overall. By putting opportunism first, the sports establishment taught the paying customers to be as cynical as it was. Exclusiveness is the core of competitive sport. To devalue it is to run the risk of making sport meaningless.

The Alouettes and the Argos were the two worst teams in the entire league, but, because of the 1955 rule change, they were actually fighting for the last playoff spot. And on the night of October 17, Montreal came into the CNE to play the Double Blue.

It was the last game in which a fan would expect anything magical to happen. By rights it was also the last game I should ever have seen the Argos play.

I got to the park early the night of the Montreal game; I'd never obtained regular press-box privileges, and I hadn't been able to break my habit of getting to the park early to buy a decent ticket from a scalper. But on this particular night I didn't have to worry. The attendance was later announced as 31,008, one of those wan, relatively tiny (for the Argos) crowds that had characterized the whole 1981 season. I bought a ticket for the open side, at the official counter, took the walk I could have taken with my eyes closed around the eastern end-zone, in the shadow of the Flyer, and then climbed to my seat half-way up on the 45-yard line. I'd only missed half a game all season, but the empty seats in the stands were still a shock: the entire western end-zone, the third-base side for the Blue Jays, was deserted, as were both extreme ends of the covered side. With the wind gusting in waves, the overall effect was to make the stadium, never cosy, seem even vaster and more open than it was, like an agoraphobic's nightmare.

It was a difficult game to handicap. The Argos were the Argos, and Montreal was trying to be. After the Alouettes' ninth game of the season — their eighth loss — Joe Scannella had been fired, and his successor, Jim Eddy, had immediately charged that Scannella's play-book had been needlessly obscure, placing an unfair burden on Vince Ferragamo. With a simplified offence, Eddy assured everyone, Vince would bloom overnight. The next game was the 62-11 loss to Edmonton. Two games later, in a 29-3 loss to Calgary, Vince was 6 for 20 with two interceptions before he was replaced in the fourth quarter by Gerry Dattilio, the talented Canadian back-up quarterback who was making approximately one fifth of Vince's salary. "We can't make the offence any simpler," Jim Eddy said. "He's operating with our basic design." By the night of the Argo game, the Alouettes had acquired Ken

Johnson, a quarterback from the Stampeders, to back up Dattilio, who was being given the starting job at last. By this time Vince had become a general embarrassment, something like a family scandal. There had even been talk of putting him and his $450,000 on the team's reserve list. Looking down at the Alouette bench, though, I could see him still there in uniform, number 15, standing helmetless with his hands on his hips and charcoal smudges under his eyes. Cosmetically he looked as professional as any quarterback I'd ever seen.

The Argos won the toss, and took the wind, and Zenon Andrusyshyn immediately kicked off through the Montreal endzone for a single point. For most of the first quarter Zenon kept the Als pinned in their own zone with his punting. Neither team seemed to be able to muster a sustained offence, but it was the Argos, surprisingly, who looked stronger. At the eight-minute mark they took advantage of a short Montreal kick to move the ball to the Alouette 20, where Condredge just missed on a touchdown pass to Martin Cox, a wide receiver who had played half a dozen games with the Argos since coming over from the Ottawa Rough Riders. Zenon kicked the field goal on the next play to make it 4-0 for the Argos. Just before the end of the quarter he added a 65-yard single to make it 5-0. The increments were coming slowly but steadily and the Argos were looking very tough. Approximately a minute later Ken Johnson launched a perfect fifty-yard parabola to James Scott, the ex-Chicago Bear, a pass so flawlessly thrown that not even the stripes on the ball could infect it with an iota of wobble. Around me the familiar sigh rose and fell —it may have been a small crowd, but it was an Argo crowd. Before the sigh could transmute to a groan James Scott was tackled inside the Argo 20. The Alouettes had to settle for a field goal. And then came a little hiatus of light, the kind of thing that in another season I would have found genuinely exciting. After the kick-off the Argos embarked on a long, sustained drive, with Condredge mixing his plays perfectly, the three downs suddenly no issue at all. It ended when Cedric Minter, who'd been outplaying David Overstreet decisively all night, started out on an end sweep from the Alouette 22-yard line, suddenly retreated a few steps, and threw a perfectly creditable pass into the end-zone to Dave Dorn, who was wide open. A halfback option, perfectly timed, flawlessly executed. Zenon added another single on a missed field goal, and the gun went off to end the half. The Argos led 13-3.

I spent half-time listening to a woman in front of me, holding a plastic cup full of rye, tell her companion a story about a priest who had murdered a transvestite barber in Chicago with an axe. It was a surprisingly dull story, but it helped keep me from thinking about the cold as I waited for the Argos to collapse. The reason I knew they were about to collapse was that I had caught myself thinking, after Cedric's unexpected touchdown pass, that maybe this time they wouldn't. I had also caught myself forgetting for long blocks of time who the Argos and the Alouettes were: two terrible teams playing a meaningless game for a playoff spot that was a mockery in itself. When it came to fandom, I thought, it was easier to understand the priest with his axe.

The Alouettes scored a single and field goal of their own at the opening of the third quarter, but it wasn't until just before the quarter ended that the inevitable Argo swoon took effect. At that point Montreal faced a third down and long yardage from their own 20, and were forced to punt. The Argos, though, were called for having too many players on the field for the kick, and the Als received a free first down, which they promptly turned into a six-minute drive that ended with a touchdown, giving them a 14-13 lead. Moving into the fourth quarter it was all Montreal; the only thing stopping them from padding the margin was their own ineptness. With about three minutes left in the game, the Alouettes drove down to the Argo 17, only to have Billy "White Shoes" Johnson fumble the ball into Jim Corrigall's hands. The Argos lost ten yards on two downs, and Zenon squibbed his punt, giving the Alouettes the ball at the Argo 33 with just a little over a minute showing on the clock.

It was at this point that a large percentage of the crowd started to file out of CNE Stadium, among them, I later discovered, the English publisher I'd met at the bar mitzvah, along with his son. It was significant, he told me, because he almost never left Argo games early. ("It's not in my blood," was how he put it.) While the publisher made his way out of the stadium, and several thousand people got up to join him, the Alouettes picked up two first downs and moved down to the Argo 10-yard line; but then, on their fourth play, David Overstreet (repeating under far less dramatic circumstances the gift of Jerry Keeling and Bernie Faloney and Bob Sandberg) fumbled the ball—and the Argos recovered.

Not that it appeared to make much difference. The Argos were behind by only a point, but there were just forty-four seconds left to play and they had to gain at least fifty yards for Zenon Andrusyshyn to be in field-goal range. At least half the crowd had left by now, and most of the remaining half was on its feet, shuffling out and glancing back, the way a crowd will, the way Argo crowds had for years. I would have joined them, but I'd never been able to leave any sporting event early, let alone an Argo game.

The first seemingly futile play of the last Argo series was a pass from Condredge Holloway into the centre of the field; it was deflected and ended up being cradled by a prone Jan Carinci, the Argo slotback, at the Argo 45. From there Condredge faded again and threw a short out-pattern, this time to Martin Cox. Cox was tackled on the Alouette 49 with only fourteen seconds showing on the clock. The Argos were still too far away for an Andrusyshyn field goal (although, with Zenon's perverse accuracy, I wasn't convinced he couldn't have hit one). The game was effectively over; at least it certainly seemed that way, when Condredge faded back for a third time and threw a pure wounded duck, a Hail Mary of a pass, towards the right sideline, aimed at a tight knot of Montreal defensive backs who had dropped back to cover the inevitable pass.

About thirty seconds earlier, on one of the exit ramps descending from the covered side, the publisher and his son had heard a sudden roar. Running back, they'd emerged into the open area behind the eastern end-zone in time to see the Argos with the ball—the roar had been David Overstreet fumbling. From behind the end-zone they had watched Condredge complete his first two desperation passes, and now they watched his unbeautiful third go up and come down towards the cluster of Montreal defenders.

On the field, at least three Alouettes were in position to make the interception. But a cornerback named Dave Dumars was in better than good position; he took one step to his right, then a little hop, and appeared to catch the ball. But he *didn't* catch it. Somehow the ball bounced off his hands and rebounded, not forwards, but *backwards*, back over his head and the heads of the little bevy of Alouettes and into the hands of Martin Cox, waiting all along at the Montreal 30-yard line.

And I like to think that at least someone in the stadium knew what it was, as Martin Cox—not known for his speed—turned like an eight-year-old boy who's just stolen a Fudgesicle and started running towards the Montreal end-zone. It was the Bounce, of course. The old Bounce. The Bounce of the old Argos. The Bounce of Clutch or luck, promise or destiny, whatever you choose to call it, beaming up through the years and making a token appearance, maybe to prove that it hadn't retired for good. In a way, Martin Cox might have been Zeke himself—they were both equally slow—pulling in Nobby's pass that day in 1952, tiptoeing down the sideline for the last touchdown. Except that in this case it was the first touchdown. It was the first time in twenty years of being a fan that I had ever seen fortune smile on the Double Blue in the dying moments of a lost cause. It was Martin Cox, for that matter, finally reaching the goal-line on nervous, rubbery legs, winning the game for the Argos.

Down on the field, the publisher watched with his progeny:

> We saw him coming right towards us, and we couldn't believe it. We couldn't even believe it after he crossed the line. We didn't know whether to laugh or cry. Was it funny, or was it marvellous? I grabbed a perfect stranger and hugged him. My son began hitting me as hard on the back as I generally hit him, which was strange, because he'd never really been an Argo fan.

It was an impossible, wonderful moment. And it almost made up for what would happen over the next two weeks. There was only one real Argo team. It was the Alouettes who would win their last game of the season and move into the playoffs with a 3 and 13 record. The Argos would lose theirs, to the Hamilton Tiger-Cats on Hallowe'en, finishing 2 and 14 on the season.

It was the worst record in their history, and their twenty-ninth year of futility.

I did a strange thing at the end of the 1981 season, even for me. I took a copy of Tony Allan's *Grey Cup or Bust*, and drove down to Varsity Stadium on a Saturday morning. There was a college game scheduled for that afternoon, and the turnstile gates had been left open beforehand for the field crews, the way they usually were. I walked through the gates on the arena side and took a seat in the stands about half-way up, and opened Tony Adams' book to his description of the 1952 Grey Cup. After a few minutes of reading I looked up. The stadium didn't appear to have changed too much in the last twenty-nine years. It had been expanded slightly to accommodate the Olympic soccer games that had been played in Toronto in 1976, and the running track and retaining wall from previous renovations were there, but other than that it was probably very much the same. Still, I couldn't help feeling that something was missing — and nothing as tangible as a winning Argo team.

For years fans and other interested parties had racked their brains for reasons for the Argos' failure, coming up with the classic and not-so-classic panoply of theories. There had been the Coach-Quarterback Mistiming Theory; the Theory of Impatience; the Theory of Lew Hayman; the Theory (Tommy Hudspeth's) of Sin; the Theory, finally, from Harry Sonshine, Harry and his fatal infatuation with American style, and the Argos' consequent laxity when it came to developing Canadian talent. But all these theories, it occurred to me, looking down at the real green grass of the old stadium, might only be camouflage. If a flying saucer full of little lime men with infinite wisdom had landed on the mid-field stripe at CNE Stadium one Sunday afternoon in the fall, or one Tuesday evening in July, their first question would not have been, "Why is this team with the large boats on their helmets losing?" Their first question would have been, "Why have all these humans come to watch this team lose?" Why were people Argo fans?

Why was I an Argo fan? Why was the book publisher? Why was the lady with her cup of rye? Why did people love any losing teams? I was convinced by then that nobody ever really wanted to see his team fail. The attraction of losing teams, I thought, was that, unlike perennial winners, their prospects closely mirrored those of human life, which after all does not have a happy ending. Under those conditions the idea of triumph acquired a very special importance.

What was one more championship for the Yankees or the Canadiens? What was another trophy for the Boston Celtics?

But if by some combination of fortune and skill a doomed team could snatch a moment in the sun — if the *Argos* could win — then anything was possible.

II The Bounce is Back

And so it should have ended—with an epiphany tempered by a strong dose of reality. After the '81 season was truly over, I was forced to admit a certain bald truth among the lyrical ones; that if the old Bounce had returned with Martin Cox's catch and run under the lights against Montreal, it had gone into hiding for the final game, and couldn't be counted in any honest assessment of the season as a whole. In fact, the '81 debacle succeeded in doing what had never before been done in Toronto football circles—it robbed the off-season of hope. I'm not referring here to the stock Argo-fan hopelessness, but true hopelessness, the utter lack of hope, a vacuum so pure it approached perfection. Cynicism, the flip-side of idealism, might have provided some relief—but cynicism was absent. There wasn't even active indifference. The feeling was more like detachment, in the Buddhist sense. After twenty-nine years of being annihilated by the Hamilton Tiger-Cats and the Ottawa Rough Riders and the B.C. Lions, the Argos had succeeded in annihilating not only themselves but their remaining link to the physical world.

I could see only one possible redeeming feature to the aftermath of 1981: it was the perfect place to look back from, the serene plain from which history could be reviewed. It was the fan's true nadir, one without the terrible burden of hope.

Five months later, the Argonauts walked onto the field at CNE Stadium to play the Edmonton Eskimos for the Grey Cup.

There wasn't a glimmer of a clue, a *scintilla*, that might have prepared me for what was about to happen. Despite my epiphany

In 1971 these Argo fans carried a sign to Vancouver
that said it all. Eleven years later, twenty-nine years is
more than long enough.

involving Martin Cox's touchdown and the return of the old Bounce, I'd never really convinced myself about the dawning of a new Argo era, and not just because of the outcome of the 2 and 14 season. For one thing, there was the sheer three-decade weight of Argo history; for another, when the Argos opened their training camp in May for the '82 season I was still writing the final draft for the hardcover edition of my book. Writing a book about something, I was discovering, tended to take it out of the present reality and dispatch it deeper and deeper into a kind of fictional past — and the newspaper items I did glance at concerning the Argos seemed like material for a picaresque novel. One, an announcement that the team was going to invite eleven quarterbacks to their training camp, I immediately slated for the epilogue. *Eleven* quarterbacks. Maybe it was a new tactic — the selection of one position for yearly emphasis. In 1982 the Argos would try to win with an entire team of quarterbacks, in 1983 with middle-linebackers.

It was a spring for thinking about mortality as opposed to beginnings — and several items in the news pointed that way. One of these was the demise of the Montreal Alouettes. Following the Als' 3 and 13 season, disquieting rumours had started to proliferate — about the club's solvency, about Vince Ferragamo's contract, and also about Nelson Skalbania's whereabouts. Skalbania had eventually been tracked down in Hong Kong, and by the middle of February George Allen, the ex-Washington Redskin coach, had arrived in Montreal and was ensconced as president and prospective owner of the Alouettes — and dedicated, he said, to resurrecting the club for the citizens of Montreal, who deserved a "better fate". Two months later George Allen was gone, leaving the team with a $10,000 hotel bill. Not long after that the Alouettes faded out of existence altogether. What rose from their ashes was a team with old uniforms, but a name taken from a less musical creature of flight: the Concorde.

The lesson was clear enough to me. The Alouettes were the descendants of the oldest football club anywhere in North America, an organization founded in 1868. One year of trying to be Argos had consigned them to oblivion for ever.

Besides the Alouettes, a pair of Argo signings during the off-season caught my eye. First, on December 30, 1981, the team announced the hiring of a replacement for head coach Tommy Hudspeth: Bob O'Billovich. A native of Butte, Montana — Evel

Knievel's home town — Bob O'Billovich had worked as an assistant coach for the Ottawa Rough Riders for six years, and had earned a reputation for total anonymity. Bob's name had always seemed perfectly reversible to me, like a parka: Bob O'Billovich, Bill O'Bobbovich.

The second signing, of a new "special" scout to monitor college and professional football in Canada and the United States, was announced less than a week later. The name of the new scout: Frank Clair. Frank the Professor himself, the last coach to take the Argos to a championship, now sixty-four and — at least till the Argos called him — retired to Sarasota, Florida. The papers ran pictures of Frank holding the Grey Cup in November 1952, while a smooth-faced Nobby Wirkowski drank Seven-Up from a squatting position in front of him. If the Argos had tried retreating to happier days with the re-hiring of Leo, I thought, they'd jumped into H.G. Wells' time machine by re-signing Frank.

All these items I regarded not only as possible endings for the book I'd written, but also as a farewell to my fandom. By the spring of '82 I was convinced I'd succeeded in cutting the umbilical cord of partisanship. The writing had been my release. I felt aloof, transcendent, almost amused.

So when, one night in June, I was struck by a new idea, exponential in nature, I tried not to take it seriously. But it was a novel thought. From 1952 to the present the Argos had fielded three outstanding teams: the '52 Grey Cup Champions, the 1961 Argos of Tobin Rote and Lou Agase, and Leo Cahill's 1971 Grey Cup losers; approximately a decade separated each of them. But it went deeper than that. In 1961, nine years after they had won the Grey Cup, the Double Blue barely lost a game that would have sent them to the championship. *Ten* years later, in '71, they barely lost in the championship game itself. *Eleven* years later was 1982. . . .

If anything the signs pointed the other way, in the direction of the traditional (although not original) Bounce. One of the eleven quarterbacks crammed into the Argos' camp in the spring of '82, for example, was a twenty-six-year-old rookie named Dan Feraday. In his last year at the University of Toronto, the year before, Feraday had broken several Canadian college passing records and had been chosen the national collegiate player of the year. He had also been selected in the twelfth round of the NFL draft by

Forrest Gregg's Cincinnati Bengals. (The Bengals' offensive coordinator Lindy Infante had called Feraday "the most accurate thing I've seen on film this year. He's calm, cool, and has a great sense of the field. If he played U.S. college football he would have been drafted among the top three quarterbacks.") As far as I could see, the strikes against Feraday—that he was slow for the Canadian game, that he was old for a rookie, that he was hobbled by the infamous Designated Import rule—were enormously outweighed by his pluses: he was an intelligent athlete, he had a superb arm, and he was a hometown boy. The PR possibilities were unlimited; in one fell swoop the Argos could reverse the American fixation that had been their albatross ever since Harry Sonshine; they could establish a laudable trend towards Canadian quarterbacks, possibly end up with another Russ Jackson, and start cultivating the kind of realistic, balanced mentality that had made the Edmonton Eskimos so infuriatingly successful in the West. Except that on June 23 the Argos released Feraday, who reported immediately to Cincinnati Bengals. The chances that he would make the NFL club were minuscule, which meant that most true Argo fans immediately envisioned him starring for Forrest Gregg in the Super Bowl.

The quarterbacks the Argos did keep were Condredge Holloway, back again from the battering of '81; Joe Barnes, the hard-nosed ex-Alouette, ex-Saskatchewan Roughrider veteran the Argos had acquired for his leadership qualities; and June Jones, a lanky quarterback out of Portland State who wore a beard. Fair or not, it would have been difficult not to have reservations about June on the basis of his name alone; with a beard added it was impossible.

But what was getting much more ink than any of the quarterbacks—and what I kept noticing in my lofty glances at the sports section—was the new offensive system the Argonauts had installed. The brainchild of Mouse Davis, the new Argo offensive coordinator, its technical name was "twin slow and motion". In the papers it was called "run and shoot", "run and gun", "gun and shoot"—nobody seemed to be sure. Other possible variations— "hit and miss", "run and hide"—seemed unavoidable. The way Mouse Davis himself described it did not exactly inspire confidence either. Basically, Mouse explained, the "run and shoot" was a flexible, improvisational offence, a kind of gridiron jazz. "It calls for fast, smart receivers," he said, "who can run proper routes, and *change* routes depending on the coverage. The quarterback, for his part, has to read the defence at the line, decide how many steps he's going to drop back, read the play while he's dropping to see which way his receivers are going to go, and then hit the open man on the run." This explanation was like a compilation of everything Argo fans had come to distrust over the years. Instead of stressing fundamentals, it advocated complexity; it was jazz for a team that had yet to learn to read quarter notes. It sported a name flashier than the worst Leo Cahill summertime gimmick, and depended on the pass more than any Argo offence since the Shotgun, Lou Agase's fan-murderer of the early sixties. Besides, the analysts were already saying it was nothing new: CFL teams had been using it for years, under duller names; it was the Calgary Stampeders–Pete Liske offence of a few years earlier; it was Joe Walsh's San Francisco Forty-Niner offence adapted to the wide field.

Who could have guessed? Using the run and shoot the Argos won their first three exhibition games, and the *Globe & Mail* printed a chart showing that teams that went 4 and 0 in the pre-season invariably had winning regular seasons. The Argos then lost their fourth exhibition game to the Tiger-Cats, and proceeded to cut Martin Cox, who had scored a pair of touchdowns in June and had been hailed as the next great Double-Blue clutch receiver. Fan reaction at this point, as far as I could tell, was mild but still relatively positive, despite the typical Argo early-season turn of events. It was masochistic but predictable: Argo fandom was a battered, exhausted institution, ready to be grateful for small mercies, and even with the loss to Hamilton the team had already won as many games by the season opener as it had the entire previous year.

Hindsight makes for terrific foresight: there are plenty of people who will claim, now, that they saw the seeds of hope in the Argos' regular season opener at Exhibition Stadium against the Calgary Stampeders. The only thing I can claim to have noticed is the peculiar tone of the game. In a contest that Calgary's head coach, Jack Gotta, later called "weird", and Stampeder quarterback Bruce Threadgill said was "berserk", the Argos intercepted five Calgary passes in the first half alone, built a 15-3 lead, and yet somehow managed to be trailing 24-16 early in the fourth quarter. At that point Condredge Holloway, who'd replaced Joe Barnes at quarterback, connected for a completion deep in Calgary territory with none other than Martin Cox—who'd been re-acquired by the Argos four days after he was released. On the next play Condredge scrambled up the middle for a 28-yard broken-play touchdown. His ensuing pass to David Newman for the two-point conversion tied the game. Adding to the flukiness of the ending were the Stampeders themselves, who worked the ball down to the Argo 39 in the dying seconds and then took a too-long-in-the-huddle penalty. Their field-goal attempt was wide, and Zenon Andrusyshyn, of all people, ran the ball out to the 3-yard line to preserve the tie.

In retrospect I admit that an unnaturally perspicacious, certifiably optimistic analyst might have detected in the Calgary game two critical reversals of historic Argo tendencies: after blowing a promising lead they had staged a successful comeback of their own; in the closing minutes of a close game *they* had displayed composure while the opposition had sabotaged themselves. By the same token, though, a team that intercepted five passes in the first half of a football game and still had to struggle to win could not really be called a paragon of Clutch.

The Argos split their next two games, a 31-12 loss to Edmonton and a 16-13 squeaker over the new Montreal Concorde. The Edmonton game was noteworthy largely because of Joe Barnes's embarrassing injury and because of the half-time discussion between the broadcast's two colour analysts, Ronnie Lancaster and Leo Cahill—which was in fact the only part of the game I watched. Joe Barnes suffered his injury in the third quarter, when I was already asleep (it was past midnight, Toronto time), but according to the papers the next day he had been caught by an Edmonton blitz and kneed heavily in the "butt". ("Severely bruised buttocks" was the bravest diagnosis I could find in print.) At half-time Ronnie and Leo had been anything but positive in their evaluation of the Argos' new offence. Between them they pointed out about seven foolproof ways of neutralizing it, not including the one Edmonton had devised. Leo in particular used several colourful expressions that I immediately wished I'd worked into Chapter Seven.

The fact is that, up to this point—three games into the season—I had yet to see the Argos actually play football. I felt as though I had, but I'd only read news reports and picked up the general rhythm of the summer. The illusion was not all that unusual. The Polo Grounds held fewer than 50,000 people in 1951, when

Bobby Thomson hit the home run heard round the world, but today at least three times that many people will swear that they were there. The 15,000-plus crowd who watched the hockey Leafs win their last Stanley Cup against Montreal in 1967 has swollen to 50,000; the 25,000 who watched the Argos win the Grey Cup that November day now run into six figures. (For that matter, I remember with crystalline clarity specific plays from television broadcasts of games that I know weren't even *on* TV.) I don't think fans lie; it's just that their hearts' desire for the surge of history is so strong that it reshapes reality to accommodate bigger ballparks.

Whatever the process, the first Argo game I actually saw was a late-night telecast of a game in Regina with the Saskatchewan Roughriders.

By now that first Saskatchewan game, along with the Edmonton game that followed it and the Eastern Final, has become a staple of the new Argo lore. Part of its fame is due, naturally, to the score—20-1 for the Argos at the half, 34-2 at the three-quarter mark, 44-22 at the end—but it was the manner in which they ran up the score that was so unusual. *Every Argo score came either on or as the result of an undeniably spectacular play.* In fact, the Argos were out-gained in total offence on the night 404 yards to 355, with Condredge Holloway suffering through what would be his worst outing of the season, completing only 10 of 28 passes. But every pass Condredge threw seemed either to turn into an explosive gain, shimmering with excitement, or to threaten to. Two of the most exciting were a 55-yarder in the first quarter to Terry Greer, who looked every bit as good to me as he was supposed to be, and a 68-yarder off a short slant pass to a "speedy" Martin Cox. After the Argos had built up their huge lead in the second half, Condredge kept going for the big play; even aborted plays had the *look* of potentially big plays. It took a while for my mind, benumbed by the hour, to realize what was going on.

It was the "run and shoot". It was like nothing I'd ever seen. It was an offence built on a precarious brinksmanship excitement— probably best characterized by the quarterback "drop" Mouse Davis had described, or at least the lack of one. On the snap of the ball Condredge would take one or maybe two steps backwards into a no man's land between the line of scrimmage and an ordinary passing pocket, and then stop, watching all the time. This meant he could get rid of the ball twice as quickly as an ordinary quarterback plus he was at least five yards closer to his receivers to begin with. Meanwhile his receivers—most of the team—were flooding zones and slanting like jets into the huge wide-open Canadian spaces left in the defences. Every play had the thrill of a quick opener. I had that once-in-a-lifetime feeling of watching something supple and revolutionary, and also so obvious I wondered why no one had ever tried it before. Not only had I never had this experience watching the Argos, I had never had it watching any game. There are fans of dynasties, Yankees fans and Canadiens fans, who have been treated to years of conventional excellence by their teams and yet denied this unique thrill. At this writing I'm firmly convinced that Mouse Davis's offence will one day be regarded as a landmark achievement in its sport, like the direct snap, or, in hockey, the Russian method of swivelling backwards to receive a pass while continuing to move forward.

Still, the question has to be asked: was I a *believer* then, as early as July 30, 1983? Not by a light-year. These were the Argos, you'll remember, and I was still convinced I had shucked off the mantle of fandom for good. Besides, the "run and shoot" was only an offence—defensively the Argos had given up over 400 yards to the Roughriders and come dangerously close to letting them pull off an impossible comeback. As impressive as the Argos' offence might have been, their defensive vulnerabilty was exactly the sort of lurking weakness that had doomed them in the past.

Eight nights later, at CNE Stadium, the Argos defeated the Grey Cup Champion Edmonton Eskimos 30-22. It was the first time the Argos had beaten Edmonton in eight years. It was also a performance of pure clutch. Leading 22-4 at half-time, the Argos saw the Eskimos pull within two points in the third quarter, then sealed the win on a 61-yard pass and run from Condredge Holloway to Terry Greer. Greer scored two touchdowns, Cedric Minter and Martin Cox one each.

But the most important thing, the thing that gave me pause watching the highlights on TV, was the response of the 38,000 people in the stands at the final gun. As the game's last second ticked away, they swarmed over the barricades and past the police, engulfing Condredge and the rest of the team in a crazed, even dangerous ecstasy. Never, not once in twenty-two years of fandom, had I seen an Argo crowd behave so hedonistically.

At this point the impossible possibility that had struck me some eighteen months earlier came percolating up and broke the surface of my consciousness: *what if this was the year . . . ?*

It was crazy. It was *insane*. Under ordinary circumstances I wouldn't have entertained the idea for more than five seconds. But there was the matter of timing: if an institution existed anywhere in the world that was perverse enough to shatter precedents at this point, it was the Argos.

It was insane, but interesting. There was my professional quandary: if the Argos did accomplish the unthinkable, if they won the Grey Cup, it would not seem to augur well for someone who had just chronicled their previous twenty-nine years of angst. On the other hand, if the Argos went to the championship, what would be more compelling than a story that put this monumental achievement into perspective? Sports fans like the ones I'd seen on TV would be willing to forgive you anything—if they didn't tear you to pieces with joy beforehand. Maybe people would just look at the pictures. Maybe I could write another chapter.

What was I thinking? These were the *Argos*.

My second and deeper conflict was all spiritual. If the Argos kept on winning, would I curse them for pulling one more incredibly inconsiderate move on me—or, worse, would I find myself rooting for them once again?

The point seemed to be growing moot when the Argos lost their next game in Hamilton to the Tiger-Cats 37-27, making it three years without a victory in Ivor Wynne Stadium and letting the Ti-Cats pull to within a game of them in the East. What followed, though, were two Argo wins: a cakewalk over Ottawa, 35-25, and a 20-19 squeaker over the highly touted B.C. Lions that was won on a safety touch and represented the Argos' first victory in Empire Stadium since 1969. The Argos were now 5-2 and 1 on the year, which meant they'd already equalled their average number of total yearly wins for the past ten years, with half the schedule still to play. Condredge Holloway was performing regular miracles of elusiveness in the run and shoot, and Terry Greer had emerged as the premier receiver in the CFL.

It seemed like the perfect time for them to swoon. I was convinced it was happening when, in front of a record crowd of 52,521 at Exhibition Stadium, the Argos dropped another close decision to Hamilton, 30-25. But they stayed inscrutable, wedging wins over Calgary and Montreal around an abysmal 46-14 loss to British Columbia. In my years as a fan the loss to the Lions would have been particularly painful. Because of the ongoing player strike in the National Football League, NBC had decided to show selected CFL games to its football-hungry fans. The Argo-B.C. game was the first one they chose. In keeping with the fascination Toronto fans had always felt for close brushes with America — from Harry Sonshine's dazzling raid on the NFL in the mid-fifties, to the exhibition games the Argos played against American pro teams half a decade later, to my own Sunday afternoon obsession with the Cleveland Browns — the B.C. game created more fan interest than any game of the season so far. To agitate things even more, the CFL had demanded that the American broadcast of the game, which would ordinarily have been seen in Ontario, be blacked out not only in Toronto but across the rest of the nation as well. The league's official reason had something to do with sponsors and exclusive advertising rights, but the situation smacked of paranoia and provincialism. It was as though the CFL moguls were afraid of what the average fan might notice about Canadian football when it was reflected through an American eye — which was, of course, exactly what I *wanted* to see. The result was that Argo fans opened their Monday papers avidly to find out, from local reporters who had driven to Buffalo, what the American broadcasters had said about the game. Scanning the articles, I was reminded of Forrest Gregg's third regular-season game as an Argo coach, when his special guest had been Marie Lombardi, Vince's widow, and the Argos had lost 31-2 to the Ottawa Rough Riders. This game was Marie Lombardi all over again — but worse. All over America, from Pittsburgh to Anaheim, hundreds of thousands of U.S. fans had been privy to the Argos' mortification. "Toronto," NBC's colour commentator, ex-NFL quarterback John Brodie, was quoted as saying, "is playing like a team that has a playoff spot clinched, and that's not good." Was this what the CFL was afraid of? Was there an Argo fan alive who needed to hear this from John Brodie?

In fact John was being premature. The Argos didn't clinch their playoff spot till the next weekend, when they defeated the Montreal Concorde 25-9. It was the first time since 1977 that they'd reached post-season play, the first time since 1976 that they'd won seven games.

And now the swoon did seem to set in. After losing a thriller 39-35 to the Winnipeg Blue Bombers in Winnipeg — a game which saw Condredge complete 37 of 53 passes for 436 yards, and Terry Greer catch a record-tying fifteen of those passes for 206 yards, and which the Argos almost won on a final-play *onside kick* from the Blue Bomber 29-yard line—the Argos came back to Exhibition Stadium and were beaten handily by the same Blue Bombers 29–16. All week Condredge had been saying how much he was looking forward to the rematch. Now Hamilton was closing fast and the Argos, I thought, could look forward to losing their last two games by large scores and then bowing out to Ottawa in the semi-final. If they happened to beat the Rough Riders there would be the Tiger-Cats again at Never Wynne. The Argos had already exceeded all reasonable expectations for the 1982 season; considering the year that had preceded it, they had been extraordinarily successful. It was time to count the winnings, strike the tents, and slip discreetly off into the night.

The second Saskatchewan game, the Argos' second-last game of the season, was the first one I attended in person in '82. My official excuse for being there was to sign books at the pre-game Argo Alumnus dinner. The experience was surreal: I stood at the back of a large room, wrote my name a few hundred times, and sheepishly handed out copies of my work to the people who starred in it. I was giving them *my* version of *their* professional lives. In a slightly giddy haze I shook hands with Nobby Wirkowski and Uly Curtis, and listened to a sweet-voiced, cuddly-looking man named Bobby Kuntz—the same Bobby Kuntz who had attacked a Saskatchewan Roughrider with his helmet in 1957, and had once *broken* his helmet on a perfectly legitimate tackle—ruefully discuss the infamous second game of the 1961 Eastern Final, which the Argos had lost on Faloney's Run and which Bobby remembered almost as vividly as I did.

I watched the game from the press box. On the Argos' first series of downs Condredge Holloway completed four consecutive passes, taking the team down to the Saskatchewan 25. His fifth pass was intercepted by a Saskatchewan defensive back, who ran it back ninety-six yards for a touchdown. So it goes, I thought, with a curious lack of satisfaction. I couldn't even work up much smugness about the way the Argos gave up two touchdowns on turnovers in the last two minutes of the first half, to go into the dressing room trailing 22–11.

And then the second half started, and in the space of six minutes the Argos were blessed by one of the luckiest series of bounces I'd ever witnessed on a football field. The first came on a fumbled Argo punt which the Argos recovered deep in Saskatchewan territory. What made it more unlikely was that the Argos' new regular punter, University of Toronto graduate Dean Dorsey (Bob O'Billovich had finally given up on Zenon Andrusyshyn's penchant for making field goals from the 50-yard line and missing them from the 5), had been injured in the first half, and the fumbled punt, a towering wicked spiral, was kicked by rover Zac Henderson, who had never punted in a pro game in his life. Next the Roughriders fumbled the ensuing kickoff, kicked by slotback Jan Carinci. A few minutes later the Argos completed a long pass on a deflection. All three breaks led to scores: within a span of seven minutes the Argos piled up 23 unanswered points. But now the Roughriders mounted a comeback of their own, scoring on their next drive to pull within a touchdown. Striking back without pause, Condredge Holloway lofted a long pass to Cedric Minter on the Argos' first possession after the kickoff; Cedric Minter caught it behind one defender, described a complete 360-degree circle around another, and ran into the end-zone to restore the fourteen-point bulge. Three minutes later the Roughriders scored again. Finally the gun sounded. I had to check the scoreboard twice to be sure who had won; it was that kind of game. The next day in the *Star*, under a headline that ran "Argo Fans Can't Handle Victory", Rick Matsumoto reported that several of those fans had responded to the game by baring their backsides to the field *en masse*, a collective moon in the afternoon. I don't blame them; it had been a totally frustrating, roller-coastering, unsatisfying win. Just to demonstrate that there are three dozen sides to every coin, Condredge Holloway called it one of the most meaningful games of the season. "We had adversity early, then the quick turnaround, then we had to hold on to win," Condredge said in the papers. "In one game we experienced things that you usually experience over a whole year."

But a win it was. Coupled with Hamilton's loss to Edmonton the night before, it meant that the Argos, now 8–6 and 1 on the season, would need only a tie in their last game, against Ottawa, to finish on top of the Eastern Conference for the first time since 1971 and the third time since 1952.

Looking back, I can see certain elements of justice in the fact that it was Ottawa the Argos met in that final regular-season game (and in another one a couple of weeks later). After coming so amazingly close to upsetting Edmonton in the Grey Cup the year before—the Eskimos had needed a last-minute Dave Cutler field goal to win—the Rough Riders had suffered through an exasperating, inconsistent season in which the only Eastern team they outplayed was the next-to-hopeless Montreal Concorde. The Ottawa fans had completed the pattern by providing one of the meagre crowds which had become something of a tradition at Lansdowne Park. It was one of those situations that struck an Argo fan (ex or otherwise) as scandalous — even in Russ Jackson's day the Rough Riders had often played to less than sellouts. But Ottawa, under George Brancato, was a team that had become known for its habit of regarding the regular season as a protracted *pre*-season, taking advantage of the ridiculously lenient playoff qualifications in the Eastern Conference that permitted third-place teams to enter post-season play despite their records (the Argos could always be counted on to finish last), and then picking up enough late NFL cuts and CFL discards to "peak" in time for the big games. Whether or not you felt that this was a blot on CFL football (as I always had), it created an interesting contrast in styles for the final game. It would be Ottawa, a team that was fuelled by relative fan indifference and had a way of rising from mediocrity to brilliance in critical games, against the Argos, a team that had enjoyed inexplicable fan loyalty over thirty years and had a proclivity for choking on an Olympian scale in the clutch.

Even in my most ardent years, I would have had trouble justifying a trip to Ottawa to attend the Argos' last game. But, in an ironic twist, my publisher had lined up a television interview for me, on the sidelines during the game. It was the first promotional trip I'd made, and I was duly nervous about it. And so, on a grey, blustery October day, my fandom and authorship came careering towards each other at terrific speeds — and the Argos played the game that I had been dreaming about for twenty-one years.

On an afternoon when the Argos needed to produce consistent offence at all costs, Condredge Holloway — who later confessed to not being "nearly as sharp" as he had been for much of the season — completed 18 of 31 passes for 264 yards; Dean Dorsey helped by kicking four field goals through gale-force winds. On an afternoon when the team had to stop Ottawa's explosive running-back Skip Walker or risk being chased out of the stadium, a swarming defence held Walker to a mere 24 yards on 10 carries. Much of this may have had to do with the first tackle made on Walker, courtesy of Zac Henderson, the Argo rover and Eastern nominee for the Schenley Award in the outstanding-defensive-player category. Henderson was amazing all day, creating percussive hits from a yard away, demonstrating the football equivalent of stroking a hundred-mile-an-hour tennis serve without the momentum of a backswing.

But the critical point as far as I was concerned came in the fourth quarter. The Rough Riders had switched quarterbacks and scored a touchdown late in the third, closing the gap to 14 points. With ample time left, their new quarterback, Kevin Starkey, moved them down to the Argo 19-yard line. In years past it would have been nothing for the Argos to let the Riders score and score again, and lose the game and first place and faith for ever. But when Kevin Starkey threw to the corner of the end-zone on first down, Jo Jo Heath, a sweet-voiced defensive back with a black belt in karate, leaped diagonally in front of the Rough Rider receiver and made an extended fingertip interception. It was a precise, gritty, big-league play at the perfect juncture of an ugly day. It was a consummately professional play. It was an American play, from the black-and-white Sunday afternoons of my adolescence; as Jo Jo went up for the ball all the colour seemed to drain out of the scene, leaving only the greys and beiges and off-whites. It was a 1962 Cleveland Browns play.

When the gun sounded a few minutes later even the final score, 28–14, had an early sixties American ring to it. In celebration the Argos now picked up the unlikely agent of that score, Bob O'Billovich, and carried him on their shoulders a short distance across the field. Mouse Davis I could have expected American efficiency from—but Obie, of the reversible name? High in the stands two lonely Argo fans let loose with the timeless, double-tone, descending cry, "*Ar-gos!*" It sounded eerily mournful considering the circumstances, but it was the only cheer they knew.

The Argos had done it. They had accomplished the first leg of the impossible. They had finished the regular season in first place.

In Toronto, the reaction for the next two weeks was difficult to describe; it was as though the entire city had drawn a deep breath. People who had given up on football years ago, people who had never even watched a game, were joining in the inhalation. I realized that the Argos' fame, or infamy, had become such a part of the daily summer-fall life of the city that a citizen didn't have to be anything close to a fan to have a feel for it, and a stake in the team's redemption. Articles by psychiatrists appeared in the newspapers discussing the psychological inability of the city to deal with success. If the Argos managed to win the upcoming Eastern final, they suggested, people would display strange behaviour. If they happened to win the Grey Cup, the pathology might be even weirder.

Meanwhile, an important portion of the Argos' fate was being decided outside their control, about forty miles to the south-west of the city. On November 14 the Ottawa Rough Riders met the Hamilton Tiger-Cats in Hamilton to decide the Argos' opponent in the Eastern final. Hamilton was the overwhelming favourite, and the nerve-racking one: the Argos hadn't beaten the Tiger-Cats in three years, and hadn't beaten them in a playoff game since 1971.

As it turned out, the anxiety was academic. In the semi-final at Ivor Wynne Stadium, Ottawa proceeded to pull one of its uncanny days out of the hat, largely with the help of Skip Walker, who gained 250-plus yards — a playoff record — rushing. The final score was 30–20, Ottawa. And it was the Rough Riders the Argos would have to defeat to go to the Grey Cup.

The thing that stays most vivid and unforgettable in my mind about the 1982 Eastern Final is the weather. It was drizzling at the opening kick-off, and dark enough for the lights to be turned on. In the second quarter the rain stopped and fog gathered in wisps between the 30-yard lines. At half-time the sky was divided evenly into portions of black cloud and sharp teal blue. For five minutes the sun shone. The only thing that was constant was the strangely mild temperature, courtesy of a kind of mistral (the legendary warm wind that induced Vincent Van Gogh to cut off his ear).

I got to the park with about ten minutes to spare, and was immediately struck by the crowd, which was generating an electricity I'd never felt before at an Argo game. The source of it seemed to be the people crammed into the western end-zone seats. Under the yellow lights they rippled and surged and were never still, like a street-section of Rio's Carnival transported to the Toronto lakefront.

One fan in particular I noticed, not in the far grandstand but in the row directly below me. He was a small, baby-faced man, wearing a plaid wool jacket buttoned to his throat and an Argo toque. It was his swearing that caught my attention. He started as soon as the Riders took the field for their introductions, emitting a sporadic barrage of intense, inventive profanity at each player's name, not in a shout, but in an intense, worried monotone, a conversation with himself. He had the haunted eyes of Slip Mahoney, from the Bowery Boys. There was something naggingly familiar about him, and his expression.

The first three minutes of the '82 Eastern Final I rank on a scale of personal recollection with only three other games: the 1958 NFL championship, the 1961 Eastern CFL Final, and the 1971 Grey Cup.

The Argos lost the toss and were forced to kick off. Ottawa took the ball and started a steady, crisp-looking drive upfield, mixing the pass and run efficiently. By an apparent stroke of luck, though, an Ottawa receiver slipped doing an out pattern, and the Rough Riders were forced to punt from midfield.

Jan Carinci, a Canadian with moves at once elusive and steely, took the punt on the dead run and returned it fifty-nine yards down the sideline into Ottawa territory. In the west end-zone the murmur had risen to an expectant grumble. Now Condredge brought the team out of the huddle for their first offensive play. He took the snap and retreated to his short-drop area in the run and shoot, looking all the while to his left. He kept looking to his left; time momentarily stood still. Then, at the last moment, he threw to his right, towards Terry Greer, who was running down the sideline, stride for stride with an Ottawa cornerback. From the moment the ball left his hand the play slowly unfolded, with that surreal crescendo of sound and action that television can never convey. The pass was slightly underthrown — Greer came back for it, the Ottawa cornerback slipped trying to. Terry caught the ball and, with a smooth ease that belonged in a practice, tumbled gently over the cornerback into the end-zone.

If the win in Ottawa that clinched first place had been a gritty 1962 Cleveland Brown memory, this was football that belonged in a fantasy. Every play the Argos ran unfolded with exactly the same slow certainty. It was hard to tell whether the ample time for each offensive play was being provided by great Argo blocking or Condredge Holloway's uncanny peripheral vision. Condredge danced and whirled and *vibrated* — elusive even while standing still — while his receivers broke into the "clear". They might have been ten-year-olds playing a game of touch. One series after Terry Greer's catch, Condredge faded back and hit Paul Pearson with a perfect 62-yard touchdown pass - - Pearson had to neither slow down nor speed up an iota to gather it in. In the second quarter,

214

after a Dean Dorsey field goal, he connected with Terry Greer again on a spot pass thrown to a corner of the far end-zone, a play as flawless in execution as Johnny Unitas to Raymond Berry. Another later pass to Pearson, deep into Ottawa territory, was memorable not so much for its immaculate timing as for the tremendous hit the Argo receiver took at the exact moment he caught the ball—and hung on.

At the half the score was 29-0 Argos. All around me the fans were going wild, holding up their index fingers, spilling beer, standing on the seats. Only the fan in the toque seemed unconvinced. If anything he looked more worried than before. He held his unsipped beer and darted his eyes nervously at the scoreboard, glancing down savagely every now and then at the fans calling "We're number one!" "Not so fast," he said, "not so *fast*." His faith was in an inverse relationship to the Argos' fortunes, I realized with surprise. The better they did, the more he agonized.

I was *sure* I'd met him before.

Ottawa finally scored in the third quarter, a successful run by Skip Walker. They got the ball back quickly and were coming on again, making me a little anxious myself, when suddenly, with the same perfect timing he had demonstrated the week before, Jo Jo Heath intercepted a pass on his own 53-yard line and ran it back fifty-seven yards for a touchdown. At the end of the quarter the score was Argos 36, Ottawa 7. At the beginning of the fourth quarter Dean Dorsey kicked a single. The score held. With six minutes left in the game Bob O'Billovich took Condredge out of the game, and the stadium rose as one to salute his finest day in a Double Blue uniform. Joe Barnes, recovered from his embarrassing injury, replaced Condredge. On his first play from scrimmage he threw a bullet over the centre to a second-string wide receiver named Geoff Townsend, who turned upfield and ran sixty yards for a touchdown.

It was at this point that I felt relaxed enough to pay closer attention to my friend in the toque. As time had ticked away in the second half, he'd stopped swearing, and now he seemed to have eschewed motion as well. He stood stock-still, eyes fixed on the clock. What I had taken for anxiety before now came into clearer focus—it was pure fear.

At the same time I realized why he seemed so familiar. I regret now that I didn't make some sort of fraternal gesture. As it was, he broke the ice, a moment after the gun sounded, looking up directly at me, down from the big board that read: Argos 44, Ottawa 7. His face was as pale as a sheet.

"Well," he said, "we made it."

I knew exactly what he meant. The old Bounce, the Bounce of 1952, was back. So, for better or worse, was I.

There's a chance I had never been gone.

To call the Grey Cup game of 1982 an anticlimax may seem like a monumental rationalization, but it's true. What else can you call a game one team is rained out of? For thirty minutes of the November classic the Argos demonstrated how a riveting offence like the run and shoot could match a first-class conventional system, touchdown for touchdown — and keep a fan wide-eyed while doing it. Then the rain fell, and it came down to a question of who had bigger hands, Warren Moon or Condredge Holloway. On such a detail is a championship decided.

Actually the Grey Cup was anticlimactic in another way. The Argo victory in the Eastern Final had been so convincing and complete that a kind of proportion or equilibrium had been achieved which the team hadn't enjoyed for thirty years. By winning the conference, and qualifying for the Cup, the Argos had abandoned their irrational world and decisively entered the ordinary one. It was a point several commentators made during Grey Cup week: although the Argos could lose the Grey Cup game in Toronto, they really couldn't lose at all.

This is not to suggest that the days leading up to the Grey Cup were devoid of excitement. The Argo-Edmonton match-up was in itself enough to fill a month's sports pages with nostalgia and coincidence. It was thirty years almost to the day since the Argos had won their last Grey Cup, also in Toronto, against another Eskimo team. Ironically, it was the 1952 Argos who were the reigning dynasty; that year the Eskimos were the great young team of the future, playing in their first Grey Cup. And just as the veteran '52 Argos had struggled through the regular season of 1952, finishing second and narrowly defeating the Tiger-Cats in the playoffs, so the 1982 Eskimos, winners of an unprecedented four Grey Cups in a row, had had their problems early in the season, losing five of their first eight games before coming back to win their last eight in a row and barely squeeze by the Winnipeg Blue Bombers into the Cup game itself. To add to the Eskimos' turmoil, coach Hugh Campbell had announced half-way through the season that he had accepted a contract for 1983 with the Los Angeles franchise in the new United States Football League (which was planning to start its games in the spring to avoid competing with the NFL). It was the kind of career advancement that in any other profession would be applauded, but that left a football fan with an unwholesome, uncomfortable feeling. Opinion was split on whether it would help the Argos or hurt them. I was trying to decipher other omens, among them the fact that of the thirty-four players on the 1982 roster, only three had been born when the Argos last won the Grey Cup.

The Friday before the Grey Cup an article appeared in the Toronto *Star* entitled "Can Argos Repeat 1952 Victory?", complete with a team photo of the 1952 team and a brief profile of "where they are now". It made interesting reading. In 1952 only three of the '82 Argos had been alive, and now that the team had reached the Cup again, three of the earlier Argo champions were dead. The vast majority of the remainder were still in Toronto, Americans included. They were doing everything from driving cab to practising chiropractic. Only Nobby Wirkowski, in the York University athletic department, had a job directly related to football.

That night Zac Henderson (who had been injured early in the Ottawa game and would not play in the Grey Cup) failed to win the Schenley Award as the nation's outstanding defensive player. But when it came to the offensive prize, Condredge Holloway, a condemned man only a year before (I hadn't been guiltless of condemning him myself), took the honours, the first Argo to win a Schenley since Bill Symons in 1969. Immediately, the omen-watchers went into action again: would Condredge's Schenley make him more or less prone to shine against Edmonton? Did the Argos consider the season a triumph and vindication already? Would Warren Moon's 5,000-plus yards passing—probably the most neglected statistic of the year—prove decisive? Could the Argos do what only one CFL team, the 1951 Ottawa Rough Riders, had done before them: come back from a last-place finish one year to a Grey Cup victory the next?

I watched the Grey Cup game on television. I had contracted a cold verging on pneumonia sitting in the rain at the Eastern Final, and besides, I was too nervous to attend in person. I watched with two friends, one who cared and one who didn't, the optimum combination.

The Eskimos scored first, on their first possession, moving

downfield with depressing efficiency and finally settling for a Dave Cutler field goal. Then the Argos got the ball back and, three plays later, created ecstasy with an instant stroke of Bob O'Billovich genius. Earlier in the week O'Billovich had announced that he was benching outside receiver Scott McGhee in favour of Emanuel Tolbert, a swift pass-catcher he had picked up on waivers from Saskatchewan in September, but who had since resided on the injury reserve list. Now, on second and fifteen from his own 26-yard line, Condredge straightened up and threw a quick outside screen to Tolbert, far to his left along the line of scrimmage. Tolbert eluded Larry Highbaugh and with the help of a tremendous block from Terry Greer ran eighty-four yards into the Eskimo end-zone. Amid the celebration in the livingroom a nagging thought kept worrying me. Condredge had just barely gotten the pass off; the run and shoot was operating on the very brink between brilliance and disaster.

As stunned as the stadium was, the Eskimos were maddeningly calm. They took Dean Dorsey's kick-off and moved quickly from their 27-yard line to the Argo 16. From there Warren Moon rolled to his left and passed into the end-zone to Brian Kelly, who pushed off Jo Jo Heath so blatantly that everyone in the ball park saw it but the nearest official. 10-7 Eskimos. The Argos took the kick-off and began to move themselves, with Condredge slipping and whirling and finally, from inside the Edmonton 25, running left and throwing right into the end-zone to Terry Greer, who made a fingertip catch over Highbaugh and spiked the ball into the turf. Argos 14, Edmonton 10. Now the Eskimos switched to offence and marched ninety-three yards the other way, the last play a forty-one yard touchdown pass to Kelly again, a pass so confidently thrown and caught it might have been taking place in a morning scrimmage. Twice more the Eskimos moved into scoring range before the half ended; once Steve Ackroyd, Zac Henderson's substitution, made a key interception in the end-zone; the second time Dave Cutler kicked another field goal to make the score at the half Edmonton 20, Argos 14.

And then the rains came, and the outcome was decided, as emphatically as it had been when the deluge refused to stop in 1971 in Vancouver during the Argos' last Grey Cup appearance. The difference was that in the '71 game the Argos had been allies in their own demise (Leon's fumble, Harry Abofs' kick) whereas in 1982 they fought heroically against it every step of the way.

Other reasons were given for the Argos' inability to score in the second half and the Eskimos' eventual 32-16 victory: the unexpected Edmonton running attack, Warren Moon's brilliant passing, Zac Henderson's injury. There was even a theory that a controversial fumble made by Cedric Minter in the third quarter, with the Argos still less than a touchdown behind, was the turning-point in the game—a kind of muted Leon's fumble. But what beat the Argos, I am convinced, was the combination of the rain and the precarious nature of the still young run and shoot. Edmonton's plays were completed with generous margins of error; the Argos' were precise burglaries carried out with split-second timing. When the rain fell, timing was a luxury neither team could afford.

But if the Argos lost the game, a greater victory had been won. Nowhere on the field, that day, had there been anything like the classic "bad" bounce. Calling Cedric's fumble a bad bounce—which some people tried to do—was inane. The football Cedric was carrying had been soaked, he'd been hit hard from behind, and even then the call had been controversial. The officials, with a quick whistle, had nullified a previous Neil Lumsden fumble that was at least as blatant. Cedric's fumble wasn't a bad break; it was more a failure to get a *good* break. The distinction is important. After the game the Argos complained about exactly this kind of *conventional* bad luck, and for once they were right. They had been beaten by factors beyond their control; they had done nothing to doom themselves.

In fact, by Grey Cup day the memory of the 29-year-old Argo jinx had already faded to the point where history was reshaping itself to fit the times. In the weeks preceding the Cup, one of the most talked about stories in the papers was a report out of Tampa, Florida, where Leon McQuay was attempting a comeback with the USFL's Tampa Bay Bandits. Asked about his infamous fumble in the 1971 Grey Cup game, Leon had offered an unprecedented explanation. "There wasn't much time left," he said, "so as soon as I fell I put the ball down and rushed back to the huddle. They called it a fumble. But it wasn't a fumble." It wasn't a bad bounce at all. *Leon was just putting the ball down.*

Granted, a fan has to live with reservations. For all their success in 1982 the Argos didn't have to meet their nemesis, the Hamilton Tiger-Cats, in the playoffs. They lost twice to Hamilton in the regular season, and have yet to break the curse and win at

Ivor Wynne. And yes, they have yet to actually win a Grey Cup.

But fortune is like that; it can't be rushed. It comes back slowly to former haunts, checking out the terrain, easing its way into new nooks and corners, taking its time before it settles in. It's been away, after all, a long time.

And then you read that the 1983 Grey Cup will be played in a domed stadium in Vancouver. No rain—

Maybe this year. . . .